Women's War Stories

Women's War Stories

The Lebanese Civil War, Women's Labor, and the Creative Arts

Edited by
Michelle Hartman
and Malek Abisaab

Syracuse University Press

First Edition 2022

22 23 24 25 26 27 6 5 4 3 2 1

∞ The paper used in this publication meets the minimum requirements of the American National Standard for Information Sciences—Permanence of Paper for Printed Library Materials, ANSI Z39.48-1992.

For a listing of books published and distributed by Syracuse University Press, visit https://press.syr.edu/.

ISBN: 978-0-8156-3772-1 (hardcover)
978-0-8156-3782-0 (paperback)
978-0-8156-5566-4 (e-book)

Library of Congress Cataloging-in-Publication Data

Names: Hartman, Michelle, editor. | Abisaab, Malek, editor.
Title: Women's war stories : the Lebanese Civil War, women's labor, and the creative arts / edited by Michelle Hartman, and Malek Abisaab.
Other titles: Lebanese Civil War, women's labor, and the creative arts
Description: First edition. | Syracuse, New York : Syracuse University Press, 2022. | Includes bibliographical references and index.
Identifiers: LCCN 2022020759 (print) | LCCN 2022020760 (ebook) | ISBN 9780815637721 (hardcover) | ISBN 9780815637820 (paperback) | ISBN 9780815655664 (ebook)
Subjects: LCSH: Lebanon—History—Civil War, 1975–1990—Participation, Female. | Women in war—Lebanon. | Women—Lebanon—Social life and customs. | Women—Lebanon—Social conditions.
Classification: LCC DS87.5 .W66 2022 (print) | LCC DS87.5 (ebook) | DDC 956.9204/4—dc23/eng/20220509
LC record available at https://lccn.loc.gov/2022020759
LC ebook record available at https://lccn.loc.gov/2022020760

Manufactured in the United States of America

For Aziz

Contents

Illustrations

Tables

Acknowledgments

This book is part of a larger project, "Women's War Stories: Building an Archive of Women and the Lebanese Civil War," funded by the Social Science and Research Council of Canada. The SSHRC provided much of the funding for the larger project and this book specifically. Our academic departments at McGill University, History and Classical Studies and the Institute of Islamic Studies, also provided support for the project, and we thank Jason Opal and Robert Wisnovsky for making that possible. We would also like to acknowledge the work and support by Syracuse University Press, especially Peggy Solic, from the beginning of our project.

We thank all of the women who talked to us and contributed to our project. This group includes not only the women we interviewed formally about the Lebanese Civil War but also those who spoke informally to us about their lives, experiences, art, and labor during the war. We also thank the women who contributed essays to this volume. Nova, Zéna, Mary, and Yasmine have been a pleasure and joy to work with, and we appreciate their participation.

One phase of the project involved hosting a commemoration of the Sabra and Shatila massacre at McGill University in September 2018, during which some of the ideas in this book were developed. We thank the colleagues, comrades, and friends who contributed to this commemoration by sharing their memories, experiences, scholarship, and activism with us: Rabab Abdulhadi, Sam Anderson, Rosemarie Mealy, Ariel Saltzmann, and Jaime Veve. Thanks also to Mai Masri and Diana Allan for their contributions.

Several researchers worked on this project with us, and so here we thank Hanine Eldiri, Ralph Haddad, Caline Nasrallah, and, above all,

Sarah Abdelshamy. Sarah's work has been central to the project generally and to this book specifically. We thank her for reading, editing, organizing, and discussing the book with us.

Michelle thanks her son, Tameem, for his patience (and participation when necessary) in all the things necessary to make this book see the light of day.

Often there are acknowledgments that bridge the intellectual and the personal, and here we would like to acknowledge the contributions of Rula Jurdi Abisaab. Rula has been with the project from the beginning, contributing to it in ways we can only begin to outline here. In a similar vein, we also warmly thank Yasmine Nachabe Taan, who is also a contributor to the volume. The book would not have taken the shape it has without Yasmine. Both Rula and Yasmine have contributed an artistic sensibility that has enriched it immensely. We also thank the Nachabes, Taans, Merhejs, and Fakihs of Ayroun for providing the space to work on so many elements of the book.

At the very inception of this project, when it was still just weekend discussions in the living room, one person in particular pushed us to develop our ideas and make it happen. Our dear friend, colleague, and comrade Aziz Choudry used to hear us talk about our idea to work together on such a project and relentlessly encouraged us to do so. He was continually supportive of our individual and collective work and believed in this project deeply. He passed away just before we heard that the book would be published; he left us much too soon. We dedicate this book to his memory.

Women's War Stories

Introduction

Women's War Stories

MALEK ABISAAB and MICHELLE HARTMAN

Stories

There is a power to stories. Stories allow us to communicate with other people; they also allow us to formulate how to express things we think and feel. They help us to record our lives and those of others; they are a way to preserve our histories and legacies. Stories entertain, soothe, and inform. Stories are also a way to work through and work out trauma. Expressing the worst of life through storytelling also ensures a truth can be told; storytelling narrates facts and events and at times also relies on invention and fiction. Though stories often combine fact and fiction, one of the reasons why we believe in stories and storytelling is that they reveal such truths.

This collection of academic essays about women's lives, work, and creative production during the fifteen-year Lebanese Civil War (1975–90), is framed by the concept of stories. We have chosen to use stories as a structuring framework here for several reasons. First, this book grows out of a larger project on the Lebanese Civil War, as we discuss later, in which we collected women's stories of this war. Second, we wanted to highlight the role of stories and storytelling as intimately connected to writing histories and understanding past events, especially as they relate to women. We privilege stories here as a feminist praxis that can uncover some of the complexities of how women experience their lives, specifically in relation to war and trauma. Another reason we decided to create our analyses within this frame is that it allows us to bring to the fore complex, diverse, and engaging ways to understand women's lives in war time—their challenges, their struggles, and their resistance.

Women's War Stories

We all have stories to tell, and in one way or another we all have "war stories." But what these stories are, how we tell them, and even how much they have to do with actual war vary. By invoking "war stories," we are consciously playing on both the literal meaning of this expression—the stories people tell about being in an armed conflict—and the metaphorical use of this phrase in everyday English to signify a story you tell about something harrowing or even just difficult you have lived through in life, something that was a challenge and that you often wear as a badge of honor. Differently than the way people relate to experiences of armed conflict and surviving war literally, we tell our metaphorical war stories all the time. They are a way to make sense of where we fit into the world, a way to work through our struggles, and a way to bond with others.

We bring out both the literal and the metaphorical meaning of the phrase *war stories* to emphasize the continuity in how stories work as a way to understand and express experience. It is striking how adding the word *women's* to *war stories* changes the expression to privilege the literal. The use of "war stories" as a way to express the everyday difficulties of life seems to be the provenance of men.[1] One of the major reasons we have put this collection of essays together is that we wanted to bring more attention to the ways in which women lived through, survived, worked, and created art during the Lebanese Civil War. All of the book's chapters focus on women who worked and produced art during this specific war, but as those stories are told, so are all of the other stories of challenges, struggles,

1. We are not setting up this contrast to reify a binary opposition between "women" and "men" as stable and fixed categories. Instead, although recognizing their inherent limitation, we are using the terms *women* and *men* with the knowledge that they can shift over time and in different contexts. We have chosen to focus this study on women defined as such to capture some of what it means to embody identities that have been excluded from writing and recounting histories, especially histories of war.

and resistance that they faced as women in society—and as women artists, writers, filmmakers, tobacco workers, and so on.

The women's war stories told here are different from each other, but all of them in one way or another narrate something as a way to cope with, understand, analyze, express, represent, or symbolize their struggles. To understand the meanings of these stories in our analyses, then, we draw upon the work of Dina Georgis. In her book *The Better Story: Queer Affects from the Middle East* (2013), Georgis implores us to look at stories and locate within them what she calls "better stories"—ways to live our lives and narrate them that can bring about better worlds than those we have. She thus proposes:

> If we have suffered from trauma and loss, it is impossible to experience that loss without symbolizing it. And, as long as the affect of loss persists, we continue to symbolize it in the writing of history and in the production of culture and identity. If we take seriously the presence of injury in our constructions, then it requires that we become different (ethical) learners and readers of history. It means that we account for the site of loss and injury in our postcolonial narratives and that we face all of the past's ruins; namely all of our postcolonial dreams and nightmares. . . . Not all responses to injury lead to the kind of "creative" survival we would wish for. Not all those injured by colonial violence resist the power of colonial domination heroically.[2]

Georgis reminds us here that not all resistance is heroic, not everyone accounts for or reacts to situations in the same way. But in our writing of history, according to her, we can change the way we read history and learn about history. The title of her book, *The Better Story*, encapsulates her argument. We all must seek out and strive not only for better ways to tell our stories but also for better ways to read each other's stories. When Georgis talks about the better story, she does not always mean the "happy ending" or a story containing only positive or good things. Rather, she suggests,

2. Georgis, *The Better Story*, 22.

we all should be looking for ways to create better stories—for ourselves, for each other, and for our world. Following this line of thinking, this collection is focusing on how we and others write our histories and produce culture and identity specifically in relation to the Lebanese Civil War.

Women's War Stories: The Larger Project

The volume *Women's War Stories: The Lebanese Civil War, Women's Labor, and the Creative Arts* shares its main title with the larger project of which it is a part. We have been working on "Women's War Stories: Building an Archive of Women and the Lebanese Civil War" since 2015.[3] The impetus for this larger project was the lack of research, writing, and attention to women in the Lebanese Civil War. There is little to no documentation of women's roles in this war—not only as fighters, militants, activists, workers, artists, writers, filmmakers, and so on but also as people living in a society affected by fifteen years of a war that ravaged the country. Histories of the war rarely speak of women except as footnotes, and there are extremely few studies of any kind devoted to women and the Civil War. Thus, we embarked on a project that first involved collecting interviews—stories of all kinds—of women who experienced the Lebanese Civil War, especially those who were politically active in various ways.

In addition to recording these stories and histories, we also transcribed, published, and made them more widely available. Although at first concentrating on women militants, fighters, workers, and others involved in organizations and politics, we soon expanded our focus to include artists and other cultural workers. The interviews led, for example, to the publication of the militant and activist Nawal Qasim Baidoun's memoir of her years in Khiam prison.[4] The publication is a direct result of her interview for our larger project. Her story, alongside others, will appear in a book we are working on now to publish the oral histories drawn from the interviews collected.

3. This project has been funded in large part by the Social Sciences and Humanities Research Council of Canada.

4. Baidoun's work is currently available in Arabic, *Mudhakkirat al-munadila fi mu'taqal al-Khiyam* (2020), and in English translation, *Memoirs of a Militant* (2021).

The project has also supported a range of other initiatives, including events, workshops, discussions, and film screenings in Montreal, where we are based, as well as in Lebanon. In 2018, we hosted a commemoration of the Sabra and Shatila massacre that focused on solidarity with Palestine and Lebanon and invited academics and activists to speak, including Rabab Abdulhadi, Sam Anderson, Rosemarie Mealy, Ariel Salzmann, and Jaime Veve. We have also mentored students and worked with them to produce their own research and creative work around women and the Lebanese Civil War—for example, the creation of 'zines in response to the war.[5] This project has been meaningful in many ways, one of which is the intergenerational work it has facilitated in relation to women's stories of the Lebanese Civil War. We believe that it is not an accident that a project focused on stories and storytelling in multiple ways would produce these conversations.

Feminist Storytelling: The Ethics of Telling Other Women's Stories

Academic work based on women telling their own war stories is not a case of simple and transparent storytelling. Because we are producing this work in our roles as historians and as literary, art, and film critics, all of the contributions in this collection are mediated versions of the stories that women tell about war. Publishing women's stories—as carefully as we pay attention to accuracy and detail in reproducing them—is never a straightforward process. For example, all of the women interviewed for our project spoke in Arabic, and most of the creative work has also been produced in Arabic. With only a few exceptions, however, the academic work we are producing is being published in English. Even as we are documenting and translating women's war stories, therefore, we shape their stories, and we ourselves are narrating another war story through them.

The issue of language is one we are particularly sensitive to and have reflected on in great detail, especially as much of the work that one of us

5. For more information about the project, see its website at https://womenswarstories.wordpress.com/, which was created and is maintained by graduate researcher Sarah Abdelshamy.

(Michelle Hartman) does is located in translation studies, the politics of translation in particular. How do we translate the stories of women from Arabic into English, from the Arabic-speaking Lebanese context to an English-speaking one in academia, from stories of war to words on a page? Language is connected to culture and society not only in relation to the politics of language but also in the ways language encompasses more than just words spoken. We have tried to ensure that all of the contributions here take language and translation into account as one of the important areas to think through carefully when we tell stories about women and war and when we are responsible for telling and talking about the stories of other women.

The question of our responsibility in (re)telling, researching, analyzing, and writing about the stories of other women is the overarching ethical question that our collection—and, indeed, our larger project—grapples with. We are extremely attuned to the fact that in making the space for women to tell their own stories, whether in the context of writing an oral history or presenting an analysis of interviews or studying film, literature, art, and performance, we are shaping and telling stories that belong to others. This delicate balance is one that we all have navigated individually in our own chapters but also one that we have worked on collectively. It was important to the integrity of our project that we ask all contributors to keep in mind their relationship to their material and their subjects as they were producing their essays.

These ethical questions about storytelling and writing the stories of others and for others are amplified in the context of war. Because war stories often recall trauma and difficult times and can trigger even more memories than an interviewer might have intended, not all women want to tell them—or even for them to be told. The final chapter in the collection, for example, explores the question of whether all stories should or must be told—or, in the words of Toni Morrison, if they ought to "be passed on." This phrase is repeated throughout Morrison's acclaimed novel *Beloved* (1987), which probes the question of stories to be passed on, specifically in relation to slavery in the United States. The parallels are remarkable: the comparison with stories of the Lebanese Civil War begs the question of why and how we tell stories, who we are telling them to and for, and how we choose to tell them.

Finally, in relation to the ethics of writing war stories, we have endeavored to think about all of the stories we are passing on through these explorations of labor/work and the creative arts as not only rooted in one time period but also having a life before and after the specific part narrated. In thinking about what came before, we follow Sara Ahmed's suggestion in *Living a Feminist Life* that "a story always starts before it can be told."[6] The collection of essays here looks to life before the war and follows along after it to give the fullest and most complete idea of what is being discussed. We hope to have identified some of the places and times where the stories we are telling here started not only to facilitate our way of telling and thinking about them but also to tell them better or, as Dina Georgis's formulation would have it, to allow the "better story" to come through. The next section offers one story of the Lebanese Civil War to give a very brief context for the chapters that follow, which we describe in the last section of this introduction.

The Lebanese Civil War: A Better Story

This volume does not contain just one single story of the Lebanese Civil War; rather, we have allowed many stories to emerge through it to help the reader piece together ways to understand women's lives, experiences, narrations, and truths of this war. To give some additional context to the reader, we have constructed here a brief story—we hope it is some kind of better story—of some elements of this extremely difficult period in Lebanon. There are academic histories of the war, though relatively few in English, and as we pointed out earlier, few make any mention of women or women's lives.[7] The lives of ordinary people in the war are largely ignored in the scholarship.

6. Ahmed, *Living a Feminist Life*, 4.

7. See, for example, Nuwayhed al-Hout, *Sabra and Shatila, September 1982*; Hudson, *The Precarious Republic*; Petran, *The Struggle over Lebanon*; Salibi, *A House of Many Mansions*; and Traboulsi, *A History of Modern Lebanon.*

Even in making a brief outline to include here, we hesitated over what we should include and leave out. How do we begin to write this brief section? What angle do we take? Let's begin with socioeconomic factors, for example. It is well known that from Lebanon's so-called golden age in the 1950s, its economic growth benefited 4 percent of the population, while the majority suffered great hardship. This meant that by 1975, when the war officially broke out, large segments of Lebanese society had been increasingly alienated from the government because they did not see any benefits from its economic plans. The structure of the economy led to increased class stratification and ever-expanding disparities between the rich and the poor, which is certainly something that should be extensively accounted for in any story of the Lebanese Civil War.

Talk of majorities, minorities, disparities, and alienation from the government suggests, however, that perhaps we should not begin this story with a primary focus on the economy but perhaps instead with the founding of Lebanon as a nation. Any talk of the Civil War and the people's discontents might be better framed by tracing back to how Lebanon came to be an independent entity in the first place. A vast simplification of a complicated story starts with how Lebanon was carved out of a region known traditionally as "Greater Syria" under the French Mandate with the fall of the Ottoman Empire during World War I. The plan to form this modern nation-state was contested by many people and groups in different ways.

One part of this story concerns the deep divisions within Lebanese society whereby a majority of Muslim groups, individual people, and political formations demanded unity with Syria, but a majority of Christians advocated a separate and distinct state that would be formed for them in particular, with a Western cultural orientation and preservation of a Christian demographic majority. The latter state was eventually formed through a sort of compromise that still largely benefited the view advocated by Christian groups and was enshrined in what came to be known as the National Pact. An unwritten agreement between elites representing different groups and communities—defined as "sects"—established a balance of power, divvying up governmental roles between them and ensuring that sectarianism would be the system by which this nation-state would be run.[8]

In fact, sectarianism is another framing that is often used to narrate the Lebanese Civil War and is the main explanatory device by which most people understand these years of conflict. In the late 1950s, the sectarian system of governance in Lebanon and the economic crisis exacerbated social and political tensions, leading to the Civil War of 1958. Then, Arab nationalism, especially Nasserism, offered a vision of social justice and Arab unity that represented the aspirations of the depressed classes many Muslims belonged to. They opposed the policies of the Lebanese president Camille Chamoun, who did not sever Lebanon's relations with France and Great Britain during the Suez Canal Crisis of 1956.[9]

But as we narrate the economic, national, and sectarian conflicts here and offer them as alternative framings, we see how closely they work together. Politics also come into play as another important framing for thinking about the Lebanese Civil War. Of course, politics and political party affiliations never line up neatly along sectarian, economic, class, or other lines, but in broad terms there are ways they do align. During the Civil War of 1958, military confrontations erupted between right and left parties that halted only when US marines landed in that same year. The marines remained until the bombing of their barracks in Beirut in 1983.

Civil war broke out anew in 1975 in similarly polarized circumstances—left and right parties clashed in the period leading up to the fighting. The demographic realities of the country and economic disparities worked together once again to make matters more pressing. Muslims had outnumbered Christians in Lebanon from at least the early 1970s, but

8. For example, a proportional system of voting was established and organized according to each citizen's sectarian affiliation through their father's affiliation. Moreover, the president of Lebanon must be a Maronite, the prime minister a Sunni Muslim, and the Speaker of the House a Shi'i Muslim, while other groups are apportioned minor roles in the administration. Parliament must maintain a 6–5 Christian–Muslim representation in seats.

9. See Hudson, *The Precarious Republic*, for more details.

a census was never taken, so Muslims were increasingly distant from the seats of power despite their rising numbers. Muslim groups—in particular those representing the more marginalized and economically disadvantaged Shi'a populations—demanded fair representation in government. Maronite power brokers repeatedly rejected this demand and sought the intervention and aid of Western countries and of the region's colonial power, Israel, to protect their interests and privileges. Muslim leaders increasingly relied on the Palestine Liberation Organization (PLO) to redress the sociopolitical balance. These tensions came to a head in 1975, and outright war unfolded rapidly from there.

Our narration of the story to this point offers in broad strokes some paths to understanding some of the major factors leading to fifteen years of war in Lebanon (1975–90). We cannot narrate a story of the war that explains the intricacies and details of the battles, massacres, and other events that make a war or a series of wars, like this one. The dizzying list of names, dates, parties, and events can tell a certain story but also prevents other stories from being told. A much less detailed summary might include the following: The war is usually understood to have begun in 1975. A year later, the Syrian army entered Lebanon to prevent the total collapse of the right-wing groups, the so-called Christian coalition, which was overwhelmed by a leftist PLO-led coalition proposing a secular-democratic strategy to reform the Lebanese system of governance. The Syrian army did not leave until long after the fighting was done, becoming a long-term dominant occupying force in the country. The war continued through the Israeli invasion in 1982 and began to wind down to a finish in 1989 with the Ta'if Accord, although it took several years for the fighting to stop completely.

How might we even choose which of the terrible events to mention and outline here? Even if we were to highlight only those discussed directly in the book's chapters, the list is still dizzying. What is mentioned and what is left out—as we discussed earlier—also speak to conscious and unconscious ways of working through war's trauma. The chapter by Malek Abisaab in this volume makes frequent reference to the massacre at Tal al-Za'tar in 1976, among other events. Several chapters in the volume—those by Abisaab, Michelle Hartman, Yasmine Nachabe Taan, and

Nova Robinson—deal directly with the Israeli invasion of 1982 and the accompanying Sabra and Shatila massacre, which is one of the better-documented atrocities of the war. The long Mountain War (1982–90) and the War of the Camps (1984–90) overlap and contain many smaller events that had much larger impacts. Though most of the chapters in this volume do not focus on the period after 1989, some of the most bitter fighting occurred at the end of the war after the Ta'if Accord was signed—the Ja'Ja'-Aoun War (1989–90), for example.

This short account gives some information about the Lebanese Civil War and tells some kind of story. But as in other writing about this devastating and long-lasting war, in this account we do not see the stories of women—women's experiences, women's roles, women fighting, women protesting, women working, women raising families, women creating and making art. We hope this collection adds to the better story of the Lebanese Civil War by focusing on just two neglected areas and the many intersections and overlaps between them—women working and women creating art.

Women's Work and Creative Production

With these considerations in mind, we present a diverse and varied series of essays that cohere around the principles and ideas we discussed earlier in this introduction. Our individual work on oral histories (Malek Abisaab) and literary expressions (Michelle Hartman) of the Lebanese Civil War came together as we met and talked to a wide range of scholars and activists involved in thinking and writing about the war, particularly in relation to women. While we were connecting to politically active women, militants, and fighters, among others, we met and spoke to so many people exploring and investigating the multifaceted lives, experiences, and creative production of women during the war. This led us to decide to put together this volume of essays that explore some facets of life around common themes.

As we put together this collection, two themes emerged as central, which we reflect in the subtitle, *The Lebanese Civil War, Women's Labor, and the Creative Arts*. All of the essays collected here touch on these themes in different and overlapping—at times intersecting—ways. One of our aims in focusing on these themes is to put an emphasis on labor and work—the work of being a woman in war, the paid work that allows for one's own or one's family and loved ones' survival, and the creative labor that itself is also work, whether paid or unpaid. We are not trying to tell one single story or advance one unified view of this labor, work, or creative production and certainly not of women's lives in the Lebanese Civil War. What this collection does instead, we hope, is to put women and women's work at the center of a story about this war. In this sense, we are writing a different kind of study and a different kind of history of the war. By focusing not only on work but also on creative production—fiction, film, the fine arts, performance art, art therapy—we are also showing the latter's importance through these essays.

Our focus on art and creative production derives in part from what we identify as the necessity of turning to art as a way to tell, express, and access stories. That great art is often produced in times of war and strife is a truism—more standard forms of language and expression do not always suffice to articulate the experiences, concepts, and ideas developed in conditions of war and violence. This connection has been recognized in the context of the Lebanese Civil War—in relation to the fictional works produced, for example. Literature, poetry, sculpture, the plastic arts, performance art, and so on are able to communicate in ways that other forms of documentation cannot. We identify the value of art as creative production and labor in the Civil War as part of our own feminist practice of telling women's war stories.

Unfortunately, it is outside the scope of our study to provide a thorough art historical frame for this book, which would allow it to tell yet another kind of story. The complexities of artistic practice and production within the period of the war and in relation to contemporary artwork outside of the few pieces discussed in this study would have provided a deeper understanding of formal, artistic, and other contextual features of the work discussed. Each chapter dealing with a different kind of art practice does contextualize that art in its own way, but this book does not provide a narrative history of art and/or creative practice in Lebanon. The discussion of artworks of different types and genres here does, however, always link back to our overall framing and method of exploring art in relation to stories and histories. Each chapter engages these questions slightly differently.

The collection opens with coeditor Malek Abisaab's contribution, "In Times of War: Tobacco Workingwomen's Experiences and Life Struggles." Much like his other contributions to the larger project, this chapter is an oral history of women tobacco workers in South Lebanon and Beirut during the Civil War. Complementing his earlier book on the subject, *Militant Women of a Fragile Nation* (2010), this chapter focuses on how women lived through the Civil War specifically. Abisaab's chapter stands out from the others in its use of the methods of oral history. As an oral historian, he draws upon his interviews of eighteen women to craft an analysis focused on the work done by women and how it is connected to their struggles during the war. This chapter is crucial to setting the stage for those that follow not only in its in-depth concentration on the specificities of these women's lives and work but also as a way to introduce how women's stories can be retold and rethought as histories. This chapter reclaims women's stories and histories to piece together elements that have been ignored, excluded, and erased in relation to the Lebanese Civil War. We consciously positioned this chapter first in the volume because it underlines how the volume probes the question of what history is and can be as well as the role of lived experience and stories about it in reshaping narratives of what counts.

This piece is followed by a second labor-orientated chapter, "The Labor of Women's Resistance: Image, Narrative, Alternative Futures" by Mary Jirmanus Saba. A filmmaker as well as a scholar, Jirmanus Saba thinks through the formulation "the most beautiful of mothers" as a way for film to depict and think about women. In her critique of the film with this title directed by Maroun Baghdadi (1978), she investigates the harm that fixed and static ideas about women do on the ground. She then juxtaposes it with the film *Wildflowers* (1986) by Jean Chamoun and Mai Masri to show feminist filmmaking as a counternarrative rooted in the labor of resistance. Tying work and labor to creative production offers new ways to think about women's political activity in wartime.

Next, Nova Robinson's chapter, "'I Was Beirut': Seta Manoukian and Art as Therapy during and after the Lebanese Civil War," picks up on similar themes of linking work and art. Robinson offers a deep analysis of the art that Seta Manoukian produced during and about the Lebanese Civil War in connection to her work as an art therapist treating children affected by its violence. An oral historian, Robinson links her interviews with Manoukian to readings and analyses of Manoukian's artwork.

The next two pieces then shift the book's focus to the production of art in a more direct way. The artist and art scholar Yasmine Nachabe Taan's chapter, "Disaster Seen by Three Female Contemporary Lebanese Artists," focuses on the fine arts, including sculpture. Like Abisaab and Robinson, Taan uses interviews she conducted with the three artists she analyzes in her chapter to build her argument. This contribution to the volume focuses on expressions of war as "disaster" and how three very different kinds of creative fine artists—Tagreed Dargouth, Samar Mogharbel, and Ginane Makki Bacho—work with this concept in their artistic production.

Zéna Meskaoui's essay "Warring Body: Art and Life in Lina Majdalanie's *Appendice*" is a close reading of a challenging performance-art piece. Meskaoui trains our attention on the ways in which Majdalanie confronts our ideas about women and women's rights in Lebanon in her performance of *Appendice*, a piece designed to provoke its audience. How a woman's physical body is affected by war and violence is a centerpiece in this show, and Meskaoui teases out the metaphorical and literal meanings of the "warring body" at its core.

We close the collection with the essay by volume coeditor Michelle Hartman, "Truth, Fiction, and Leaving the Page Blank: Women and the Sabra and Shatila Massacre." Mentioned earlier in relation to the ethics of storytelling—what should and what should not be passed on regarding times of trauma—this chapter focuses on an analysis of how four novels by Arab women narrate the Sabra and Shatila massacre of 1982. As in the history of the Lebanese Civil War, women's fiction that depicts this massacre is rarely discussed or studied. This essay highlights specifically how the four novels—Radwa Ashour's *The Woman from Tantoura*, Susan Abulhawa's *Mornings in Jenin*, Jana Elhassan's *The 99th Floor*, and Adania Shibli's *Touch*—express how women and children experienced the massacre.

This final piece locates and questions the subtle lines between fact and fiction, literature and history, especially in the telling of women's war stories. It draws upon Toni Morrison's now famous statement about what she felt these lines are: "Therefore the crucial distinction for me is not the distinction between fact and fiction, but the distinction between fact and truth."[10] What we hope to offer in our collection of essays about women and the Lebanese Civil War is glimpses of this truth. Although we do offer "facts" and "documentation" of the ways in which this war affected women and how they reacted by means of their labor, work, creative production, and daily life, these things are not our focus. All of the chapters here document stories and tell their own stories. We hope that some of these stories are the "better story" of the Lebanese Civil War and might become someday the basis upon which to build not only better stories but also a better world.

10. Morrison, *What Moves at the Margin*, 72.

1

In Times of War

Tobacco Workingwomen's Experiences and Life Struggles

MALEK ABISAAB

When the Lebanese Civil War broke out in 1975, women workers constituted no less than 40 percent of the labor force in various branches of the country's tobacco industry, the Régie co-intéressée libanaise des tabacs et tombacs, widely known as the Régie.[1] By that time, Israeli assaults on southern towns had already resulted in a fragile security and livelihood for thousands. The Israeli occupation of South Lebanon from 1978 to 2000, in turn, brought a greater radicalization of the youth, many of whom joined leftist and nationalist parties as well as the Palestinian resistance movement. New waves of migration from the countryside to Beirut followed. Experiences of displacement and impoverishment among the rural migrants living in Beirut's suburbs in turn encouraged labor militancy, unionism, and communist opposition to the state.

Some of the same socioeconomic grievances and deep political divisions that contributed to the outbreak of the war absorbed the tobacco women workers during the 1960s and the 1970s. As the war grew worse, they faced great challenges, ranging from staying alive and ensuring the

1. The percentage of female workers in the population of Régie workers changed from 43 percent in 1969 to 41 percent in 1981 and 42 percent in 1987 (Abisaab, *Militant Women*, 29).

safety of their families to overcoming hunger and displacement during work stoppages for male members of their families. The loss of salary for many families was the result of injury or the impossibility of reaching the workplace due to warfare, the threat of death and kidnapping, and the closing down of plants and stores, some of which were demolished. Communal rural-based circles and urban social arenas provided vital services for the lower classes in the absence of state-sponsored programs. Within these circles and arenas, family, in addition to civil and sectarian organizations, played a crucial role. Working-class families suffered from inflation and consequent devaluation of the Lebanese currency, and the only way they could cope during periods of crisis was to rely on food rations and relief packages from international organizations such as Caritas Internationalis, Red Cross, and Red Crescent as well as from local political parties, charitable organizations, and Arab countries. Several religious organizations, sectarian associations, and political parties administered the distribution of food and medical packages to families living in war zones. Families received flour, dates, canned meats, raisins, oil, and powdered milk. In this context, the agency of the Régie's workingwomen and the range of activities and positions they took to deal with the war illustrate how their class situation and religious-sectarian affiliation worked both with and against each other in various contexts. The women's relationship to their families and their roles and powers also underwent a further shift during the war.

In this chapter, I shed light on workingwomen's experiences during the Civil War and their daily struggles to survive, preserve their source of livelihood, overcome the ravages of migration and displacement, and maintain the safety and development of their families, all while navigating new expressions of patriarchy and, more frequently, resorting to religious- and family-based networks of support. Workingwomen's experiences are conveyed here through their own words, which give us a unique perspective on their agency at a time when the state broke down and local political organizations took over the social and economic organization of daily life. Gendered adaptations to, shaping of, survival of, and understanding of wars have rarely made their way into national accounts of Lebanese history of the nineteenth and twentieth centuries. Men's public and formal activities are relatively well documented, but it is rarely understood how wars evoke or authorize ways of being a woman, especially within the domestic unit and at the workplace; what modes of survival and productivity women adopt during crisis; and what ways they reorganize priorities and assign value to everyday activities. We need to understand the ways in which the female subject conforms, partially subverts, or resists power generated by the cultural and economic institutions that are responsible for igniting wars and that justify various types and levels of violence. A close look at women's roles in sustaining or disrupting war and at their survival strategies also gives us rare insight into nonnormative facets of Lebanese society.

I focus attention on eight tobacco women workers from the two major plants of the Régie in Hadath and Ghaziyya. The largest and most diversified was the Hadath plant, located at the heart of a major war zone that divided Beirut into two areas: the East, inhabited mostly by Christians from various denominations, and the West, predominantly Muslim. The Ghaziyya branch was located in a rural area to the east of Saida and was surrounded by a number of villages that witnessed heavy fighting during the Israeli occupation and throughout the Civil War. Through the voices of the Lebanese workingwomen at those two geographically and religiously diverse plants, we encounter unique and complex narratives about the way war shaped their lives and how relations between class and patriarchy unfolded. Their stories, moreover, destabilize male-dominated narratives about the connections or disconnections between patriarchy and class during the Lebanese Civil War.

Collecting Data: Oral History

Oral history can help fill in the gaps of what we do not know about the experiences of Lebanese women during the Civil War, especially given the absence of statistical records and quantitative data. The ever-changing social and political environment of the subjects in question and the effect of these changes on memory produce limitations for the oral historian, of course. The significance of a particular event or experience changes over time alongside the perceptions, values, attitudes, and perspectives held by the subject. Indeed, thinking of the past from the prism of the future is a challenge for writing an historical account based on oral histories. Moreover, a subject's willingness to narrate her own story may be limited. To overcome these obstacles, I asked several questions on the same topic in very different ways and in connection to other distinct topics to try to obtain more spontaneous and less calculated responses. An advantage of the passing of time is that more tobacco workingwomen were for various reasons willing to be interviewed and to revisit their experiences; by 1997, the trauma of the war had begun to seem more remote.

I first distributed a questionnaire to determine who, among the female and male Régie workers, had a story about the Civil War and was ready to tell it.[2] Second, I aimed to interview a representative number of workers—about one-sixth of the total workforce of the Régie (1,681 in 1997). The Régie did not have an elaborate census for the year 1997, so I used the census of 1995: "Listing du personnel par matricule, 1 Octobre, 1995." This census provided several variables and categories, the most important of which was the sectarian representation of the total workforce. The Régie censuses, however, did not record the demographic dislocations or forced eviction of workers from their pre–Civil War residences. As a consequence, strategies of survival for women workers could not be discerned through the census. It did offer another important variable, though: notations of seniority, which helped in selecting senior female workers who had long work and life experiences at the Régie and had witnessed or even participated in the Civil War. With the help of Mr. Hayik, a key manager in the Personnel Department, I selected 356 workers listed in the census, who later agreed to participate voluntarily in the research project and answer the questions. I conducted unstructured interviews with 77 of these 356 workers. Of the 77, 19.4 percent were male, and 80.3 percent were female, with 0.3 percent unaccounted for. This was a fair representation of the workforce in 1997, especially in the productive departments, such as the Leaf and Factory Departments, where most workers were female. The selection process also addressed the sectarian composition of

2. I thank Ms. Layla al-Khalil and Ms. Sana' 'Awadah for assisting me in filling out the questionnaires.

the tobacco workforce. The respondents to the questionnaire broke down as follows: 49.4 percent Muslim Shi'a; 24.7 percent Christian Maronite; 11.2 percent Muslim Sunni; 6.7 percent Christian Orthodox; 6.2 percent Christian Catholic; 0.3 percent Muslim Druze; 0.8 percent Armenian; 0.3 percent Syriac; and 0.35 percent unaccounted for.

Before proceeding, I met with the interviewees individually for two hours on average to explain the purpose of my research, ask them to fill out the questionnaire, and explain the signing of the consent form. Most of the interviewees, especially the women, were illiterate, so I asked the questions orally and recorded their answers on tape, then wrote my reflections on them. It is important to note that not all the Régie branches were suitable for conducting fieldwork. The Hadath and Ghaziyya branches were ideal, however, mainly due to their location within the war zones and the concentration of the workforce in them. I also prepared an alternative list of workers, also chosen randomly, in case the earlier ones chosen were absent, sick, or unwilling to continue participating in the study. It was also important to obtain data on the year the workers were hired to assess one of the central aims of the study: the impact of the Civil War on women's lives and on their productivity both at the Régie and outside of it. I targeted the Leaf, Factory, and the Sanitary Departments because they have the lowest-ranking unskilled workers and, as such, the most vulnerable in terms of security and salary during the war.

Workingwomen at the Hadath and Ghaziyya Plants

During the presidency of Fuad Shihab (1958–64), the Régie had seven branches across the country: Hadath in Beirut; Bikfayya and Khinshara in Mount Lebanon; Tripoli and Batrun in North Lebanon; and Nabatiyya and Ghaziyya in the South. The Hadath plant was the central one and the largest because it held the full production line: sorting, preparing, manufacturing, packaging, and storing tobacco. It also had the largest percentage of the Régie's labor force. It exhibited a highly mixed and heterogeneous sectarian composition of both female and male laborers before the war. During the war, women tobacco workers at the Hadath plant experienced critical challenges, such as work disruptions, dislocation from their homes, tensions and instability at the workplace, salary fluctuation, and safety, especially during the commute between home and work. In addition, numerous Muslim women could no longer stay employed at the Hadath plant, and Shi'a Régie workers were forced to leave their residence in the Fanar, a neighborhood in East Beirut's poverty belt, and move to western Beirut.[3]

At the Ghaziyya and Nabatiyya plants in the South, the majority of the workers were Shi'a women.[4] The Ghaziyya plant, founded in 1964, has been a major station in South Lebanon for sorting the Régie's raw tobacco harvest. After the Israeli invasion of Lebanon in 1982, villages and towns surrounding the Ghaziyya Régie branch became the battleground on which various Lebanese combatants fought each other, and in 1985 militias, in particular the Shi'a military group Afwaj al Muqawama al Lubnaniyya (AMAL, Lebanese Resistance Regiments), launched a war against Palestinian camps in the South. As a consequence, it became arduous and perilous for Christians in general and for the Régie laborers in particular to continue living and working there. They left their homes, moved to eastern Beirut, and joined the Hadath plant.

During the first phase of the war (1975–82) the production of tobacco in Hadath fluctuated depending on the intensity of the military confrontations between, on the one hand, the Phalanges, a right-wing, largely Christian, militia group and its supporters, stationed in the town of Hadath itself, and, on the other, the leftist militia groups allied to the Palestine Liberation Organization (PLO), based in Beirut's southern suburbs and at Choueifat in Mount Lebanon. Work at the Hadath plant stopped intermittently until October 1976, when the Syrian army entered Lebanon with the declared aim of helping end the war. Tobacco production resumed steadily for a while after that but stopped again in 1977 due to military confrontations between the Syrian army and right-wing militias.

3. Lebanese Christian Maronites formed 85 percent of East Beirut's overall population of 125,000 between 1976 and 1978. See Khalifa, *Al-Shi'a fi Lubnan*, 67–71.

4. For more information on the history of the Régie, see Abisaab, *Militant Women*.

During the Civil War, the Régie accumulated a debt of around US$200 million, owed mostly to Franca Bank.[5] Production and revenues continued to dwindle until 1985, when the Régie's debts threatened to end its monopoly altogether, putting the income of thousands of workers at risk.[6] To avert the crisis, the administration came up with a plan in early 1985 to compete with smugglers, pay off the debt, and maintain the salaries of the workers and employees. However, to sort out the raw tobacco and operate the machines at the factory, the new plan needed workers, but their number had decreased rapidly due to the war. Christian workers were prevented from crossing into Muslim territories and vice versa.[7] The Régie building complex at the time of the war, as the secretary-general of the Régie, George Hobeika, described it, resembled a military fortress, and workers felt that they were coming "not to work but to a battle ground."[8]

The Régie decided to pay the Christian workers, who were not as at risk as their Muslim counterparts, a bonus in addition to their salaries in order to encourage them to continue to come to work. The workingwomen and men were, however, to undertake this extra risk by commuting on dangerous roads, thus exposing themselves to injury, kidnapping, and even death. Meanwhile, Régie workers who could not come to work continued

5. George Hobeika, interviewed by Malek Abisaab, Feb. 18, 1997, Hadath, Lebanon; all translations are mine. Mr. Hobeika claims that the Régie lost its control over the tobacco market and remained a monopoly only on paper.

6. The total number of the Régie labor force in 1981 was 2,974, out of which 41 percent were female workers. In 1987, the number of workers went down to 2,608, 42 percent of which were female. See "Listing du personnel par matricule, 1 Octobre 1981," and "Liste des rubriques de paie, 13-12-1987," Régie Company Records, Hadath.

7. Hobeika confirms that before hiring new workers, he consulted with the steward of the Union of the Régie Workers and Employees, Kamil Hijazi, to see if he were in favor of sending buses that would be protected by the Lebanese Forces, who were in control of Hadath, to safely transport Muslim workers willing to come to Hadath to work. Hijazi, according to Hobeika, did not support the proposed plan because he feared the transportation facilities and the life of workers could be jeopardized when clashes broke out between West Beirut and East Beirut.

8. Hobeika, interview. Hobeika asserted that the militiamen that controlled Hadath also had a military position on the Régie premises.

to receive their salaries without any change, as the Régie administration had promised they would. The supplementary bonus offered by the Régie was based on piecework, meaning the more cigarettes a worker produced, the more money that worker received. The working hours were also flexible; workers could come at any time of the day and work an indefinite number of hours to produce the desired amount of cigarettes per day.[9] Most importantly, to avoid legal problems between those temporary workers and the Régie, the company resorted to the *al-iltizam* system, which meant that the new hires would not be given the benefits extended to permanent workers.[10] The company was thus able to achieve a considerable increase in production—making fifteen thousand boxes of cigarettes per month, which seems to have met the growing demands of both the Lebanese market and the newly accessible Syrian and Jordanian markets.[11]

Most of the workingwomen I interviewed were major contributors to their families' income. Around 51 percent were married, 25 percent single, 4 percent divorced, and 20 percent widows (see table 1.1).

9. Lebanese cigarettes had gained access to the Syrian market, which was able to absorb no less than twenty thousand boxes of cigarettes (each box containing fifty cartons) per month—thus the need for additional hands at the Régie plants. Hobeika asserted that the new plan allowed the Régie to sell American cigarettes along with the new Lebanese brand of cigarette, Cedars. The advantage of this policy, according to Hobeika, was to curtail the smuggling of American cigarettes during the war, which constituted a strong challenge to the Régie monopoly of cigarettes in Lebanon, and it eventually helped the Régie regain its authority.

10. The *iltizam* system is based on giving the work to a *muta'ahhid* (contractor), who would hire workers to do the job, meaning that there would be no direct relationship between the workers and the administration of the Régie. At the time, through the *iltizam* system the Régie hired five hundred female laborers only for sorting out raw tobacco. A few became permanent workers after the war.

11. Hobeika, interview. When I asked Hobeika whether the plant encountered any problem with the Israeli occupying army, he replied: "When the Israelis came, they did not like the Cedars cigarette; they did not take any Lebanese [tobacco] products because they considered such an act not to be good for them [i.e., not good for their reputation]. They look at us as inferior, this is real; . . . we are a backward country, and they think of themselves as better than the Americans, and we were proving to them that we were mediocre."

Table 1.1
Marital Status of Régie Women Workers, 1997

	Frequency	*Percentage*
Married	147	51
Single	70	25
Divorced	12	4
Widowed	57	20
Total	286	100

Survey of 286 Régie women workers conducted in 1997. Figures are rounded to the nearest whole number.

Both married and widowed women played a significant role in sustaining their families during the Civil War (see table 1.2), owing to men's loss of work in war zones, new economic burdens caused by displacement, and/or the loosening of patriarchal constraints on women's movement and salaried labor in wartime. The contribution by single women was no less important and seems to have increased when male breadwinners lost their jobs or lives. In fact, only 13 percent of the respondents' husbands had a steady job during the war, and 24 percent of the spouses did not work at all. In 1 percent of the cases, the husband had retired, and in 12 percent the husband had died. Around 1 percent of the respondents were divorced. Fourteen percent of the respondents' husbands worked in unstable and temporary jobs, which meant the wages earned by mothers, sisters, and daughters who worked at the Régie were necessary for the survival of the whole family.[12]

12. For independent professional workers, the survey I conducted in 1997 reported the following categories: farmers; school bus drivers; public bus drivers; taxi drivers; landscapers; bakers; farm dealers; shopkeepers; teachers; sandwich makers; chauffeurs; truck drivers; vegetable peddlers; fishermen; car mechanics; technicians; welders; construction workers and painters; ice cream peddlers; stone cutters; locksmiths; realtors; contractors; furniture makers; household-item cleaners; tailors; shoe menders; tractor drivers; car dealers; shop owners; livestock dealers; accountants; carpenters; barbers; hospital workers; TV technicians; tourism workers; rentiers; horse racers. As for employees,

Table 1.2
Job Status of Régie Women Workers' Spouses during the Lebanese Civil War, 1975–90

	Frequency	*Percentage*
Worked during the war	37	13.0
Did not work during the war	69	24.0
Retired	4	1.0
Died	33	12.0
Not married	97	34.0
Divorced	4	1.0
Independent professional work	41	14.0
Temporary job	1	0.3
Total	286	100.0

Survey of 286 Régie women workers conducted in 1997. Figures are rounded to the nearest whole number.

Workingwomen dealing with the ravages of war found themselves at times shifting between accommodating certain forms of male protection and control and effectively negotiating other forms. The example of Fatima A. is illuminating in this respect. From a rural Shi'a family, she joined the Régie in 1958. She was living in Laylaki, a southern suburb of Beirut, when the war broke out. She was thus forced to leave Beirut and return to her rural hometown, 'Almat Jubayl in Mount Lebanon, with her husband and their nine children. Her husband was a carpenter, suffered from heart disease and diabetes, and eventually went blind. He stopped work and could not contribute to household chores or even basic childcare. Fatima then started a home-based bakery and tilled the land around

the survey noted the following categories: army personnel; public employees; municipality workers; Régie workers; state telephone company workers; factory workers; seaport company employees; tire company workers; airport employees; police; security workers; bank clerks; printing-press workers; state water company workers; postmen; American University of Beirut workers; pharmaceutical company workers; customs officers; municipality police.

her house to grow vegetables for the family to eat. Under these conditions, the children shared the burden of the crisis with their mother—all of them stopped going to school and started to work on the land and at the bakery to make ends meet. Meanwhile, their urban residence in Laylaki was looted and destroyed, which forced the family to permanently relocate to 'Almat.[13] Fatima became the main decision maker in the family and throughout this period relied on several of her male children to take up the domestic tasks she used to carry out. It took long, labor-intense years for her to achieve the security she and her children needed.

Other women at the Régie started to work in small trade despite the competition from experienced businessmen, the collapse of the state, and obstacles to implementing commercial transactions and contract laws protecting business partners' legal rights. The experiences of Georgette H., who started work at the Régie when she was fourteen, shed light on this type of situation. Born in 1934 to a Maronite Christian family from Jezzine in South Lebanon, she married a municipal worker at the age of twenty-three and had three children. They lived in a small, rented apartment in Achrafieh in East Beirut until 1978, when they were forced to flee their bombarded apartment and move to Jounieh on the northern coast during one of the military confrontations between the Syrian army and the Lebanese Forces.[14] She kept going to work at the Régie's Hadath plant intermittently despite the danger both near the factory itself and on the journey between home and work. Georgette's family managed to survive on her salary alone for a while. But when their economic hardships increased, she decided to start a small business in Jounieh.

Georgette borrowed some money from the church in her neighborhood and opened a café overlooking the Mediterranean Sea. Her husband, sister, and brother-in-law helped her expand the café, and she began selling sandwiches and salads. Meanwhile, she faced social pressure from her coreligionists, especially the older residents of the city, who treated

13. Fatima A., interviewed by Malek Abisaab, Feb. 18, 1997, Hadath.

14. This is the Hundred Days War between the Syrian army and the Lebanese Forces, which started on July 1, 1978. The Syrian army used a policy of heavy bombardment of the eastern part of Beirut, especially Achrafieh, to pressure the Lebanese Forces to surrender.

her at first as a stranger (*ghariba*) because she was a *muhajjara* (displaced woman) who was competing with them economically and thus placing more pressure on the fragile economy. The way they labeled her an outsider, she felt early on, would kill her small enterprise in the long run. She did not give up, however. She was quick to reduce the prices of everything she was selling to attract and keep her clientele. She endured social marginalization and tough competition for four years. Her strategy, which was to ignore the residents' discriminatory attitudes and to offer great service and low prices for the city's families, paid off.[15] Georgette and her family lived off this business until the end of the Civil War.

Workingwomen's Strategies: Patriarchal Constraints and the Ravages of War

The tobacco workingwomen, whose narratives I am working with here, talked about the types of personal and social freedoms they embraced when they started working at the urban Régie plants, away from their families' homes. They often mentioned how they navigated patriarchal constraints. Georgette B., for example, believed that the job at the Régie allowed her earn to money, which in turn helped her feel independent: "Instead of asking my husband to give me money to buy things, now I can buy everything I want."[16] Fadwa A. escaped from working at her parents farm and joined the Régie labor force "because it is easier than working in the field."[17] For Tamam A., working at the Régie allowed her to become free and to assert herself because "women could also take up jobs other than [the ones] in the kitchen." "It helped me," she continued, "become more conscious with respect to the role of women in society and that I have the courage to stand up and perform two jobs: at home and outside of it."[18] Working at the Régie transformed Khadigeh S. fundamentally. She joined the Tripoli branch of the tobacco monopoly as a worker after she completed secondary school. The job then allowed her to earn a bachelor's

15. Georgette H., interviewed by Malek Abisaab, Mar. 21, 1997, Hadath.
16. Georgette B., interviewed by Malek Abisaab, Feb. 11, 1997, Hadath.
17. Fadwa A., interviewed by Malek Abisaab, Feb. 10, 1997, Hadath.
18. Tamam A., interviewed by Malek Abisaab, Jan. 28, 1997, Hadath.

degree in Arabic literature, which in turned helped her be promoted to the head of the Personnel Department at the Régie.[19]

The Civil War also undermined the expectations of many workingwomen in Lebanon, though—because of both their increasing financial burdens and their closer proximity to their family members, especially when they returned from the capital city to their rural hometowns. To be sure, several families of these tobacco workingwomen underwent urban–rural migration to find safety away from war zones. In other words, whereas the economic changes of the 1950s and the 1960s had brought an influx of rural immigrants into the city of Beirut and other urban centers, the war led to a reverse migration process at times. This reversal brought workingwomen in closer proximity to communal sect-based and family-based relations that frequently accentuated male authority. Notwithstanding this situation, workingwomen manifested their agency in many ways as they tried to minimize the ravages of the war, the loss or interruption of work, and worries about personal security, displacement, and social instability.

Fatima and Georgette, discussed further later in this chapter, in particular demonstrate how workingwomen devised new strategies for seeking supplementary sources of income, drawing upon the assistance of their families, including their children, to make ends meet, although the degradations of war forced all of them to work longer hours in mixed domestic and subsidiary waged work. The women I spoke to were also able to achieve a few important practical aims, such as asserting greater control over domestic labor and shifting gendered boundaries. Male relatives, spouses, and sons were forced to take up tasks that women had typically done so that the women could generate income from waged work. The workingwomen also stabilized their life patterns, creating homes for themselves and their children wherever they were displaced to. They thus became key decision makers.

The intensification of the Civil War and the Régie's reliance on temporary workers for a steady production of cigarettes created strenuous conditions for workingwomen. Those who worked at plants close to or in the

19. Khadigeh S., interviewed by Malek Abisaab, Mar. 5, 1997, Tripoli, Lebanon.

middle of the war zones experienced uncertainty not merely in terms of long-term planning but also in terms of being reassured that they would keep getting paid during the days and sometimes months when they could not cross into the war zone to work. The fear of losing their jobs was at times as serious as their fear of getting wounded or killed, which pushed a few of them to cross into the war zone once in a while.

Political Affiliation and Attitudes about the War

A slight minority of tobacco workingwomen expressed a clear identification with one or another of the political parties engaged in the Civil War (see table 1.3). These women in interviews tended to defend their parties' political outlook and the military activities of their representative warring group(s). Around 80 percent of the workingwomen surveyed for this study, however, noted that they did not have any political affiliation. The three main Christian political groups in Lebanon—the Phalanges, the Lebanese Forces, and General Michel Aoun's followers—did not have a substantial representation among the Christian workingwomen of the Régie. The same can be said about Muslim groups' representation among Shi'a workingwomen, who did not express a political involvement in the two most influential Muslim parties, AMAL and Hizbullah.

These results can be interpreted in various ways. First, the workingwomen may have perceived the notion of "political affiliation" to mean a long-term commitment or actual membership in one of the main warring political parties in Lebanon. Many of the workingwomen did not consider themselves active in this sense. Second, the bylaws of the Régie, which is a governmental institution, prohibited workers and employees from joining political parties, and thus the workingwomen I surveyed may have been apprehensive about disclosing such affiliations in questionnaires and interviews. Third, in the case of the Christian workingwomen, the figure may reflect also a mood of *ihbat* (disappointment), apathy, and withdrawal from politics, which characterized the phase succeeding the promulgation of the Ta'if Accord in 1989 near the end of war. Under this agreement, Maronite Christian leaders lost some of their prerogatives and the overall political power they had enjoyed under the prewar government. People tended to blame this decline in power on internal Christian–Christian

Table 1.3
Political Affiliation of Female Tobacco Workers, 1997

	Frequency	*Percentage*
Phalangist Party	5	2
Ahrar	3	1
AMAL	12	2
Hizbullah	19	7
Nasserite	1	0
Syrian Social National Party	7	2
Kamil As'ad	2	1
Tayyar	2	1
Rashid Karame	2	1
Michel Murr	1	0
Albert Mkhayber	1	0
Rafic al-Hariri	2	1
No affiliation	229	80
Total	286	100

Survey of 286 Régie women workers conducted in 1997. Figures are rounded to the nearest whole number.

factionalism (such as between the Lebanese Forces and the brigades of the Lebanese army loyal to General Michel Aoun in 1990).

Only a small group of Shi'a workingwomen in the survey associated themselves with Hizbullah, possibly because the latter was new on the scene in the late 1980s, having been founded in 1985. During that period, Hizbullah was perceived in part as an extremist Islamist group supported by Iran. The older and more established party, AMAL, was engaged in several military struggles: against the Palestinian camps and against Hizbullah. Over the years, AMAL lost much of its moral standing due to accusations of corruption and its only lukewarm defense of the South against Israeli occupation.[20] Following the military skirmishes between AMAL

20. As Hizbullah established its grassroots movement in South Lebanon and in the southern suburb of Beirut, it, in collaboration with various nationalist and leftist groups,

and Hizbullah, the latter emerged as the stronger party, and a new alignment between the sectarian interests of Shi'a leaders and political ideology was formed. After the assassination of Prime Minister Rafic al-Hariri in 2005, the two parties formed an alliance in defense of the *muqawama* (armed resistance) against Israeli occupation and international threats.[21] Nonetheless, there is no reason to believe that some of the Shi'a workingwomen did not sympathize and even identify with AMAL during this period, given its weight and strong involvement in the Civil War.

Even if many workingwomen had no formal political affiliation with any group—or did not wish to disclose any affiliations they might have had—they nonetheless expressed a wide range of political attitudes and preferences. Workingwoman In'am A., for one, noted that she closely followed political developments and incidents in the country but that she did not support any of the existing political parties. She also expressed something contradictory when she noted her prewar allegiance to the right-wing politician Dori Chamoun and how she kept supporting him even after the war.[22] Another woman worker, Therèse H., who had been elected to the executive board of Syndicat des employés et ouvriers de la Régie libanaise des tabacs et tombacs (Union of the Régie Workers and Employees) in 1995, had a disappointing political experience. In 1960, she joined a right-wing organization, the National Liberal Party, but her initial political enthusiasm started to diminish after the war mainly owing to the spread of sectarianism. During the war, Therèse's single political activity was to assist the Women's Committee of that party in founding a health clinic to help civilians and treat fighters injured during the war with the Palestinian refugee camp Tal al-Za'tar in 1976.[23] Therèse said that

---

gradually liberated the South from Israeli occupation. The occupation, one should note, was a detrimental economic force in the lives of Shi'a workingwomen and men. Hizbullah also gradually established a network of medical, educational, and socioeconomic services to help the Shi'a poor. For more on the conflict between AMAL and Hizbullah, see Abisaab and Abisaab, *The Shi'ites of Lebanon*, 130–31, 139–40.

21. Abisaab and Abisaab, *The Shi'ites of Lebanon*, 178–79.

22. In'am A., interviewed by Malek Abisaab, Feb. 20, 1997, Hadath.

23. Therèse H., interviewed by Malek Abisaab, Mar. 3, 1997, Hadath.

she believes that sectarianism came to Lebanon with Egyptian president Gamal Abdel Nasser's rise in popularity among Lebanese. Politics became contentious after the war, she noted, as sectarian polarization took root among the tobacco workers, whose loyalty was to Lebanon and to their own interests as workers before the war. The Régie became, in her view, "tribal," so that if "I cherish [Nabih] Berri [the Shi'a president of the Parliament] or Shams al-Din [the vice president of the Supreme Shi'a Council of Lebanon after the war], then I get the job at the Régie."[24]

Other workingwomen also followed the war's development through daily battles, skirmishes, and military campaigns, which unfolded across different war zones in the country. They consistently read the news or listened to it on the radio and on TV to stay informed about the regional, national, and local developments tied to the Civil War. At times in the interviews, they conveyed their political preferences indirectly when discussing their religious practices. Fatima N. supported the Socialist Democratic Party, a right-wing organization founded and led by Kamel al-As'ad (1932–2010), who intermittently presided over the Parliament between 1964 and 1984. Fatima justified her affiliation to al-As'ad's party by drawing attention to the bad reputation of other parties and organizations (hinting at AMAL), labeling them "thugs and thieves who stole food rations" during the war. Fatima, who regularly prayed and fasted during the war, hoped to perform Hajj when she retired and to wear Islamic dress.[25]

The majority of the workingwomen at the Régie, however, articulated a general aversion to and disillusionment with all Lebanese political parties and factions (see table 1.3). They appeared almost indifferent to questions of political affiliation, as explained earlier. They tended to express quickly their love of their homeland (*watan*), to blame "foreigners" (*al-ghuraba*) for igniting the war, and to reject sectarianism outright. Yet even as they nurtured a strong work ethic on the shop floor and solidarity with other women workers during demonstrations and campaigns

24. Therèse H., interview.

25. Fatima N., interviewed by Malek Abisaab, Feb. 6, 1997, Shayyah, Lebanon.

to raise their salaries and improve their working conditions, sectarian difference was an important feature of their activities, experiences, and performance. The war undoubtedly contributed to sectarian tensions at the workplace, but it was obvious from the interviews I conducted that these workingwomen saw themselves as responsible citizens who to the best of their ability should keep the peace and manage any tensions that might arise. It seems that there was almost a tacit agreement to keep their potentially divisive political views and affiliations outside the Régie plants. Given this norm, the outlook, activities, public assertions of political affiliation, and sectarian awareness of one particular workingwoman, Najla J., deserve a closer look.

Najla was born in Dayr al-Ahmar (Biqaʿ) to a Maronite family in 1931.[26] She did not complete elementary school because, as she put it, "I did not like to study." With her father's encouragement, she joined the Régie in 1950. She insisted that her family of nine was not desperate for her income but that she, like other "girls," wanted "to move to an area different from the one [she was] born in." Najla grew up with a memory of family rivalries and Muslim–Christian struggles unfolding between her townspeople and neighboring Shiʿa families, which turned at times into bloody feuds. Thus, a steady job in Beirut offered her an escape from her more precarious and tumultuous village life. During the Civil War, her town became a battlefield between the Left–PLO coalition and the Lebanese Forces. Scores of people from Dayr al-Ahmar were killed.[27]

Najla was proud of her family and identified with their sectarian politics, noting that Maronites had values and a way of life superior to those of their Muslim neighbors. She described her experience at work as quite pleasant:

26. After changing several jobs and killing a man accidentally, Najla's father finally found a job with the help of a political leader from his family and stayed in that job until his death.

27. Najla J., interviewed by Malek Abisaab, Feb. 6, 1997, Achrafieh, Lebanon; all quotations from Najla and details of her experiences come from this interview. For more on Dayr al-Ahmar, see al-Durar al-Shamiyya, *Nar al-ʿashaʾr tashtaʿil fi Lubnan*.

> I liked my work and my managers from the Sawaya family. The tasks were clear, and the work systematic and well organized. There was no smoking, and no one had perfume on. But when the Régie grew larger, the management started to hire *al-matawila* [a pejorative term referring to Shi'a Muslims] and others from the [Shi'a] Zu'aytir family from Ba'labak, whose demeanor was quite distinct from ours [the Maronites].

Najla became a permanent worker and was promoted in 1958 to operating one of the machines. She described an incident in which she refused to be yelled at by her supervisor, emphasizing to him that she was "not a refugee, not a Palestinian." She demanded his respect as a fellow Lebanese, using Palestinians as a contrast. On the one hand, her attitude underscored her strength and resolve, but on the other she positioned herself as superior to Palestinians and Muslims to do this. She saw herself and the other Christian workingwomen as "clean, nicely dressed, and good looking" in comparison with fellow workers who were Shi'a from Ba'labak and gave this difference in appearance as a reason why the Christian workers received better treatment from the Régie's management. Even though she readily referred to the patronage that some of her family members enjoyed through a prominent parliamentarian, she criticized how the Shi'a workingwomen were hired through the patronage of Sabri Himadeh, who was Speaker of the Parliament intermittently from 1943 until 1970: "Their girls often curse, scream, and we constantly had problems with them." The "Zu'aytir girls were troublemakers," she noted, and she felt that they tried to dominate her and her fellow Christian workingwomen. She did not hesitate, as she noted, to "hit one of them after she cursed at me."

During the 1960s, Najla had opposed the Arab nationalist affiliations of her Muslim coworkers. She denounced Arabism as championed by Gamal Abdel Nasser and described it as disloyalty to the Lebanese nation. She talked about how it had led to deep divisions and struggles among the Régie workers. In one incident, Najla and her supporters tore down a picture of Nasser hanging in the elevator, insisting that they would not accept that a "stranger" rule them. The Régie administration penalized Najla and her comrades by deducting a day's pay from their salaries but also subsequently prohibited the posting of any pictures at the Régie. Najla counted that incident as a victory. The steady increase in Shiʿa workingwomen created new anxieties, which were at times expressed in public confrontations. She recalled an incident in which she exchanged insults with a Shiʿa colleague at the Régie: Fatima "cursing the Christian Cross and [Najla] returning the profanity by cursing Prophet Muhammad." Najla perceived her competition as brutal, which made her and her fellow Christians turn into "wolves." She was not merely commenting on the rapid increase in the number of Muslim workers at the Régie but also describing systematic attempts on the part of managers to prevent the promotion of Christian workingwomen and men.

This account would be incomplete, however, without Najla's significant regulatory comments and interventions in her own narrative. She discussed all the other ways in which she maintained her solidarity with the Shiʿa Muslim workingwomen as well as her leadership role in solving problems and building ties of mutual aid with them. She noted that she "maintained good relations" with her colleagues "no matter what their sectarian identity was" and that she helped even the Shiʿa (*matawila*) without their knowing about it. She had mixed feelings of pity and responsibility when they were treated unfairly. She recalled one illuminating incident:

> We founded a secret saving scheme during the war to help each other, only for the Christian women workers. Each one of us would put in [twenty] Lebanese pounds [around US$6.50] or more if she could afford it. We used the fund to support any one of us who needed hospitalization or was to give birth. Sometimes we sent money to an injured woman or one who had a permanent disability. In one case, a woman had her hand deeply cut. The Shiʿa who worked with us [in the same section] did not come up with these aid plans like us. Yet we were good-hearted and helped some of them even if we did not trust them. The daughter-in-law of Fatima, one of the Shiʿa workingwomen, needed help one time after being hospitalized at Hotel Dieu in Beirut. We could not give her money from our fund, but we collected three hundred Lebanese pounds [around US$98] for her daughter-in-law. Even though I did not like Fatima, I still wanted to help her daughter-in-law. The latter recovered, and Fatima returned the money three years after. All the workers loved

> me. I used to solve problems among them; even the Shi'a used to come to me, complaining about issues and asking me to help settle their problems. But the Shi'a have sectarian biases; the managers sell sectarianism to the workers, which causes disunity. But at some point the workingwomen and workingmen discovered the management's manipulations.

Najla noted insightfully that the management manipulated the workers' sectarian fears and rivalries and did not attempt to reconcile them.

The Civil War did not seem either to accentuate or to diminish the faith or patterns of religious practice among most of the tobacco workingwomen. In this respect, the case of Georgette B. was unique. Born in Rashayya (Biqa') in 1932 to a Christian Greek Catholic family, she believed that the Virgin Mary cured her of a chronic health condition that started during the Civil War.[28] She joined the Régie in 1959 and in 1971 married a grocery-store owner in Verdun, West Beirut. The couple had one son, who was only thirteen days old when the war broke out. They were living close to the war zone in Achrafieh, East Beirut, and had to flee their house several times during clashes between West and East Beirut. Her husband's store was pillaged, so the family started to rely exclusively on her salary to survive. Despite the hazards of commuting between Achrafieh and the Hadath plant, she continued to go to work until the plant was bombarded. Her health deteriorated in 1980, when she experienced severe pains in her legs and arms. She had started crying and praying to the Virgin Mary intensely, fearing that a bomb would hit her son's kindergarten. Then she had a vision, after which she noticed an improvement in moving her limbs. A week later, she was able to walk slowly again.

The majority (71 percent) of women workers expressed their faith openly and practiced it publicly. The Muslims prayed, fasted, and engaged in the activities of their local mosques. The Christians, prayed, fasted, and attended Sunday Mass. Around 26 percent of all the workingwomen were nonpracticing but expressed their belief in God (see table 1.4). Only 1 percent was secular, and another 1 percent, though secular, participated

28. Georgette B., interview.

Table 1.4
Religious Practices of Female Tobacco Workers, 1997

	Frequency	*Percentage*
Observant believers	204	71
Nonobservant believers	75	26
Secular-atheists	2	1
Secularists who participate occasionally in religious social activities	3	1
No answer	2	1
Total	286	100

Survey of 286 Régie women workers conducted in 1997. Figures are rounded to the nearest whole number.

in relgious ceremonies as part of socializing. Another 1 percent did not answer the question.

The prolongation of the Civil War and the resulting erosion of infrastructure and deterioration of the standard of living created episodes of despair among workingwomen and men. The diminishing hope that basic economic and health benefits could ever be enjoyed again in the middle of political violence pushed many of them to seek refuge within religious institutions and those institutions' affiliated social welfare associations.

Tahjeer: Forced Displacement, Human Loss, and the Degradations of War

The war had a long-lasting effect on the lives of numerous female Régie workers and their families. Multiple incidents of dislocation as well as permanent displacement were referred to by the Arabic term *tahjeer*. The displaced *muhajjareen*, or emigrants, faced not only an abrupt deterioration of their standard of living but also an adjustment to the cold and even hostile receptions they experienced. *Tahjeer* thus came with a severe rupture in the normal flow of work and life patterns for women workers who lived in neighborhoods with a mix of religious groups. A change of regions and neighborhoods also meant an interruption in access to educational,

Table 1.5
Displacement of Female Tobacco Workers and Their Families during the Lebanese Civil War, 1975–90

	Frequency	*Percentage*
0 displacements	82	29
1 displacement	81	28
2 displacements	89	31
3 displacements	24	8
4 displacements	6	2
5 displacements	1	0
6 displacements	1	0
7 displacements	2	1
Total	286	100

Survey of 286 Régie women workers conducted in 1997. Figures are rounded to the nearest whole number.

health, and other social facilities. It also led to a change of schools for children or even a discontinuation of schooling, especially if new working hands were needed for the family to make ends meet. The hopes of going back home remained alive for the *muhajjareen*, who thought they were enduring these hardships for a short while until the war ended, and they could return to their villages or towns. Two stark examples of tobacco workers who bore the brunt of such degradations of war are the Régie's Christian workingwomen of Sharq Saida and the Shi'a workingwomen of the Fanar in East Beirut.

More than half of the tobacco workingwomen experienced dislocation during the Civil War, with 31 percent being forced to leave their places of residence twice to move to a safer location; 8 percent having to leave three times; 2 percent having to leave their abode fourtimes; and, finally, 1 percent changing their living place seven times (see table 1.5).

The *muhajjareen* had to abandon most of their belongings, including their furniture, utilities, and other amenities, so looting was common, followed by the burning of empty homes. It was also common to plunder the infrastructure of a home by tearing down the walls and ceilings to steal steel rods, electrical wires, tiles, as well as kitchen and bathroom appliances. The targets of plunder ranged from makeshift rooms in Palestinian refugee camps to small homes built illegally in the poverty belt around Beirut and even the brick homes in the Christian villages of Sharq Saida and Mount Lebanon. At times, homeowners left notes and letters to militiamen before leaving their homes to find refuge in another part of the country, pleading with them to use the home and stay in it but to preserve its structure.[29] A man from Maghdousheh who left his house after the fighting broke out between AMAL and the Palestinian fighters in 1988 wrote a note for the militiamen and temporary settlers describing how he and his wife, a schoolteacher, had toiled to build the house and buy its furniture. He directed them to the *muneh* (stored provisions), such as lentils, dried figs, raisins, olive oil, sugar, tea, tomato paste, and cooked meat, that his family kept for the winter and for times of climatic crisis and war.[30]

Therèse A., one of the Maronite workingwomen at the Ghaziyya plant, was displaced with her family three times, and each time the home they had to leave was looted and demolished. Her husband lost his bulldozer, his only source of livelihood, after the war. Her children lived through constant interruptions in their living and educational environments.[31] Therèse and her family fled the town of Darb al-Seem in Sharq Saida, moved to Aytaneet, and then fled from there to the Nabatiyya in the South. After the war, the family finally settled in Sin al-Fil in East Beirut. Therèse worked at the Ghaziyya plant from 1976 to 1987, but when the war grew more intense, she joined the Hadath plant in the city.

Hayat M., another Maronite from Tamboreet in the South, faced a similar destiny. She had three children with her husband, a farmer, whom she had married and settled down with in Maghdousheh in 1983. She had fond memories of her social life and workplace at the Ghaziyya plant, where she worked from 1979 to 1985. The work, she recalled, "was very good; workers loved each other, production of tobacco was good, too, and

29. Nofel, *Maghdusha*, 268, 338, 341.

30. Nofel, *Maghdusha*.

31. Therèse A., interviewed by Malek Abisaab, Feb. 26, 1997, Hadath.

work in general was stable. After the war broke out, it became extremely dangerous to commute between my home and the factory." When a new wave of battles broke out between the Lebanese Forces and the leftists, Hayat and her family were forced to flee to Sin al-Fil in East Beirut. Their house in Maghdousheh was looted and destroyed, and a close member of her family was killed. The family continued to live in Sin al-Fil, and Hayat joined the Hadath plant.[32]

Women workers at the Régie who lived in the eastern and southern suburbs that formed Beirut's "poverty belt," such as Fatima Z. and Khadija M., faced life-threatening conditions. Before the first phase of the Civil War (1975–76), many working-class shanty towns in the eastern suburb, such as Borj Hammoud, Sin al-Fil, Dikwaneh, Mkallis, Bushiryyeh, Jdaydeh, Fanar, and Zalqa, encompassed a mix of ethnic groups, sects, and both Lebanese and non-Lebanese communities.[33] All these towns were the target of focused attacks by right-wing militia groups aiming to marginalize leftist parties and the supporters of the PLO.[34] Neighborhoods closely attached to Tal al-Zaʿtar, such as Fanar, Nabʿa, Maslakh, and Karantina, were eradicated.

The Phalangists launched their ethnic-cleansing campaign against the Palestinian refugee camp Tal al-Zaʿtar in December 1976.[35] Thousands

32. Hayat M., interviewed by Malek Abisaab, Feb. 27, 1997, Hadath.

33. Nasr, *Susyulujya al-harb fi Lubnan*, 90. Salim Nasr finds that after 1970 Greater Beirut embraced more than 40 percent of the total population of Lebanon, 11.4 percent of which lived in al-Dahiya al-Sharqiyya.

34. On December 9, 1975, al-Inʿizaliyyin (the Isolationists) started an attack on Hart al-Ghawarina, a slum in the vicinity of Antielias, five kilometers north of Beirut. The attack ended the presence of what had been 150 Muslim families in the Hara and involved the killing of thirty persons, the burning of three hundred homes, and the abducting of scores of women and children. See *Irth Lubnan*, 12–13, and *Yawmiyyat al-harb*, 1:288. Then on December 16, 1975, another attack was launched by the military gangs of the National Liberal Party (established in 1958 by President Camille Chamoun [in office 1952–58]) against Sibnay, a poor neighborhood between Hadath and Bʿabda, the administrative capital of Lebanon. The assailants evicted 450 Muslim residents from their homes, who fled to West Beirut. See *Irth Lubnan*, 12–13.

35. The Phalangist Party started the Civil War, claiming that the Palestinians forced the eviction of Christians from Jisr al-Basha (a Palestinian camp), Dikwani, and Qalʿa.

of Palestinians were killed, along with several Lebanese and Syrian civilians.[36] Umm 'Aziz, a Palestinian woman refugee, described the carnage in Tal al-Za'tar following the 1976 campaign and how she walked barefoot with her wounded children to try and reach the nearby post of the Popular Front for the Liberation of Palestine, even as young Palestinian men were being killed, sometimes in front of their mothers.[37]

Tal al-Za'tar was originally established in 1950 on an area of 295 donum (0.295 square kilometers) owned by the Maronite Church and private landowners. In 1968, the industrial area surrounding the camp encompassed 29 percent of Lebanese factories, 22 percent of the workforce in Lebanon, and 23 percent of the industrial capital. Palestinian working-women and men staffed the floors of several plants and operated their machines. They offered inexpensive labor for business owners who were looking to pay wages below the minimum standard. Because the Palestinians had an illegal status as workers, they could not organize trade unions and consequently could not enjoy union protection or health benefits, let alone any other social or life insurance.[38]

Women tobacco workers who lived in the eastern suburbs of Beirut were spared the mass murder and ethnic–religious cleansing witnessed in Tal al-Za'tar and Jisr al-Basha. They escaped to the southern suburbs, where many other Shi'a Muslims from the South and the Biqa' lived. In the case of Khadija M., tragedy hit home when she lost three of her children. A Shi'a worker at the Régie, Khadija was born in al-Hirmel in 1932. She married when she was fourteen years old. After her husband died, she married a man who worked at a telephone company. She started working at the Régie in 1960 to provide for her children from her first marriage. Her second husband then lost his job at the telephone company, forcing

Then the Phalangists confiscated several trucks loaded with food supplies on their way to Tal al-Za'tar and another truck going to Nab'a, which signaled the beginning of a siege of the poverty triangle, Tal al-Za'tar, Nab'a, and Maslakh-Karantina. See *Yawmiyyat al-Harb*, 1:10–12.

36. Mundus, *Tariq Tal al-Za'tar*, 119.

37. Mundus, *Tariq Tal al-Za'tar*, 64.

38. Mundus, *Tariq Tal al-Za'tar*, 26–28, 25, 36, 48–49.

the whole family to rely on her salary. Before the war, the family lived in Tal al-Zaʿtar, but they were forced to leave the camp for her village in the Biqaʿ. Her home in the Biqaʿ was then destroyed, and Khadija lost three children. The remaining family members moved to Hay al-Silum, a slum in the southern suburbs, when the war ended in 1990. Even more critically, her husband later divorced her because she did not give birth to any male children. She has six daughters.[39]

The case of Inʿam A., who joined the Régie in 1958, sheds light on some of the worst consequences of the war for workingwomen. She and her family had left her hometown Yuneen in the Biqaʿ to live in Borj Hammoud, where she could be close to her job at the Régie. Her house was destroyed during the war, and she lost her brother and his wife. She became the only breadwinner for the extended family's twelve children, including not only her own children but also her nieces and nephews. She stayed in Borj Hammoud until the fall of the Nabʿa on January 18, 1976.[40] Her family could not offer her brother a proper burial in his village because they had long had a feud with another family there. Her brother was buried quickly at a nearby cemetery. Soon after that, her maternal uncle was kidnapped, and his family retaliated by kidnapping an engineer and a lawyer from a rival Christian family, the Rahmis from Dayr al-Ahmar. After some negotiations, the kidnapped men were released. Meanwhile, Inʿam's house in Borj Hammoud was plundered, and she stopped going to work at the Régie. She had to go back to her rural village. She started working on the farms in Yuneen and the neighboring villages, planting and harvesting lentils, wheat, barley, chickpeas, and fruit. However, she kept receiving

39. Khadija M., interviewed by Malek Abisaab, Feb. 17, 1997, Hadath.

40. In her book *The Struggle over Lebanon*, Tabitha Petran describes the fall of Nabʿa as follows: "On August 6, after a fifteen-day siege without food and water, the town of Nabaa—close to Tel al-Zaatar and crucial to the camp's defenses—fell to Lebanese Front militias. A group of Shiʿa leaders including Musa Sadr and Kamel Al-Asaad surrendered the quarter without consulting the defending garrison, which battled on for another two days before being overcome. Lebanese Front militiamen then 'cleansed' Nabaa of its inhabitants and fought each other over the spoils in two days' looting. The poor Armenian Christian quarter, Badawi, was the next to be 'cleansed,' the crime of its inhabitants having been to try to help the people of Nabaa" (208–9).

Table 1.6
Family Member(s) Lost to Régie Women Workers
during the Lebanese Civil War, 1975–90

	Frequency	*Percentage*
No members lost	179	63
Husband	27	9
Son	8	3
Daughter	2	1
Father	5	1
Mother	2	1
Brother	13	4
Sister	2	1
Nephew	8	3
Niece	1	0
Permanent disability to self	2	1
Family or more than one person	32	11
Kidnapped	3	1
The woman worker herself was injured (exact level of injury not specified)	2	1
Total	286	100

Survey of 286 Régie women workers conducted in 1997. Figures are rounded to the nearest whole number.

a salary from the Régie. She was able to send eight of her siblings to the Musa al-Sadr school for orphans and resumed her work at the Hadath plant when the first phase of the Civil War was over. When Israel invaded Lebanon in 1982, she fled to East Beirut again and from there went back to her hometown, Yuneen.[41]

Around 37 percent of the women workers surveyed were directly touched by human tragedy: death in the family or/and a debilitating injury from the war (see table 1.6). Around 11 percent lost more than one member of their family, 9 percent lost their husbands, 3 percent a son, 4 percent a

41. In'am A., interview.

brother, and 3 percent a nephew. Fewer of them lost a sister, a mother, a daughter, a father, or a friend or close neighbor to war. There were also a few incidents of kidnapping and injury suffered by relative and friends. The war also left two of these women workers with permanent disabilities.

Samira M. and Zahra D. suffered the loss of more than one member of their families, in addition to their homes and most of their belongings. They described the phase that followed their loss as marked by additional loss of personal space and aspirations, which made the struggle for survival during the war as much psychological as physical. They responded differently to the ravages of the war. Samira preserved her sense of well-being and safety through the church, and Zahra did so by becoming staunchly apolitical, losing faith in all the ideologies and existing political groups.

Samira M. was born to a Maronite family from the rural town of Shlifa-Ba'labak. She lived with her family in Achrafieh in East Beirut. At the age of fourteen, she started working at the Régie to overcome poverty. She noted that her parents controlled her salary and activities. She envied those of her fellow workingwomen who enjoyed certain "personal liberties." The war made her situation only worse. She lost most of her family—her father, mother, and two of her brothers. The tragedy pushed her to live with the remaining brother, and although she was quite unhappy with this arrangement, she did not have a choice. Her movements and whereabouts became restricted even further. She was keen, however, on presenting herself as a pious woman who was at church every Sunday and who observed all the religious holidays and events. Politically, she supported General Michel Aoun and the Lebanese army and approved of his aims and role in the war.[42] This was a period when many Christians were looking for an alternative to the fascist Lebanese Forces and were growing weary of the Forces' internal fighting over the control of East Beirut.[43]

42. Samira M., interviewed by Malek Abisaab, Mar. 5, 1997, Hadath.

43. From the inception of the Lebanese Forces in the late 1970s, there was always discord and competition among its founding groups and leading members. Most, if not all, of the issues of dissent that ended in violent confrontations centered on control over the decision-making power in areas held by the Lebanese Forces and divisions of the Lebanese army, mainly East Beirut, northern Matn, Jbeil, Keserwan, and segments of

Zahra D., a Greek Orthodox workingwoman from Dayr Mimas in South Lebanon, expressed a clear detachment from the ideals of the warring factions and saw the war as a calamity. She joined the Régie workforce in 1956, when she was nineteen years old. She noted in her interview that she was forced to do so because her "family needed the money." She took her work seriously and thus felt unsettled by the disorganization at the Régie caused by the Civil War. As the war grew more intense, commuting from her house in Achrafieh to the Régie complex at Hadath became dangerous, and she stopped going to work. Achrafieh, too, became unsafe when internal fighting broke out not only between factions within the Lebanese Forces but also between the Lebanese Forces and the national army of Michel Aoun.[44] Her house in Achrafieh was seriously damaged, and she had to move with her family to a safer place in Sin al-Fil in East Beirut. Her father died during this episode. Her sister was so traumatized

---

North Lebanon. Military campaigns to wipe out opponents began on July 7, 1980, when the Lebanese Forces eliminated the presence of the Numur al-Ahrar (the military wing of the Liberal Party) in Safra (coast of Keserwan), which ended in the killing of fifty fighters. Then between 1983 and 1988, the countless clashes between divisions of the Lebanese army and the Lebanese Forces were driven by struggles for power over the Christian enclave. Another round of violence erupted on January 15, 1986, between the followers of Samir Ja'ja', the current chairman of the Lebanese Forces, and Elie Hbeika (1956–2002), the chairman who preceded Ja'ja', and his supporters over the Tripartite Agreement to end the Civil War in Lebanon. It was a ferocious battle as the forces commanded by Ja'ja' attacked the residences of Hbeika's men, arrested those men, and condemned them to summary execution. A few months later, Hbeika and his troops attempted to regain their positions in East Beirut and started an attack on Achrafieh. The attack failed, and the forces fighting for Ja'ja' started a witch-hunt against the followers of Hbeika. They immediately killed anyone they found or "would tie them to cars and drag them through the streets of Achrafieh. Others had their feet tied up to rocks and hurled to the sea" (*Irth Lubnan*, 67). The grand battle between Christians, or the War of Liberation, took place in March 1989 between divisions of the Lebanese army loyal to General Michel Aoun (b. 1935) and the Lebanese Forces, which caused the deaths of thousands of civilians and hundreds of fighters from both sides. For a chronological record of these battles, see *Irth Lubnan*, 67–72.

44. For a brief description of the war between Ja'ja' and Hbeika and the war between Ja'ja' and Aoun, see note 43.

by the internal fighting that she died shortly afterward from heart failure. Zahra attributed her father's and sister's deaths to immense fear and uncertainty. She lost her faith in all political parties and ideologies and became staunchly apolitical, stating in her interview that "politics ruined the life of Lebanese people."[45]

Finally, the case of Zaynab Z. offers us a close look at the way the Civil War greatly restricted women's personal choices and ignited sectarian and ethnic divisions that undermined their ability to maintain a safe and stable experience at the workplace. Zaynab was born to a Shi'a peasant family from Knayseh in Ba'labak in 1938. She was ten years old when her family moved to Furn al-Shubbak in East Beirut. She started working at the Régie around 1959. In 1961, she married a man who had been married twice before. He could not earn a living, even though they had five children to support, and he never helped her with household chores or looked after the children.[46] At one point, he committed a crime and was sent to prison; she gave him half of her salary and used the other half to provide for her family, including a daughter with a disability. He spent several years in Saudi Arabia but came back penniless. She threatened to divorce him when he started drinking, but she reported that she could not do it due to her love for her children. As one hears of Zaynab's efforts, activities, and struggles during the Civil War, one wonders whether the option of getting a divorce and changing her domestic conditions were severely undermined by the Civil War.

After being displaced from Fanar, Zaynab used her social and political connections to find a place to move to. She stayed with her family for seven months in the West Beirut neighborhood of al-Ramla al-Bayda.[47] They

45. Zahra D., interviewed by Malek Abisaab, Mar. 3, 1997, Hadath.

46. Zaynab Z. interviewed by Malek Abisaab, Feb. 13 and 17, 1997, Lebanon; all quotations from Zeinab and details about her experiences come from this interview.

47. The reason the family left Fanar was the fall of the Palestinian camp Tal al-Za'tar. Zaynab and the members of her clan who remained alive as well as many other Muslim families left the area as a cautious move because they were threatened by the Phalangist militia. Shaykh Muhammad Da'as negotiated with Camille Chamoun their safe evacuation from Fanar. Zaynab asserted "that no less than ninety of our members [unclear if

inhabited the lower floor of an empty building whose European owners and tenants had left and entrusted her with taking care of their apartments and belongings. She was keen on emphasizing how well she took care of these apartments and the valuables in them.

Zaynab and her children later moved to the building of the Faculty of Social Science at the Lebanese University, along with other displaced groups, including Kurds. Sectarian–ethnic tensions surfaced there, too, though, eventually reaching the point of open conflict. Zaynab noted that she could not reside with Kurdish people, describing them as "very dirty." She remembered that the Kurds denigrated the Shi'a, calling them "Metawli." To threaten them, she tried to fire a Kalashnikov but ended up hitting the ceiling and hurting her hand. She and her family left that building in 1987 when the "war of the two flags" broke out between AMAL and the Druze-based Progressive Socialist Party, led by Walid Jumblat. They moved this time to Dawha in Mount Lebanon and then left Dawha for Knayseh.

During this period, Zaynab remained close to her extended family in Knayseh, seeking their help to survive. She received various food staples from them and rations of flour from the PLO. She often had to stand in a long line with her disabled daughter for up to ten hours to receive these rations. One day she started cursing and yelling until they gave her flour. She challenged the PLO by claiming that their enemies, the Phalangists, used to distribute flour and wheat more efficiently. The distribution of rations became better organized with time, and the PLO offered her medical help for appendicitis as well. She also borrowed money from her Palestinian neighbors and returned it whenever she could. To supplement her salary from the Régie, she worked on a farm in Knayseh seasonally. Despite her husband's opposition, she eventually bought forty acres of land and made it arable with the help of her family. She noted that she wanted to stay connected to the land and be buried there when she dies.

---

they were from her family or were Shi'a in general] were killed during the battle of Tal al-Za'tar."

Around two hundred women from the Zu'aytir family were at the Régie when Zaynab began working there.[48] In the interview, she noted that she was disillusioned by the sectarian and gender discrimination in the Sorting Department, where she was placed. According to her, Christian workers were promoted more quickly, and their Muslim counterparts had to fight at every step for advancement. Christian workingwomen and men did not have to stand in line even to enter the company or leave it. She was convinced that the Muslim workingwomen and men were *mbahdaleen* (treated poorly as inferiors) compared to their Christian counterparts: "Christian women workers were sacred in their [the Régie's] eyes. We [Muslims] were not."

During the Civil War, the workers kept going to the Régie factory in Hadath after the Israeli invasion even though there were Israeli patrols in the area. Zaynab noted,

> To terrorize us, the Israeli soldiers would shoot over our heads when we left the building at the end of workday. Many workingwomen panicked and hid behind the walls and poles of the building. I was not frightened and started encouraging the girls [*sic*] to stay calm, saying that the Israelis just want to terrify us. I was not scared because I believe in God. Many times the Israeli tanks would attack us when we were in cars on our way home after work.

48. The major characteristic of the Zu'aytir tribe and other tribes is the way they live in neighborhoods shaped by social and political kinship structures. The kinship factor is so decisive that you can find a member of the tribe simply by looking for him in a village or urban slum inhabited by people who belong to the same *jibb* (subsection) or the tribe at large. During the Civil War and the consequent displacement from Fanar and other neighborhoods in East Beirut, one could easily recognize that the displaced Zu'aytiris were clustered along the *jibb* in one building or in one community or lived together on a certain street in West Beirut. The same configuration could be discerned in working patterns, so if a member of the *jibb* mastered a trade, then many relatives who belonged to the same *jibb* would follow suit. This could explain the existence of the large number of the Zu'aytir laborers in the Régie workforce. See Zu'aytir, "Aal Zu'aytir in History, Geography, and Politics," 52.

News of dead Syrian soldiers who had been headed to the Beirut–Damascus highway created an atmosphere of fear and panic among the Régie's Muslim workers in particular because the Lebanese Forces' power increased greatly during the Israeli invasion. No less than "six hundred Syrian soldiers were killed by the Lebanese Forces in Hadath," stated Zaynab. She simply could not quit her job, however. She feared the Régie might fire her and the other Muslim workingwomen and men if they did not show up for work. Therefore, she sent her family to Knayseh because it was safer, and she continued to work. But the atmosphere was tense. She recalled that a Christian workingman, Joseph Mazraʿani, pulled her gunny sack, which she used as a prayer rag, from beneath her knees and said, "There is no praying here." She did not reply and continued praying silently until she reached the Qura'nic verse al-Fatiha, which she read aloud angrily: "Not the path of those who have brought down wrath nor of those who wander astray."

Zaynab described herself defiantly as *ukht al-rijal* (strong as a man), which allowed her to survive the war. She feared that Joseph Mazraʿani would have someone kidnap her, the same way a Muslim male coworker, Muhammad al-ʿArabi, disappeared on his way home, presumably kidnapped. She clearly relied on the support of several Christian workingwomen and men, especially from the Jaʿjaʿ family, to help her. The day after al-ʿArabi's kidnapping, she went to work carrying a sharp knife, with the plan of defending herself even if she ended up injured. She hoped to gain the respect of her coworkers, especially those from her family. She let people know that she was carrying a knife because she did not feel safe. Christian workingwomen and men from the Jaʿjaʿ family stood behind her and reassured her that no one would hurt her. There was an old, strong alliance between the Jaʿjaʿ and Zuʿaytir families that drew upon traditional tribal codes. The gendered features of this alliance were such that women who needed protection in either family could count on the family men to defend them because the men were obligated to defend the women's honor. Workers from the Jaʿjaʿ family protected her all day, and the Zuʿaytir workingwomen at the Régie also rushed to stand by her.

The support of the Jaʿjaʿ family's workers was decisive. They warned Mazraʿani to stop harassing her. Nonetheless, the incidents of kidnapping and death increased, and the Ja'ja's were afraid that their protection might not extend beyond the gates of the Régie. They urged Zaynab to leave the Régie, so she took her salary, six hundred Lebanese pounds, and left. During the interview, she cried bitterly when she mentioned her departure, and she said she cries whenever she remembers the incident. She stopped working at the Régie after the uprising on February 6, 1984, but kept receiving her salary.

'Itaf T. experienced a different type of sectarianism.[49] A Sunni born in 1933, she was eleven years old when she was engaged to a man from Beirut who knew her parents, although that engagement lasted for only one year. In 1948, Palestinian refugees started to come to Saida, and 'Itaf was once again engaged, this time to a Lebanese man who was a nurse in a hospital in Palestine, whom she married. His mother was a Palestinian, and his father had died in Palestine. He took a course in nursing in Sur (Tyre) but could not find a job in a hospital. With the help of 'Itaf's neighbor, he started to learn carpentry. They then moved to Beirut and lived in the Hamad neighborhood of Tariq al-Jadida for nine years, where 'Itaf's husband was a carpenter. When 'Itaf was seventeen years old, she gave birth to her first daughter. Then they moved back to Saida to receive government compensation because of the earthquake in 1956, which destroyed her father's family's home. Her husband died in 1968, one year after rebuilding their house. 'Itaf had also joined the Régie that year, before he died. He had opposed her decision because he had felt that working at the Régie work would exhaust her and prevent her from giving sufficient attention to their children. She insisted: "I used to read women's magazines, in which I read essays about women's work and the ideal lady of the family, ideal mother, etc." She decided to work to become like the women the magazines described. She had five daughters and two sons when she started doing Régie work. Her husband changed his mind about her job thanks to the *wasta* (nepotism) of Ma'ruf Sa'd (1910–75), a popular political leader in Saida.[50]

49. 'Itaf T., interviewed by Malek Abisaab, Feb. 15, 1977, Saida, Lebanon; all quotations from 'Itaf T. and details of her experiences come from this interview.

50. 'Itaf appealed to Sa'd as a deputy representing Saida in the Lebanese Parliament of 1968. Sa'd then telephoned the minister of finance, the custodial power of the Régie.

The Régie job was good for ʿItaf. When Israel invaded Lebanon in 1982, her salary was two thousand Lebanese pounds per month, which was an excellent amount of money at the time (around US$650). In her interview, ʿItaf recounted, "We used to save money, but when Israel pulled out, the value of my salary started to diminish." The work at the Régie gradually started to recover, though, and her salary reached up to five hundred thousand Lebanese pounds per month (US$330).[51] ʿItaf complained about the sectarian basis of the Régie's promotion policy, though. She claimed that a group of women belonging to AMAL were promoted because of *wasta*. "One manager gave a promotion to his wife," she remembered.

> Another one promoted a woman he knew [implying he had an affair with her]. A lot of promotions took place here; they got a salary increase and joined the Control Department. They joined the Régie eighteen years ago, unlike us, who joined work thirty years ago [implying seniority]; I am sixty-four years old now and still working; I should get rest, [and] they still ask us to work doing the same thing since we started at the Régie. They [the managers, who belong to AMAL or are Shiʿas] had no manners; they yelled at an old woman a lot; they registered names of workers whom they favor. He [the manager] was free to do whatever he pleased; he was bad-tempered and bullied the girls. If an old woman was a few minutes late to work, he would start yelling at her. She was sixty-five years old. I tried to soften his attitude a little bit, but he did not care. He said, "I don't care at all about the girls here." He was callous, from Jbaʿ; I don't think he was from AMAL, but I really did not know, and he wasn't from Hizbullah because at the time there was no one from Hizbullah who joined the Régie in 1982. This guy made me hate the job. Before the war, there was a man from Iqlim al-Kharub [implying a Sunni] in his place. No one [the Shiʿa] complained about him; if I wanted to complain to the administration, I would be alone; girls were not united. Before the war, girls were all united; after the war, they became atomized. After the war, everyone started to be identified

51. The value of one US dollar went up to 1,514 Lebanese pounds after the withdrawal of Israel from Lebanon in 2000.

> by her or his sectarian background: this is a Shi'a, this is a Sunni, and this a Christian. You started to find workers split into sectarian groups, sitting together with their own sect members. We were from Saida, so they started to curse Rafic al-Hariri in front of us: "Go tell Hariri that we are cursing him." We refused to reciprocate. Rafic al-Hariri is from my town [Saida], and I defended him. I loved him, and I loved Mustafa Sa'd [also a Sunni leader from Saida] because they were from my country. Why would we curse Nabih Berri [a Shi'a Speaker of the Parliament] and not anyone from Hizbullah? Then in the end I stopped retaliating.

'Itaf found that politics caused disunity and problems at the Régie. She asserted in her interview that before the Civil War the high-ranking administrative staff were very good. When the Ghaziyya plant was administered by a Christian director, the women workers "were united and showed solidarity with each other; we used to visit each other's villages, make tabbouleh, and go on picnics." Even during the dangerous times of the war, 'Itaf never stopped visiting her Christian colleagues in Maghdousheh. The Régie family was happy then, but after the war workers started to fear each other: "It became boring at work; we had nothing to talk with each other about," 'Itaf lamented.

During the Civil War, 'Itaf did not stop going to work, but when the factory was shelled by the Israeli army and its allies, work stopped altogether, and everyone stayed home. During an intense episode of the Civil War called the "War of Sharq Saida," leading to the displacement of the area's Christians, 'Itaf didn't go to the Régie for three years. The Régie used to send her salary, as it did to other workers in other branches. The Ghaziyya plant did not close, however, because the workers who lived in Ghaziyya Town, who were mostly Shi'as, kept going to work. Female workers from Kfar Rimman also did not stop going to work. 'Itaf related, "Christian workers were forced out of their villages and moved to East Beirut. The Régie kept giving them their salaries. I started saying to myself: 'I don't have to go to work.'"

When Israel invaded Lebanon and started bombing Saida, 'Itaf and her family escaped to a nearby shelter. They initially thought the bombing would be temporary, as it had been previously, when Israeli jets attacked the Palestinian camp Ayn al-Hilweh and Palestinian military positions. ʿItaf remembered that this time the bombing lasted longer, throughout the entire night. Then a person from Haret Saida (mostly Shiʿa) came to the shelter and asked them to leave because the Israeli army was going to attack Sirop, another neighborhood in Saida. But when the pro-Israeli Lebanese Forces came to the area in the wake of the Israelis, the inhabitants of ʿItaf's neighborhood suffered even more. An atmosphere of terror was created when anyone who supported the PLO was persecuted and roadblocks were set up to arrest non-Christian and leftist pro-PLO people. She says, "Al-Miyyi wa-Miyyi [a Christian village] had a higher geographical position over our heads. Our young people were afraid that the Lebanese Forces would attack al-Hara [the Shiʿa slum]. Our people started building barriers, used barrels, and guarded the place. I made them sandwiches and tea, and other neighbors did too. We could not sleep at night until the men started to guard the neighborhood."

ʿItaf's house was damaged during the invasion and the subsequent War of Sharq Saida. Her furniture was looted; although aid institutions sponsored by al-Hariri indemnified her, the compensation was not adequate. The municipality of Saida also later helped post–Civil War reconstruction efforts, providing stones and cement to help renovate ʿItaf's house. Although she suffered a great deal, none of ʿItaf's children was hurt during the war, but her sister and her family were injured when their residence in al-Miyyi wa-Miyyi was damaged.

When ʿItaf's husband died, she was responsible for their five children. She could not rely on her Régie salary alone, especially because her children were very young. She did not ask anyone for help, neither her brother nor her deceased husband's family. To keep up with inflation and the devaluation of the Lebanese pound, she instead started a business. "I like commerce and trade," she declared in her interview. She began her career in trade in the early 1970s, going to Damascus on Sundays and when she had breaks to buy cloth, and later at home she would display the cloth on the ground floor of her home with the help of one of her sons. Her friends and colleagues would ask her to buy cloth for them. She would buy it in Syrian pounds, and they would buy it from her in Lebanese currency because the Lebanese pound was worth more. Then she started to take a bag full of cloth to the Régie and sell it on the factory premises. "Thank God," she sighed with relief but articulated proudly, "I didn't need any help from anyone and managed for my family to live decently. I sent my kids to school." 'Itaf saved for an honorable retirement: "I'm waiting for my pension; I plan to build an additional story onto my house and live off of the rent. I did not want to put my pension in the bank because it is haram to take interest. Because I went on pilgrimage [to Mecca], interest is haram. Even if I did not go on pilgrimage, it's haram to take interest."

After the death of her husband in 1970, 'Itaf joined the Organization of Communist Action (OCA). Her son-in-law and another person, Salim al-Mamluk, persuaded her to join this group, which was, according to 'Itaf, a very good political organization in terms of supporting workers' rights. The OCA did not participate in sectarian killing or slaughter anyone, she argued: "It did not loot; I do know that they used to receive financial aid from outside Lebanon—Arab countries such as Libya and Iraq." 'Itaf's sons did not join any political party. However, when one of her children joined the OCA, the organization sent him to a military camp for training. She vehemently opposed this and threatened the neighbor's son one day, shouting, "If you don't bring back my son, I will take a gun and shoot everyone in the office [of the OCA]." According to 'Itaf, the political environment at the time was not good, and AMAL attacked the OCA office in Sour, killing everyone who happened to be there. 'Itaf affirmed, "I used to know one of the people killed there. They killed him. I had no man at home other than my two sons, who were supposed to help me when I grow old." Her perception of her life began to change in the early 1990s. She began wearing a veil in 1991 and believed that when women become "elderly in our religion, it is haram not to cover their hair."

Conclusion

During the Civil War, Lebanese women tobacco workers faced direct threats to their lives, which affected their physical and psychological well-being and influenced their socioeconomic productivity inside and outside the workplace. They employed various strategies to overcome fear, hunger, displacement, insecurity, and loss of income. The collapse of the state and its municipal administration as well as the absence of state-sponsored relief programs changed gender relations and authorized new ways of being a woman within both the domestic unit and the workplace. The distance between the household and the factory shrank. Productivity and salaried labor seeped into the family household as well. Women devised strategies to raise money by doing the same things they have always done domestically at home, especially cooking. As the cottage industries of the late nineteenth and early twentieth centuries show, women were part of a long history of unrecorded, unwritten, and unseen labor. Much of their salaried and unsalaried work typically went unnoticed. But during the Lebanese Civil War, workingwomen became aware of how important their economic roles were, especially in maintaining the social fabric of the family and society at large. Their contributions also became a matter of life and death. The Lebanese women tobacco workers articulated an awareness of their own contributions and the dependence of so many persons on them. As they narrated their wartime experiences, they expressed a new relationship to their labor and to other people that reflected a sense of social empowerment.

Almost all the women I interviewed emphasized that they turned to themselves first to see what they could do to survive and to help their families survive. They also looked to local—rural and urban—communal resources as well as to family members, influential community leaders, and sectarian associations for assistance, be it to find temporary residence, to relocate, or to seek out sources of income. During this period, a woman's class position and sectarian affiliation might work together to improve her situation, but they might also work against each other. Within the Régie, for instance, a combination of both was present and entangled with political divisions, as in the case of the conflict between Najla and Fatima.

Workingwomen's multiple survival strategies were an immediate reaction to the alarming decrease in their salaries during the war and their vulnerability. On the one hand, they were overworked and underpaid at the Régie and so started to work intensively outside it, too, which must have been taxing on their health and overall well-being. On the other hand, their social impact on their families and their decision-making power increased dramatically. They strongly felt this power, as did those around them, who openly expressed how much they depended on these women.

This dependence in turn recast gendered relations within the family and allowed women to renegotiate patriarchal restrictions and values more effectively. Workingwomen's relationships to their societies thereafter underwent a further shift with the active roles they came to play in postwar public arenas.

2

The Labor of Women's Resistance

Image, Narrative, Alternative Futures

MARY JIRMANUS SABA

In the early weeks of Lebanon's unprecedented mass protests in 2019, a Twitter post and video tagged "Ajmal al Umahat" (The Most Beautiful of Mothers) spread across the internet.[1] In it, there is the image of a woman, apparently in her sixties, who struggles valiantly not to lose grasp of a bearded young man whom Internal Security Forces (ISF) officers[2] are trying to detain. She holds two wrapped sandwiches in her hand as she beats off the ISF officers with the other. They manage to wrest the young man from her hands, ultimately dragging him away. She became an instant celebrity, newspapers reporting on this "most beautiful of mothers" for her auxiliary support of the young revolutionaries.[3] News reports checking back in with her several months later painted an image of a matriarch defending her children's protest, a goal the press framed as secondary to her own support of the contemporary movement's demands or her personal history of resistance.[4]

The same phrase, *ajmal al-umahat*, was also the title of a poem by Hassan Abdallah, a song by Marcel Khalife, and a film by Maroun Baghdadi.

1. Jaber, "اجمل الأمهات" (The most beautiful of mothers).

2. The ISF is essentially a Lebanese state police force.

3. Annahar.com, "أجمل الأمهات ‘مشهدٌ ’أيقونيٌ‘ جديد في انتفاضة تشرين" (The most beautiful of mothers, a new "iconic" scene from the October Uprising).

4. Shabaro, "لينا بوبس . . . أجمل الأمّهات الثائرات من أجل وطن" (Nina Boubos: The most beautiful of mothers, militants for the nation).

Although a common phrase with multiple possible interpretations in everyday parlance, Abdallah's, Khalife's, and Baghdadi's works popularized a particular version of "the most beautiful of mothers"—a woman who mothers the resistance, which echoes in this present day. In fact, this phrase and the concept underlying it have proven a surprisingly resilient framework for explaining women's political action in Lebanon, though the role of cultural production around the question of motherhood—and women's political action—has been limited.

At least since the Lebanese Civil War, if not before, a wide range of women's political activity has regularly been flattened into mothering and more often articulated as women "mothering the resistance." Across the political spectrum, competing nationalist discourses have maintained remarkably similar options for women: either "muscular nationalism," a gendered binary that constrains women's role to "chaste woman," or devoted motherhood.[5] Thus, in exploring an archive of news images from the Lebanese Civil War (1975–90), we might just as easily pull images of distraught Palestinian women searching for their children as we could of Christian-nationalist women holding crosses and photographs of their sons, their gazes confronting the camera in defense of their political project. Such representations have often come at the expense of more nuanced portrayals of the rich landscape of women's political action in Lebanon both during the Civil War and beyond it.

This point has been no truer anywhere than in the genre of documentary cinema in Lebanon, which for the past decades has been dominated by narratives of the Civil War and its reverberations in the present. Perhaps reflecting the militarized and deeply hierarchal forms of struggle characterizing war and the aforementioned limiting nationalist frameworks, very few films have rarely made room for alternative social histories or narratives of collective action and even less frequently for collective action by women. Notable Civil War–era works by Jocelyne Saab and Randa Chahal, which feature women as political actors, focus largely on those women in exceptional leadership positions or as social deviants, exhilaratingly enacting

5. I have drawn this concept from Banerjee, *Muscular Nationalism*, 2.

their refusal of social norms in isolation.[6] In both cases, these individuals are abstracted from a more popular or collective context.

For the most part, thus, searching for stories of women's collective struggle and resistance in times of war has often meant reading between the lines of the documentation we have available and at times excavating narratives of militant motherhood and other forms of social reproductive labor for different potentialities. Doing so allows us both to defy the narrative and material practices that have sought to constrain women's political action and to seek resonances across texts and moments that might provide new horizons beyond the most beautiful of mothers.

Documentary Film: Women's Resistance, Political Agency, and Struggle

I attempt such an undertaking here, reading Baghdadi's newsreel film *The Most Beautiful of Mothers* (1978) alongside Jean Chamoun and Mai Masri's documentary *Wildflowers: Women of South Lebanon* (1986). Both films are set amid the resistance to Israeli occupation of South Lebanon, a decade apart; both focus on women, with distinct stylistic approaches. Baghdadi's newsreel eulogy was commissioned by the Organization for Communist Action (OCA), a member of the largely secular Lebanese National Resistance Front (LNRF), which brought several organizations together in resistance to Israeli occupation of South Lebanon, and the film thus is often popularly discussed in this exceptional light. It is composed largely of direct addresses by women—for the most part mothers but also wives and sisters and one father—speaking of their lost fighters, interspersed with a scene of teenage men heading into a military operation. *Wildflowers*, in turn, mixes vérité and same-person reenactment to explicitly narrate women's role in the same struggle at a distinct political moment, just as the role of the secular LNRF is being eclipsed by the Islamic Resistance.[7] The film tracks a central real-life figure, Khadija

6. For a discussion of these films, see Khatib, "The Voices of Taboos."

7. For a discussion of Hizbullah's role in the Lebanese resistance, see Daher, "Hezbollah's Military Apparatus," and Frangie, "The Anatomy of a Crisis."

Hariz, imprisoned for her political activity and later becoming a prominent Hizbullah member, as she discusses her own involvement in the nationalist resistance.

Whereas Baghdadi's film is in many ways emblematic of its eponymous title, Chamoun and Masri's work directly centers women as political agents in different moments of one ongoing struggle. Consequently, both reflect the subsidiary role frequently proffered to women within the movement even as the movement changed over time. Yet, as I attempt to show, when read together the two films open a set of questions and possibilities about distinctions and continuities across these two moments of nationalist struggle and about women's presumed role within them. What kinds of images of women's resistance and political agency have been available to us? Within what frameworks do they operate, and have they been constrained? How does the legacy of these narratives carry forward to the present, and how can we read around them and in the margins to recuperate a more complex and politically tenable and productive version of women's radical action? Which stories reach the camera and our subconscious, and which must we unearth? What role has political motherhood played in popular struggle in Lebanon, and how might an expansive reading of representations of mothering and social reproductive work reveal alternate horizons for coordinated action on the ground?

This chapter reads these two now-classic films against the grain of their typical interpretation by critics. They are commonly understood in Lebanon to be part of a descriptive archival record of a sparsely documented secular resistance, in contrast to Hizbullah's deliberate efforts to mis-historicize the resistance to Israel as exclusively religious and exclusively its own. In part because of the paucity of audiovisual documentation of that secular resistance struggle, the content and context of "militant films" such as *The Most Beautiful of Mothers* and to a lesser degree *Wildflowers* are read for the "facts" that they show but not for the kinds of narratives they enable and promote or for those they eschew. Part of what I draw out of my readings of these films is how an explicit version of women's agency is limited to their participation in a nationalist resistance projec and thus subject to the deeply gendered constraints inherent in nationalism as a frame.[8] But my reading goes beyond this argument, and I propose that we can literally re-view them to find a parallel hidden narrative, as if to organize images in lieu of people—to continue and expand a historical-political project unduly truncated.

I contend that these films document and amplify a movement politics that, although structured to replace the ruling political system with another system, is in many ways indistinguishable from that which it opposes, at least as far as women's lives are concerned. I have argued elsewhere that the failure on the part of progressive and revolutionary movements to take women's political and intellectual labor seriously greatly contributed to those movements' ultimate downfall.[9] By shifting toward a sharper reading of women's labor and the labor of care work or social reproduction, I extend this argument here to consider the radical potentials lost by an oppositional politics that relegates women to a subsidiary political role. Put another way, these films address mothering but do not take the actual labor and work of mothering into account in their critique and thus miss an important potential nexus of political coordination. The limited version of women's labor in the two films—confined to raising martyrs and supporting the indeterminate ends of a nationalist resistance project—both reflects and further confines our political imaginaries as well as the possible horizons of social transformation. At the same time, this adjusted lens through which I am re-viewing these films allows me to propose an alternative reading of moments in them that reach affectively toward different logics and offer different paths to a new political future. I conclude this chapter by speculating on ways to think through these films as stories or histories of the Lebanese Civil War in order to imagine alternative narratives that may in turn create alternative futures.

8. Feminist scholars have argued extensively about the myriad ways in which anticolonial nationalist projects have circumscribed women as unequal or subsidiary political subjects, and they locate this circumscription in the limitations of nationalism as a framework. See, among other works, Bannerji, "Projects of Hegemony"; Smith, *Conquest*; and Stoler, *Carnal Knowledge and Imperial Power.*

9. See my film *A Feeling Greater Than Love* (Beirut Tricontinental Media, 2017).

Poetry across Time: *The Most Beautiful of Mothers*

Hassan Abdallah penned his poem "Ajmal al-umahat" upon witnessing a heartbroken mother in South Lebanon whose son had been martyred in the resistance against Israel refuse to succumb to her sorrows. Instead, with all the surreal intertextuality of everyday life, she blasted Marcel Khalife's nationalist tunes from a loudspeaker on her roof, fighting back pain with a gesture undoubtedly aimed at raising her own and local public morale and proudly showing her defiance to the Israeli occupiers.[10] The rest of this story, including the woman's other political efforts and the effects of her public intervention, is, sadly, lost to the archives. Yet this backstory provides us with rich content we can use to read Abdallah's poem and the music and film it gave rise to. Perhaps missing or deliberately sidestepping the organizational function of the grieving mother's anger, Abdallah penned "Ajmal al-umahat," a poem that lauds her steadfastness, talking about the most beautiful of mothers who waited for her son and how he returned only as a martyr while she waited.

Like the woman who inspired him, Abdallah's protagonist continues to turn her grief into beauty:

> so she cried
> two tears and a flower
> and didn't isolate herself in mourning clothes.[11]

Indeed, Abdallah hints at his protagonist's public action but pauses only briefly on her politicization of that grief. Rather, he quickly moves on to affirm the justness, the eternalness, of her son's cause:

> the war did not end
>
> but he returned
> his rifle wilted
> his hand, neutral.

10. Habib Sadek relates this narrative in the supplement to the release of Maroun Baghdadi's film *Ajmal al-umahat* on DVD (see *Maroun Baghdadi Documentary*).

11. Abdallah, "Ajmal al-umahat"; all quotations of this poem come from this source. All translations of Arabic are my own.

The martyr's political project continues, his agency enacted, even after his death. His mother's action, however, is restricted to vigilance: "her eyes do not sleep." The cause is instead taken on by an unspecified collectivity: "We will not retreat from his blood that is soaked in the land. / We will not let go of our love for the mountains that drank his soul." Abdallah subtly promises retribution, enacted on the occupied land: "We will remain steadfast, here." Conflating land and landscape with cause and country, he subtly subsumes the grieving mother's sadness and rage into that natural fabric that becomes her contribution to the movement—"she cried . . . a flower." Beyond this, her ability to do anything more than watch and wait is subsumed into the collective "We" who will enact vengeance.

Shortly after this poem was published, the iconic Lebanese performer Marcel Khalife put the lyrics to song and recorded them. Not long thereafter, Maroun Baghdadi's newsreel film of the same title appeared. Through Khalife's and Baghdadi's works, Abdallah's words produce a powerful version of nationalism that reduces women's resistance and political action to "merely" mothering.

Baghdadi's documentary *Ajmal al-umahat* opens in silence with a slow-motion telephoto shot of a simple metal coffin, which is held aloft by five pairs of hands, their owners not visible. Far in the distant background, there is a verdant mountainside; closer up, treetops. The camera focuses on a young woman's distressed, contorted face. She is walking within the procession. She cries—also in slow motion—and waves a white handkerchief, her hair underneath a loosely wrapped scarf flying in the wind.

The procession's synchronous sound is removed, replaced with the melancholy strains of an oud and Khalife's voice repeating the line: "The most beautiful of mothers is she who waited for her son."

The same shot of the anguished woman repeats. She waves her handkerchief, again in slow motion. Khalife continues with the familiar line about her waiting and about the soldier returning as a martyr.[12] The screen then goes black and cuts to an older woman, her head covered by a black scarf. She affectionately describes her son, Ali, as "blond like his father,

12. Khalife and al-Mayadeen Ensemble, *Of All the Beautiful Mothers*, CD.

tall after his mama." Hearing herself repeat this perhaps once oft-spoken phrase causes her to pause. She squints as she fights back tears.

This haunting image of a woman speaking of her lost son in the present tense and the accompanying sensation of collective mourning and anger remained with me long after I first viewed Baghdadi's film a decade ago. As I revisited the film, reflecting critically on present-day reverberations of the same reductive narratives of political motherhood, I was overcome by what I can only call the *surplus* of sensation invoked by this clip in particular and by the film more broadly. This sensation is the affect that allows the frames of Abdallah's poem to become amplified so effectively through the film, functioning at various sensory levels: discursive, sonic, visual. The film proceeds as an accumulation of story after story told by mothers, widows, and fathers, all of whom aspire to camera-appropriate composure as they detail their loved ones' characteristics, reasons for joining the armed resistance, and deaths.

Many of these narrators convey an excess of affect or emotion in relaying their stories. A young woman, one of few who appear without their heads covered, chokes back tears as she describes being newly pregnant at the time of her husband's death. She describes dismissing friends and family's recommendations that she terminate the pregnancy because she wished to honor his strong desire to have a child. In this context, the young woman's story of her personal decision to have a child is transformed into a continuation of the political project outlined in the song—giving birth to the resistance. Women's contribution becomes literally the production of new soldiers.

And yet, feminist criticality aside, the cumulative impact of these stories is devastating. The repetition and the fragility of each story, delivered with relentless urgency, work at a visceral level. This impact is akin to what Joshua Hirsch has called a "traumatic afterimage" insofar as it formally produces or accesses in the viewer the sensation of loss associated with a traumatic or visceral memory, evoking "an experience of suddenly seeing the unthinkable"—in this case occupation and violence.[13] But this excess

13. Hirsch, *Afterimage*, 19.

of emotion also produces other kinds of possible connections and conclusions—beyond those to which Baghdadi would so meticulous direct us. In particular, the longer stories from which the women's interventions are cut create a narrative thread linking women's experience of war and resistance to each other and to other stories beyond the screen. The pregnant widow is on-screen for barely two minutes, and yet she relates her memorable predicament with apparent candor: deciding to give birth after her husband's death is not only an emotional decision but also a material one. We are left wondering about the kinds of labor through which she sustained life under occupation, about who (certainly other women) helped her, about how she fared. Even when Imm Ali, the charming and devastated mother with whom I began, returns to tell us, "I felt I lost my heart. How should I feel? I lost my son," we wish her at the least solace, community. That at some level we might want to allow the characters in such humanly similar situations to comfort one another, to speak, to scheme, suggests a way in which their narratives reach beyond the film as text, beyond the screen even toward each other and to others.

Yet the film's rapid and charged pace succeeds largely in redirecting our sympathies toward the cause of the fighters. As with other newsreel films, the propagandist structure of *Ajmal al-umahat* seeks to transfer this afterimage into a political end—support for the OCA's and LFNR's political projects and legal protection against the Israeli onslaught. Indeed, the film's DVD slip tells us that the film was shown at the United Nations and contributed to that body's legislation deeming the invasion of South Lebanon illegal.[14] For those viewers with direct or proximate memories of that violent occupation, the message is hard to avoid. Thus, as the film moves on to introduce us to some of these young soldiers, seated in a barebones rural encampment, the young men, some barely teenagers, articulate their motivations for joining the resistance—not only to free their villages but also to fight for equality and a dignified life for their fellow citizens.

14. The film's screening was "a major influence in the issuance of [UN] Resolution 1425, concerning the withdrawal of Israeli occupation forces from Lebanon" (Sadek, in *Maroun Baghdadi Documentary*). Like numerous UN resolutions, though, 1425 had no binding effect.

Intercutting among these teenage fighters and their charged testimonials, Baghdadi creates an increasingly heightened feeling of urgency across the twenty-nine minutes of the film. Thus, when the film culminates in the excursion of the military resistance, it is difficult not to be overcome by a sense of enthusiasm for this action and for some kind of solution. The film plays on invoking this feeling and seeks to transfer it explicitly to support—moral, financial, or otherwise—for the OCA's military actions in South Lebanon during the Civil War. More specifically, our concern as viewers is transplanted from the situation of the film's women (the majority of the characters we meet) to the situation of the young boys who will take military action to secure justice. The film simultaneously and subtly reinforces the ideologies of the gendered division of political labor as articulated by Abdallah's poem, frameworks that assuredly preceded the poem and definitely have outlived it. The film ends with a rapid series of images of faces. They are the party's fallen fighters, including one woman, and are associated here with the various regions of Lebanon. The film leaves no doubt about its message—ours is a nationalist cause.

This ending comes at the expense of any narrative around women's political action or lives more generally. In framing the activities of resistance in this way, the film—and perhaps the movement itself—manages to successfully bracket out all other forms of struggle aside from the military. Labor, agrarian, feminist, political intellectual struggles are subsumed into the all-important or superseding and here purportedly more important uncritical national attempts at liberation. The unaddressed afterthoughts here are: Whose liberation? By what means and to what consequence will this liberation come?

Wildflowers

In sharp formal contrast to Baghdadi's newsreel-style film, Jean Chamoun and Mai Masri's film *Wildflowers: Women of South Lebanon* (1986) fits primarily within the genre of cinema verité, intermixing observation with interview and reenactments of various genres that depict women and at times children resisting the Israeli occupation of South Lebanon. The film attends to how gendered roles function across different situations in the occupied South, including what it is like to be a woman prisoner.

The narrative centers on the life story of Khadija Hariz, a former political prisoner and now prominent member of Hizbullah. Through a mix of interviews and observations at important sites of her struggle and domestic life, she tells the story of her political involvement in the resistance, imprisonment, and eventual release.

The film opens with a long shot of a landscape in the countryside. We see a woman in the distance; she calmly crosses a tobacco field, a large burlap sack balanced atop her head. Women of various ages perform a variety of domestic tasks, tending to plants, milking a sheep, gathering water, sifting cracked wheat. Children play around them. While paring small squashes, one woman kindly chides her daughter about how much easier household chores have become: mechanized food preparation is much easier, but the food is less delicious than when it is homemade. By opening the film in this way, Masri and Chamoun locate their characters' resistance in a relationship to the land, community, and daily life, aspects of women's lives that are far more marginal in Baghdadi's portrayal of the resistance. Through women discussing not only their attachment to the land but also the tedium of traditional housework and agricultural labor, we observe the complex relationship they have with their lifestyle. This relationship is crucial to the ways in which actual rural women characterize their position vis-à-vis the occupation of their lands, villages, and country. This discussion is decisively not nostalgic but rather practical. This nuance is conveyed visually through the recurrence of rural landscapes and the frequent interjection of household and agricultural work and discursively through the specific story of the film's main subject, Khadija, a story of resistance also rooted in gender-based inequity.

We are introduced to Khadija as she finishes changing her young child's diaper and then carries the child to where her husband and other child are relaxing on the grass near a riverbed. Seated peacefully under a tree, Khadija reads to the camera and to her husband, Mohamad, from her memoirs, where she has written about deciding to attend her first demonstration against the occupation on her wedding anniversary while he was imprisoned: "I decided to celebrate in my own way and called for a demonstration demanding the prisoners' release." She likens the mixed emotion of anger and collective power to a personal joy: "I fought them with sand and stones, jumping up and down as if I were dancing at my wedding anniversary." This intensity of emotion that mixes personal feeling with political commitment assuredly carries throughout Khadija's narration, complicating the more straightforward narratives of injustice and nationalism proffered by Baghdadi's shorter film.

We witness documentation of Israeli aerial attacks and tanks plowing along rural roads as Khadija relates the rage and powerlessness that she felt during the occupation. Articulating and simultaneously undermining a narration where woman equals nation, she laments, "I felt as if someone were raping my daughter in front of me; I could do nothing." She clearly describes ways in which the violent occupation targeted *all* residents of the South in varying gendered fashion: men being taken from their homes and tied up, women and children being forced to wait for hours in the village square without food or water, a tactic likely intended to increase a sense of powerlessness and dependence. For Khadija and the women who work with her, however, this injustice had the opposite effect. She decided to get involved in the resistance that emerged rather organically from a gathering of women whose husbands or sons were imprisoned at Ansar, an infamous prisoner-of-war camp. Meeting at first to comfort one another and ask news of each other's loved ones, the women decided to organize: "We decided to do something about it. To rebel." This flipping of the woman-as-nation paradigm, in which the woman becomes defender of the nation, is subtle but insistent in the film. Indeed, the collectivity of women whose impassioned accounts parallel Khadija's own story echoes and amplifies this ambivalence. Indeed, Khadija's narrative of involvement, imprisonment, release, and reinvolvement throughout the film provides a focal point from which a collective narrative resonates.

Amid Khadija's relating of a pivotal demonstration at Ansar, we are introduced to the intergenerational group of women with whom she has worked. As they gather together on a hill with their children, each relates her own action during the Israeli onslaught, her steadfastness (to borrow a term from Abdallah's poem) in the face of unimaginable violence. An older woman takes center stage, telling of her response as her son was arrested: "We all are going to resist. Men, women, and children." Another interjects, "We are going to continue resisting Israel until there are none of us left." A third tells of Israeli soldiers coming to her house to take her son: "I had a pot on the stove, I was going to throw it at them! . . . I told them, 'Shoot, I'm not afraid of you!'" A fourth mocked the Israeli soldier who tried to enforce a curfew: "I told him, 'You are so scary! I'm going to the store,'" eliciting smiles and laughter from the group. Early on in the film, we understand not only that the women used a variety of spontaneous tactics to respond to their occupiers but also that this spontaneity was manifested in relation to one another and to a broader struggle.

And yet even as we begin to understand the women's political work as essential to the resistance, women's formal role within that struggle appears largely contingent and not necessarily consistent. In sharp contrast to Baghdadi's organization-specific portrait, we never understand from *Wildflowers* with which organizations Khadija worked. She describes being violently arrested and tortured, taken first to a prison inside occupied Palestine and later to a women's prison in South Lebanon, where she was interrogated for information on resistance activities, which she refused to divulge, only vaguely alluding to participation in a formal organization. Masri and Chamoun represent some of this as reenactment. The violence she faced is decisively gendered, as is her resistance to it. She recalls that after days of isolation, exhaustion, and beatings, she responded to a soldier's threats of rape by playing on his own gendered sense of decency, "I don't have anything to tell you. And before you do anything, remember that there is God as our witness." This argument was apparently convincing, so he instead pulled her by the hair and threw her into a holding cell before she was transferred to another prison. This concealing of organizational details is the product both of Masri and Chamoun's decision to remain independent from all Lebanese political parties and of the need to establish a security measure for a film made amid an ongoing struggle.[15] Certainly, as in other instances throughout Lebanese history (and

15. The machinations of international geopolitical battles, the internal power struggles, and the practice of violence—for example, political assassinations and intra-resistance front struggles that led Hizbullah to subsume the secular Front for National Liberation—are elided in *Wildflowers*. Khadija has spoken publicly about her involvement with the PLO and her transition to a prominent role within Hizbullah—two groups

global history more broadly), the lines between organizational belonging and spontaneous participation were often blurred during the occupation. As Malek Abisaab diligently shows us in his research on workingwomen, since the inception of the Lebanese state, women participated actively in the labor movement but rarely joined the leftist and communist parties.[16] Yet in the absence of such an explicit discussion of women's participation in particular resistance organizations, we are left with a sense that women's resistance is contingent and even temporary, and so we are bereft of the opportunity to think more explicitly about women's often subsidiary position within those organizations.

Rather, the film attempts to maintain a broad setting and understanding of resistance within a collective of women and children and, again, emerging from a direct connection to the land. Portrayals of landscapes—transient, moving, and contemplative—recur throughout the film. In many ways, it appears as if the land itself is engendering the resistance or, at the very least, as if the women's political activities are in an active relationship to the land of South Lebanon. At stake in Chamoun and Masri's work is a constant challenge to the Zionist narrative. The land itself, in this case South Lebanon under Israeli control, therefore must be established as deeply rooted in the people to counteract the terrorism of the settler-colonial forces.

Khadija explicitly articulates this connection early on in the film. When she takes us to the remains of the Ansar prison, in rubble after the

---

with distinctive visions of social transformation but with equally rigid hierarchical power structures. During the early 1980s, when the film was shot, the resistance that the women are discussing in the film had not yet been solidified as *al-muqawama*, "the Resistance," and it was a more collectivist and fluid moment of response than the one we perhaps are in today. Of course, the film and filmmakers were explicitly trying not to detail that political landscape in detail. Indeed, Masri and Chamoun deliberately evaded mentioning political parties in their films, a decision that could be interpreted as a critique of all parties. Like Baghdadi's newsreel film, their wartime films aim to be an urgent reflection on a developing and critical situation. Certainly, both *The Most Beautiful of Mothers* and *Wildflowers* offer rare insight into women's roles in a moment of history that they otherwise are written out of.

16. See Abisaab, "'Unruly' Factory Women in Lebanon." Malek Abisaab's contribution to this volume, chapter 1, also touches on this issue obliquely.

Israeli military destroyed it following a prisoner swap in 1985, we have a vastly different landscape from the one Baghdadi shows. In *Wildflowers*, women react, scheme, and actively resist as part of the liberation struggle. Khadija articulates this resistance as emerging from and in relationship to the South and its people as one united body. She relates a women's march to Ansar, where she was essentially identified as an instigator: Israeli soldiers chased her with whips and guns, and she stood on a hilltop and yelled to her husband, Mohamad, and the other men inside the camp, "We are a women's march here." The women and children below and the men inside the camp joined her, yelling, "God is great," and calling to their loved ones. The prisoners yelled, defying the violence of their capturers by coming out to the prison yard and responding to their loved ones outside. In this brief moment as she relates this event, Khadija is swept away with emotion; "forgetting Mohamad," she identifies her own suffering with that of the land and of the occupied South as a whole, "as if the South itself was one suffering mass of women children and land, and I stopped thinking of just Mohamad." This weaving of life, land, and resistance together continues throughout Khadija's narration and structures Masri and Chamoun's visual approach.

As a result, the film's most dramatic scenes depict a collective resistance that appears to emerge from or even blend with the landscape. In one such sequence, we follow two young women as they walk through a field at dusk. They crouch behind trees and then stand up again, moving about decisively and fluidly. We begin to see a cable that they are carrying. Slowly we understand the women are planting a bomb, and they eventually explain to us their routine procedure of arming the landscape to prevent Israeli advancement. It is unclear if we are witnessing a reenactment or if the filmmakers are accompanying actual operatives on a mission. The blurred lines between fact and fiction make the moment all the more resonant.

In another similar moment in the film, children and women (men are conspicuously absent) run, yell, and throw stones as they repel an Israeli onslaught. The camera fluidly accompanies them as they dodge and weave behind large rocks and trees, standing on a hill above the road and leaping back down excitedly. Once again, a scene so close temporally to the actual event, located within the continuation of the same occupation, appears to be as much a reenactment as it is a training for future and continued actions. Women excitedly gather to relate their different encounters with occupation soldiers and the myriad forms of their resistance to them. One describes trafficking bombs under her pregnant belly—even feigning that she was going into labor if she was threatened with capture. In doing this, she fused the work of social reproduction with resistance work, simultaneously contributing to population growth while actively contributing to this population's means to defend and sustain itself. There is no shortage of such stories within the reenactment of the invasion in 1982. In another moment, an older woman stands on a rooftop: "I had a boiling pot of oil on the stove, [and] as the soldiers passed," she pauses dramatically, "I threw the oil from the window onto their heads." Other scenes hint at a direct link between women's household labor and political-intellectual work as well as at disruptions of gendered divisions of labor. In a third instance, two women in a garage appear to be cooking something in an old pot. As they discuss their work, it becomes apparent that they are heating materials for explosives—in essence, cooking a bomb. These explicitly political sequences are always followed by interludes of agricultural and household work: women stringing tobacco leaves, baking bread in a wood-powered stove, caring for children.

The film subtly politicizes these other forms of labor—household work, childrearing, political-intellectual labor, education—and yet these forms remain secondary to action in response to the national question. Indeed, toward the end of the film, Khadija explicitly articulates her own predisposition to reflect on the world, to question social structures, and to evaluate right and wrong in terms of her family experience and gender inequity. In a final sequence, seated with a friend and seamstress who sews as they speak, she tells the story of how her father couldn't justify spending money on a girl's education and so removed her from school as a child. Her love for knowledge was much stronger than his discipline, however, and she continued to learn by sneaking in on her brother's lessons. She later worked overtime at a sewing factory to put herself through school, lying to her parents that the instructor was teaching her for free. She states, "I'm not the kind of person who takes for granted that you should obey your parents without questioning. I would obey, but I would always question internally. . . . I was living a constant rebellion." The film might thus be subtly leading us to interpret her later decision to join the resistance as rooted in her sense of injustice as a child—patriarchal injustice here is linked to colonial injustice.

Yet the film leaves this subtle link unexplored, omitting, for example, the story of an abusive previous marriage and Khadija's separation from her children.[17] Although Khadija's persona as a militant actor in her own right undermines Sikata Banerjee's "chaste woman, militant man" binary, the filmmakers' decision to sidestep and even erase these personal details that complicate the portrait of Khadija's defense of the land are also significant. They limit the film's potential to frame the conditions under which women took active part in the resistance to Israel in light of a continuity of resistance and political action, uniting home with work with nation. Similarly, they miss the chance to consider more clearly the ways in which women's participation—say, through intellectual work—at times challenged those clear divisions of labor.

While *Wildflowers* creates a defiant vision and version of a landscape of people's resistance, it simultaneously leaves many questions unanswered, which leaves it open to some of the same critiques I made of Baghdadi's newsreel. By making the resistance appear purely as a product of personal experiences of exploitation—class, gender, colonial—the filmmakers extrapolate who participates in what kinds of decisions and at what level from our understanding of the broader political context that guides the form of resistance.

Wildflowers gestures toward explicitly linking a gendered critique of women's social, reproductive, and intellectual-political labor to a broader critique of settler colonialism and occupation, but it ultimately leaves this tension unresolved. This lack of resolution is indeed both an explicit product

17. Khadija relates these details as the subject of a later documentary, *Women of Hizbullah* (2001), by the filmmaker Maher Abi Samra. Like many of her generation, Khadija trained militarily with the PLO, which was based in Lebanon until 1982, a detail that she related to Mai Masri but that did not make it into *Wildflowers*, likely for the same reasons that Masri and Chamoun generally omitted political affiliations from their films.

of the film's verité form and assuredly a reflection of the resistance movement itself. Undoubtedly, both Baghdadi's as well as Chamoun and Masri's films reflect actual divisions of labor inherent in militarized forms of struggle almost everywhere, with their strict hierarchies, secrecy, and the virtual absence of women in leadership positions. Simultaneously, by glorifying women's auxiliary roles in anticolonial armed struggle, the films reinforce this military model of political action at the expense of other models. Certainly, though, as the films themselves suggest, that militarized model has never been the entire story. In a moment late in *Wildflowers* that could be broadly interpreted as reflecting an awareness of this point, a young woman discusses her role in planning military operations and adjusting the plan for an attack on a military facility so as not to "hurt civilians." This important documentation of rural women's political-intellectual work should not be understated. And yet the question regarding under what coordination or leadership the bombs are placed becomes secondary.

With these contexts and questions falling to the side in *Wildflowers*, we fall short of being able to imagine a different possible future—one that might have avoided the historical pattern of sidelining women's labor from political movement once the revolutionary moment subsided. Because the film omits this explicit critique, we do not end up questioning what follows from the exceptional moment of communal coordination and collective action that it shows. What other futures might have been? What other kinds of films might we imagine, recuperate, or make that would engender different kinds of frameworks for action? In sum, what does a feminist reading of *The Most Beautiful of Mothers* and *Wildflowers* together provide as a method or model for future work?

Beyond the Most Beautiful of Mothers

I first viewed *The Most Beautiful of Mothers* and *Wildflowers* in 2010 in the makeshift screening room of the film-production house and cinema association Beirut DC. At the time, I was doing preliminary research for what became my film *A Feeling Greater Than Love* (2017). This meant I was explicitly searching for specific images—those depicting labor strikes, farmers organizing, and women's political action in general. A few of the participants in the social movements of the 1970s whom I had previously interviewed recalled such images within Maroun Baghdadi's films, and some perhaps thought there were some in Chamoun and Masri's films as well. Ten years ago Beirut DC's impressive archive of VHS transfers was the only way to view Lebanese *cinema badila* (alternative cinema) of the 1970s and 1980s. Over several weeks, I watched Beirut DC's entire collection of Baghdadi's films, from fiction to documentary; Masri and Chamoun's slightly better-circulated works; and a handful of other films by Joceleyn Saab, Randa Chahal, Borhane Alaouie, and others.

To my disappointment, none of these beautiful and rich films contained the images of popular labor struggle that had been described to me as being shown in them. My interlocutors' impressions were thus likely based on their own limited viewings due to the lack of films' availability decades earlier. Significantly, their memories of the broad-based and multilayered social movements overlapped with the films' production, but they still remained largely unpictured and merged into their memories of wartime cinema—much like those alternative narratives of struggle subsumed into war.

The scenes they imagined are a kind of archive of a broader and more complex movement landscape that intervenes in more regimented versions of politics. Finding those counternarratives, ellipses, and erased gestures can open new terrain for both the study and the production of Lebanese cinema—an archive still much in need of excavation. Certainly, the past decade has seen exciting experiments in investigating hidden narratives of women's experience in and around war. Works by Zeina Daccache, Rami Nehawi, Eliane Raheb, Mai Masri, and the history lab Knowledge Workshop are just a few examples of contemporary filmmakers doing such work in Lebanon today. Yet there is much work to be done to create a fuller picture of the varied horizons of women's political action and of the obstacles to that action during the Civil War and beyond it. Still more work is required to mobilize those histories into forms useful to present-day struggles. I would also like to suggest that a third, more nebulous, and exceedingly ambitious path emerges from viewing these films side by side, one that could situate women's everyday experience and varied forms of labor in relation to these narratives of struggle as well as provide means for a broadly transformative feminist cinema and politics.

Searching for those elusive scenes while viewing *The Most Beautiful of Mothers* alongside *Wildflowers*, I quickly began to read the latter as a response to the former, despite the fact that Chamoun and Masri had not seen Baghdadi's film before they made their own.[18] The two films' narratives began a conversation, an affective montage between past and present, across space and time—between the South Lebanon of the late 1970s and early 1980s and the independent cinema-production house in which I viewed the films decades later. A set of questions arose through this conjuncture. Baghdadi's particular politicization of motherhood brought into sharp focus Chamoun and Masri's expanded landscape of political action and much subtler treatment of social reproductive labor. Together, the films called into question the possibilities of everyday linkages between women's labor and explicit political struggle in what remained beyond the screen. Some of those questions indeed echo persistent, if muffled, debates from the period surrounding women's circumscribed frames for political participation.[19] As I was looking explicitly for images of women in social movements, beyond the military struggle, I began to question why those images did not exist.

Similarly, the time–space gap between the films, which were made in South Lebanon some seven years apart, each with a distinct funding structure, raises another set of questions about the political economy of funding and distribution. Baghdadi's film was produced by a political organization, the OCA, and shown at the United Nations General Assembly; Chamoun and Masri's film in turn was funded by European and American television and shown in film festivals and on European television. My experience of these films is similarly situated in relation to the physical space of Beirut DC, a hub for independent cinema production financed largely by European Union Development Grants and occasional

18. Indeed, the inaccessibility of the two films amid the broader condition of civil war, which complicated collective viewing, meant that filmmakers were often unfamiliar with one another's work (Mai Masri, personal communication to Mary Jirmanus Saba, April 2019).

19. See Daou, "Feminisms in Lebanon," and Ribas-Mateos, "Women and Left in the Middle East," 284.

service provision, such as equipment rental.[20] Although political-party-sponsored and hodgepodge-funded Lebanese cinema of the 1970s and 1980s has given way to a more systematized international funding scheme, the latter scheme, too, has incentivized the production of certain kinds of films but marginalized others.[21] Attentiveness to this political-economic context is essential even as we try to uncover other kinds of past narratives that might be useful to our future imaginings. Most crucially, however, it is this relation among films, narratives, and missing images that opens up a space to think about both what kinds of films we lack as well as the kind of films that are allowed to be made and are relatively easily funded, distributed, critiqued, and seen. Here again I pose the question about what a critical feminist cinema might do for contemporary Lebanese politics more broadly. This is the work of imagining different futures as well of beginning to construct them.

This relational method, inspired by my own serendipitous viewing of these two films in dialogue with one another (and with what they did *not* show), is informed equally by the various theorists and practitioners of the Global Women's Strike, a proposed international general strike by unwaged workers inspired by Selma James, Margaret Prescod, Silvia Federici, and others' theorizations around an International Wages for Housework Campaign in the 1970s.[22] The strike has the aims of achieving a wage for caregivers and presenting "a way of organizing from the bottom up, of autonomous sectors working together to end the power relations among us."[23]

20. In fact, in 2016 I finalized the edit for *A Feeling Greater Than Love* in Beirut DC's backyard editing suite, at the time being rented out to Goethe Institute Beirut. See also Farine, "Imaginaire cinématographique du 'dialogue euro méditerranéen.'"

21. Although surprisingly little has been written about the funding and festival landscape's impact on the kinds of films that are produced and circulated, the preference for "character-driven narratives" that has articulated by funding bodies globally at least since the late 1990s has assuredly had an impact. See Farine, "Imaginaire cinématographique du 'dialogue euro méditerranéen,'" and Ross, "The Film Festival as Producer."

22. Global Women's Strike, "Global Women's Strike Demands"; Federici, *Wages against Housework*.

23. Global Women's Strike, "Global Women's Strike Demands."

As the Argentinian scholar-activist Verónica Gago has argued, the aspiration for and practice of such a strike are profoundly relational. Writing to promote the Feminist Strike of 2018, she connects our ability to assimilate or comprehend knowledge of the most extreme kinds of violence and oppression enacted on women by global capitalist patriarchy. She gives the example of what she calls the world "femicide capital"—Ciudad Juárez in Mexico—and the everyday experience of life and work under that system, arguing "there is no international women's strike without the expanded geography of Ciudad Juárez, without our fears and our desires, which are all mixed up there, to the rhythm of flexibilized production and the border, escapes, and conditions of exploitation that we never would have imagined we would be able to handle or confront."[24] She is speaking from a Latin American context but reaching beyond it; Ciudad Juárez is likewise indelibly linked to past histories of women's struggles across time and space, including strikes from the 1920s in which women were central, if marginalized, protagonists. All of this together creates an understanding without which we cannot link our own experience to a broader analysis of exploitation and the possibilities of collective action. Tithi Bhattacharya clarifies: "The fundamental insight of SRT [social reproduction theory] is, simply put, that human labor is at the heart of creating or reproducing society as a whole."[25] To think about the disruptive and generative potential of halting *all* social reproductive labor is the proposition from which the women's strike takes off. Its proponents suggest that the women's strike and reproductive labor are far from marginal to a transformative class struggle but rather essential to its liberatory potential.

These expanded affective geographies are likewise relevant to the off-camera story of Hassan Abdallah's inspiration, the mother of a martyr who sought to mourn and inspire her neighbors by blasting loud nationalist music from her home, thus making herself a target to the occupiers. They relate to the stories of women who persisted and carried on life in their villages despite some twenty years of Israeli occupation. These

24. Gago, "WeStrike," 678.

25. Bhattacharya, "Introduction," 2.

internationalist feminist reverberations are also linked to the gendered torture women have suffered in Israeli prisons, as Khadija describes in *Wildflowers*, thus associating herself with female comrades of many political persuasions. Together, these stories open enormous space not only for critique and cinematic production but also for a politics that links everyday experience with a rich tradition of women's political action. This relational method of viewing and making feminist cinema also offers directions for politics itself. Women's stories in cinema can be so productive for understanding what to do now because we cannot make new what we have not yet understood. To create a movement, we must act as we would in making a critical historical film: reflexively, reflectively, with attention to the productive contradictions that are opened between efforts, as they are between films.

What might filmmaking in this relational mode look like? How and through what collective production processes might films be made? Where and how would they be displayed? And what kind of alternative horizons could they open? Perhaps such films will not be "new" at all but rather excuses for gathering across distance and generation. How else might we create a cinema that does not seek to memorialize and does not consecrate already-existing inequalities but rather explodes them? Such a turn in our thinking, filmmaking, and political work is essential today as the paths leading us out of the Lebanese uprisings of 2019 appear murkier and as the financial crisis and COVID-19 pandemic highlight the need for a politics in Lebanon and beyond that integrates care, mutual support, and radical (re)imagination in a historically informed praxis. Only in this way can *ajmal al-umahat* become not a foreclosing trope for women but a means toward centering women's labor into an integrated and radically open cinema and politics.

3

"I Was Beirut"

Seta Manoukian and Art as Therapy during and after the Lebanese Civil War

NOVA ROBINSON

A young girl sits with a paintbrush between her thumb and forefinger. She had just dipped the brush into black paint and was contemplating where to drop it on the blank piece of paper before her. She settled on the upper-right corner and started to press her brush to the page. The young boy to her right was carefully painting a building, while a girl a few years her senior was hunched over in concentration, working on a painting that tried to capture the gradated blues of the sea. A calm energy suffused the light-filled room in an abandoned Armenian neighborhood center in Zokak al-Blat, not far from the Green Line, which divided East and West Beirut. Living so close to the epicenter of the fighting in the Lebanese Civil War, the neighborhood's children needed a creative outlet to process their experiences with the war. A teacher in her thirties with thick brown hair and a simple beige blouse circulated among the children, praising their paintings. Her name was Seta Manoukian (b. 1945).

Manoukian, now known as Ani Pema Tsultrim Drolma, is a Lebanese artist for whom art is a healing, spiritual outlet. Indeed, she has described the "arts as a spiritual quest."[1] During the Lebanese Civil War, Manoukian

1. In Svetlana Darsalia, dir., *Mother Sela: Artist and Buddhist Nunn* (documentary film) (Three Point Landing, 2012).

chose to share the healing properties of art with children in Beirut. In doing so, she pioneered the use of art as a therapeutic outlet for children. In the makeshift art rooms she created, she gave children paint and paper and then encouraged them to produce free-form paintings, a hallmark of art therapy. In the late 1970s and early 1980s, many children in impoverished and middle-class West Beirut neighborhoods produced paintings under Manoukian's guidance, which provide an enduring record of the war through children's eyes.

Some of the children's wartime paintings captured the playful whimsy of children given the opportunity to create—irregularly drawn flowers, people dancing—but most of them depicted graphic content—dead bodies, bullets, and bombs—thereby serving as a record of the children's wartime anguish. The images the children produced with Manoukian were collected into two books. The first, *Lebanese Children and the War* (1977), was published in Arabic, English, and French. The multilingual nature of the volume indicates that Manoukian and her collaborators wanted to use it to broadcast stories of children's wartime experiences to an international audience. A second title followed in 1983: *Traces rouges et bleues: Exprimées par les enfants durant l'occupation* coupled reproductions of the children's artwork with photos of the children at work producing the images during the Israeli invasion of South Lebanon and the bombing of Beirut in 1982. Pairing photographs of the children's rapt attention while painting and the resulting artistic images that documented the violence of the war highlighted the war's psychological and spiritual impact on civilians, especially children. The children look peaceful, but the images they produced are detailed accounts of the war's toll on young civilians. Both books contain paintings by children as young as five that convey an understanding of the general outline of the war unfolding not far from where they lived, played, and in the summer of 1982 cowered from bombings.

This chapter chronicles Seta Manoukian's path toward using art therapy techniques with children in Beirut between 1975 and 1983. It also puts Manoukian's use of art therapy into regional and global context before exploring how her own artistic practice served as a therapeutic salve for her own experiences of war. Manoukian's wartime oeuvre and the paintings produced by children in her art room produce a record of the conflict and offer a window into women's and children's war stories, which are often sidelined in the wider official history of the Lebanese Civil War.

Seta Manoukian's "White Period" and the Eve of War

Manoukian was born into a wealthy and artistic Armenian family in Beirut in 1945. Her grandfather, an Orthodox priest, had fled the Armenian Genocide and ended up on the outskirts of Beirut. Her father, Avedis Manoukian (1915–2011), was an industrialist in the aluminum sector who appreciated and supported the arts; he became a painter at the age of eighty-four. Manoukian's mother and grandmother (a silk artist) cultivated her creativity. They weaned her on art books and enrolled her in ballet and Armenian folkdance classes. At twelve, she discovered painting. She was naturally talented, so her family arranged for her to take classes with the famous Lebanese Armenian painter Paul Guiragossian. His imprint on her artistic development is visible in her early work, especially in her vivid color palette.

In 1963 at age eighteen, she won a painting competition sponsored by the Italian Consulate in Beirut that included a scholarship to study painting in Perugia, Italy. Enamored with Italy, she stayed and continued her studies at the Fine Arts Academy in Rome. In 1967, after graduating, she was drawn back to Beirut. Upon returning there, she was alarmed by the "spiritual absence" she sensed in the Arab world, which had recently gone to war with Israel and had lost.[2] Preparing for a solo exhibit at a gallery in Beirut restored her vitality, though. Her sister recalled that the entire Armenian community turned out for the exhibit to make sure she had returned "safe and sound."[3] They likely enjoyed the bright portraits and abstract paintings, too. In 1973, Manoukian went to London to study silk-screen printing. Both sojourns abroad shaped her evolving artistic style and enhanced her use of color and form.

After years of playing with color, Manoukian started painting images of her bedroom, which turned into the "Inside the Room" series. The walls of Manoukian's bedroom, captured with deep, angular shadows and sharp

2. In Darsalia, *Mother Sela*.

3. A. Manoukian, "Seta Manoukian," 166.

lines, convey an intense foreboding and are more evocative of a prison than of a place of rest. When viewed as a whole, the bedroom images capture Manoukian's sense of being trapped by circumstance, which for her included several overlapping factors: class, gender, religion, ethnicity, location. After painting her room in a series of menacing, distorted angles, Manoukian moved from painting the physical environs of her room to painting her bed. The images, such as *First Atom of a Dream on Trauma* (1970), evoke a person trapped in the sheets, unable to break free, yet they do not feature any body parts. The unseen bodies struggling to escape convey the tension swirling under the surface in Beirut in the early 1970s.

Manoukian's "White Period" images chronicle the buildup to the Civil War and document the toll that the uncertainty in this period took on Beirutis' psyches. Manoukian's impulse to use her paintbrush to capture her mental anguish as political and economic forces drove her country apart likely helped others understand they were not alone in despairing about the future. She described the "whole country as traumatized" on the eve of the war.[4] She found an artistic and intellectual community at the Horseshoe Café in Hamra, where artists gathered over strong coffee and packs of cigarettes to discuss the specter of war in Lebanon and the state of Arab politics in the region more broadly. Like her friends the playwright Ziad Rahbani and the filmmaker Maroun Baghdadi, Manoukian was sympathetic to the social and economic suffering of Palestinian refugees, especially Palestinian children. Her artistic profile in Lebanon continued to rise, and in 1975, just as the political and economic fracas erupted into war, she secured a position teaching art in the Fine Arts Department at the Lebanese University.

Art as an Antidote to Wars in Lebanon and Palestine

Much of the fighting in the early stages of the Lebanese Civil War happened in densely populated urban environments, so civilians lived close to and sometimes on the front lines of the conflict. Many civilians stayed home, but Manoukian did not want to shut herself in because "if you stay home, you end up being paranoid. If you are in the streets helping, it is

4. Ani Pema Tsultrim Drolma (Seta Manoukian), telephone interview in English by Nova Robinson, Aug. 5, 2019.

better for everybody."[5] In reflecting on how she could help as an artist and a teacher, she settled on teaching art because "art was the only way I knew how to help."[6] She brought tempera paints and blank pieces of white paper to children living in the umbra of the war.

Manoukian distributed the materials, and the students instinctively knew what to do: paint. John Berger, author of the seminal text about how to look at art, *Ways of Seeing* (1972), has observed elsewhere that children all over the world paint in similar ways. Of course, there is variation in what they paint; a child surrounded by desert in Libya will depict the world differently than one surrounded by verdant mountains in Lebanon or the sea in Bahrain. Berger notes, however, that "what is similar is the way young children make intuitive marks on the paper—a question of space, gestures, proportion, even color." He adds, "The first early language of painting appears to have a biological rather than a cultural basis."[7]

Manoukian did not give any directions to the children gathered in the abandoned factory in Zokak al-Blat or in the abandoned school in Wadi Jamil, nor did she direct the children in poorer suburbs. She said she gave students artistic freedom because she "wanted the images to be totally genuine, without interference from grownups. I did not want to spoil their expression."[8] As a consequence, the images are unfettered, reflecting the innate language that painting brings forth. All of the paintings, even those of the sea, are powerful records of the emotional and psychological toll of the war on young children. Some of the paintings are more overt war narratives that feature guns, militias, and bombs. Manoukian observed, "I saw the hand of the teachers" in other books about war. "The [teachers] were correcting and instructing too much. I hated that. This is war. This is trauma. You cannot tell students what to do."[9] It appears Manoukian defined "trauma" in this case as an experience that overwhelmed the children and had a lasting psychological impact. This framing of "trauma"

5. Drolma, interview.

6. Drolma, interview.

7. Berger, foreword to Boullata, *Faithful Witnesses*, 9.

8. Drolma, interview.

9. Drolma, interview.

aligns with recent scholarship that defines it as "an autonomic, physiological, and neurological response to overwhelming events or experiences that creates a secondary psychological response."[10]

Giving children art materials and encouraging them to express themselves without much intervention, as Manoukian did, falls within the parameters of art therapy, which is defined as an interdisciplinary mix of the arts and therapy.[11] Art therapy emphasizes the notion that expression through the arts can "circumvent the limitations of language," which are especially pronounced in young children whose language capacities are not fully developed.[12] Manoukian's use of art therapy with vulnerable, traumatized children in Lebanon was novel for the Lebanese context. Manoukian was not a trained art therapist, but such credentialing was relatively new in the United States and was not available in Lebanon in the 1970s. The emphasis placed on securing the right credentials to be a practicing art therapist today is admirable but should not be projected on the past to discredit the healing work Manoukian did with children during the first decade of the Lebanese Civil War.

A growing body of research has investigated art therapy's ability to help children who have experienced various forms of trauma, including war. The first book to display children's experiences during conflict in the Middle East, *In Time of War: Children Testify* (1970), was produced by the

10. Rothchild, *The Body Remembers*, 4.

11. According to the American Art Therapy Association (AATA), "art therapy" is "an integrative mental health and human services profession that enriches the lives of individuals, families, and communities through active art-making, creative process, applied psychological theory, and human experience within a psychotherapeutic relationship." The AATA further emphasizes that art therapy can be "used to improve cognitive and sensory-motor functions, foster self-esteem and self-awareness, cultivate emotional resilience, promote insight, enhance social skills, reduce and resolve conflicts and distress, and advance societal and ecological change." Finally, the AATA observes that "art therapy engages the mind, body, and spirit in ways that are distinct from verbal articulation alone. Kinesthetic, sensory, perceptual, and symbolic opportunities invite alternative modes of receptive and expressive communication, which can circumvent the limitations of language" (American Art Therapy Association, "About Art Therapy").

12. American Art Therapy Association, "About Art Therapy."

Jordanian sculptor Mona Saudi.[13] A year after the 1967 Arab–Israeli War, Saudi produced art with Palestinian children in the Baqa'a refugee camp in Jordan. She later reflected, "I was able to give these children the opportunity to express themselves freely using just paper and wax colors." She was "fascinated by their creations" and decided to turn them into a book, "in which children, through their drawings and words[,] expressed political conflict, the war, exile, and their dreams and hopes."[14] The resulting images were accompanied by poems written by the children and by narration of the students' experiences.

Saudi's editorial voice comes through in the juxtaposition of text and images. For example, a painting of a woman in *qabbeh*-embroidered *thob* picking apples from a tree, with rolling hills in the background, was paired alongside a poem by eight-year-old Nawal Ahmad:

> The trees were laden with fruit.
> The enemy's airplanes came and
> bombed the camp and the trees.
> The green leaves burned, the roses
> fell, the apples fell, and the
> neighbour's daughter also.[15]

Guns and planes featured prominently in the book's images of the war. Two sociologists who studied the reasons for the exodus in 1967 found that planes were crucial in compelling many Palestinians to flee the West Bank.[16] The prevalence of images of planes in the children's art captures the psychological trauma experienced by some of the war's young refugees. The children's frequent paintings of the bombers led Saudi to write, "The cry of the poor, of a suffering people, will ultimately always be a call to revolution for a new and purer world where a Palestinian child will draw a house under a sky free of bombers."[17]

13. Mona Saudi, telephone interview by Nova Robinson, Aug. 28, 2019.
14. Saudi, *Forty Years in Sculpture*, 35–36.
15. Saudi, *In Time of War*, xx.
16. Saudi, *In Time of War*, xx.
17. Saudi, *In Time of War*, xx.

Since the publication of Saudi's volume in 1970, children's wartime images have been showcased during each period of conflict in the Middle East. Collections of children's artwork were produced in Lebanon during the Civil War, in Palestine during the Intifadas, and in Iraq during the Iran–Iraq War of 1980–88 and then during the US invasion and occupation in 2003. A recent volume showcases art produced by children living in refugee camps on Syria's borders.[18] Both Saudi and Manoukian worked to get the children's images into global circulation.[19]

Manoukian knew of Saudi's work but did not set out to replicate it in Beirut during the Civil War. She said she was motivated by a desire to help children create and find peace through art. Manoukian's friends came up with the idea of producing *Lebanese Children and the War.*[20] The second book chronicling children's wartime experiences during the Israeli occupation, *Traces rouges et bleues*, was produced in collaboration with the League for Lebanese Women's Rights. In addition to the book, the images were put on public display in abandoned buildings. Calendars with the children's work were also produced to raise funds for war victims. Manoukian recalled that the exhibits and the books were "received tremendously well—everyone wanted a copy."[21]

A Paintbrush and Love: Art Therapy with Children in War Zones

Both Saudi's and Manoukian's use of art therapy with children during periods of war preceded the theory of art therapy. Since the late 1970s, the formal academic field of art therapy has flourished, though its practice has a longer history. Therapists used art with psychiatric patients as early as the 1920s, but this art was produced primarily for its aesthetic

18. Syrian refugee children's art has been featured in many news outlets. The Australian artist Ben Quilty compiled a series of images in *Home: Drawings by Syrian Children* (2018).

19. Saudi's and Manoukian's books produced about children's wartime experiences in Palestine and Lebanon in the late 1960s and early 1970s are presently out of circulation.

20. Drolma, interview.

21. Drolma, interview.

value rather than for its potentially therapeutic or diagnostic properties.[22] Using the therapeutic aspects of art has roots in Freudian psychoanalysis and stretches back to the 1940s in the United States and England.[23] Freud's theories of the unconscious and the power of dreams were explored and adapted by social scientists in the Arab world.[24] Carl Gustav Jung, following in the Freudian tradition of analyzing the subconscious, asked his patients to draw their dreams, observing that "to paint what we see before us is a different art from painting what we see within."[25] After the trauma of World War II, there was an increased appreciation in Europe and the United States of "art as an expression of a person's inner mind."[26] However, the arts have long been recognized for their healing powers, historical records indicate that Navajo sand painting and some forms of sculpture found in sub-Saharan Africa were developed and practiced with a therapeutic effect in mind.[27] Therefore, even prior to the development of the formal field of art therapy, as the psychologist Jeanne Achterberg observes, "the use of image and imagination in the context of healing [was] prevalent in both Western and non-Western cultures."[28]

Using a patient's drawings as the basis for psychological tests emerged in the first half of the twentieth century. These tests were designed to let a person respond to ambiguous prompts or stimuli. According to this branch of art therapy, asking a patient to draw a "house-tree-person" or to have her analyze an inkblot—as in the famous Rorschach inkblot test, which was developed in 1921 and popular in the 1960s but widely criticized since then—would reveal her unspoken or hidden internal conflicts.[29] The art projects Manoukian and Saudi developed with children

22. Junge, *The Modern History of Art Therapy*, 8.

23. Junge, *The Modern History of Art Therapy*, 7.

24. On Freud in the Arab world, see Omnia El Shakry's book *The Arabic Freud* (2017).

25. Jung, *Practice of Psychotherapy*, 253.

26. Junge, *The Modern History of Art Therapy*, 8.

27. Junge, *The Modern History of Art Therapy*, 7.

28. Achterberg, *Imagery in Healing*, 7.

29. Debate about the diagnostic validity of the Rorschach test continued through the late 1990s. See, for example, Wood and Lilienfeld, "The Rorschach Inkblot Test," and Weiner, "Some Observations on the Validity of the Rorschach Inkblot Method," 206.

experiencing war in Lebanon and in Palestinian refugee camps in Jordan did not engage in this diagnostic form of art therapy. Rather, they tried to share with children the therapeutic properties of art that they themselves experienced as artists in their work with oil paint and stone to capture and convey meaning. Saudi and Manoukian were using art therapy for its therapeutic qualities, not for what it could reveal psychologically.

The field of art therapy formalized in the United States with the creation of the American Art Therapy Association in 1969; the association's journal, *Art Therapy*, followed in 1983. Thus, Saudi and Manoukian used art as therapy in Jordan and in Lebanon alongside the formalization of the field in other parts of the world. However, most scholarship focuses on art therapy in Europe and North America, thereby perpetuating the notion that it originated in the "West." Such an origin story occludes the fact that art therapy spread organically and seemingly simultaneously throughout the world in the 1970s. In fact, some aspects of "Western" art therapy were borrowed from "non-Western" artistic traditions. For example, some art therapy practitioners have used the mandala, a circular figure representing the universe in the Hindu and Buddhist traditions, as a therapeutic outlet. The first scholarship on using art therapy with children in conflict zones was published in the early 1990s, many years after Manoukian and Saudi had children express themselves through art during periods of conflict in Palestine and Lebanon in the late 1960s and early 1970s.[30] A whole subfield of art therapy has emerged to help civilians, children in particular, process war trauma.[31]

Manoukian's therapeutic work with children predated but predicted the best practices of art therapy for children traumatized by war and its aftereffects. Her instinctual practices align with the theory that has been established since the late 1980s by practitioners operating in the United States and Europe. Much of the scholarship on art therapy asserts the importance of creating a safe space for children, or "clients," so they feel

30. Tanay, "Croatian and Bosnian Children's Art in Times of War"; Byers, "Children of the Stones."

31. See McKray, *The Psychological Impact of War Trauma on Civilians*; Baker, "Art Speaks in Healing Survivors of War"; and Jones, *Art-Making with Refugees and Survivors.*

comfortable producing art that captures their feelings.[32] This safe and supportive space is most important in diagnostic art therapy settings but is also essential in other settings that wish to use the therapeutic properties of art. Cathy Malchiodi, a social scientist who studies art therapy, emphasizes that when therapists encounter children who have experienced trauma, they must "form a productive relationship with them to enable them not only to revisit painful experiences, but also to overcome intrusive memories, make meaning, and find hope."[33] In such an environment, art becomes a tool for processing trauma and a creative outlet that provides relief. Manoukian recalls the children running up to her and hugging her whenever she arrived with art supplies. She remembers they "were extremely enthusiastic. They loved to paint and draw."[34] The first children who painted with Manoukian also recruited other children to join them in making art, another sign that they felt comfortable expressing themselves with paint in Manoukian's presence.

Another tenet of art therapy suggests that children should produce work without much direction, although they should be given age-appropriate materials. This freedom of expression allows for "multiple possibilities and provides the opportunity for multiple levels of narrative to unfold."[35] Manoukian instinctively, perhaps based on her own artistic practice, gave students the materials to paint their feelings and fears without much intervention. Such free forms of expression help children, who, owing to age or trauma or both, are not as able to communicate verbally. Manoukian had children work with watercolors and tempera paints, which are widely regarded an age-appropriate media for children as young as two. In addition, the literature on art therapy suggests avoiding a close reading of the art in the presence of the child or client. Manoukian said she did not analyze the work, just showed support, compassion, and love

32. Many academic resources emphasize the importance of creating a safe, supportive art therapy environment for traumatized children; see, for example, Farrell-Kirk, "Secrets, Symbols, Synthesis, and Safety," 88.

33. Malchiodi, "Neurobiology, Creative Interventions, and Childhood Trauma," 3.

34. Drolma, interview.

35. Kalmanowitz and Lloyd, "Art Therapy and Political Violence," 27.

with comments such as "Whoa, beautiful."[36] Such forms of verbal support de-emphasize the final product and emphasize the production process, an emphasis that is heralded as essential in art therapy environments.

Contemporary scholarship on art therapy further underscores that therapists should know the community they are working with, so that the interventions are culturally sensitive.[37] As a resident of Zokak al-Blat, Manoukian knew the children's cultural context, if not their families. Furthermore, scholars who study art therapy encourage practitioners to avoid stereotyping foreign cultures and to understand the meaning of art in the communities in which they are working.[38] This intervention emerged after US art therapists working in the Balkans experienced some cultural misunderstandings with the communities they intended to help.[39] Since Manoukian was living through the war and was working with poor and middle-class children in her own neighborhood, she was well acquainted with the needs of the community she was working with. Even when she was working with children in other neighborhoods, she always shared a language—Arabic—and an overarching national identity—Lebanese—with the children, who were from the Orthodox, Sunni, Shiʿa, Armenian, Kurdish, and Palestinian communities in Lebanon.[40]

She remembered that the children were "very thankful," perhaps because someone gave them a tool to express their deepest fears about their security and that of their loved ones.[41] Manoukian's goal was to build community for students who felt alone, especially during bombardments. She said that children instinctively knew that even if they sought refuge on their mothers' laps as bombs fell, their mothers could not protect them.[42]

36. Drolma, interview.

37. Art therapists frequently emphasize the importance of cultural sensitivity. See, for example, Westlich, "Art Therapy with Culturally Different Clients," and Malchiodi, "Ethics, Evidence, Trauma-Informed Practice, and Cultural Sensitivity."

38. Chebaro, "Cross-Cultural Inquiry in Art and Therapy," 229.

39. Kälin and Murphy, "'The Moment in and out of Time.'"

40. Drolma, interview.

41. Drolma, interview.

42. Drolma, interview.

After seeing the positive effects of Manoukian's work with children, other artists and art teachers joined her in bringing art to children caught on the front lines of war.

Manoukian believes that "if you deeply love children, they love you." Through sharing the language of art, Manoukian was able to share this message of love and give the children an outlet for their feelings, which might lead to healing. She is quick to assert that although she saw that what she was doing with the children was art therapy, her sessions with them were "too short to engage in a healing process."[43] Yet she also asserts that "art is a healer, always."[44] As a traveling art teacher, Manoukian transformed abandoned rooms into healing spaces full of therapeutic artistic production. The paintings the children produced under Manoukian's guidance helped them process their feelings about the war; the images provide an arresting and affecting visual record of children's wartime experiences.

Children's Visual Testimonies of the Lebanese Civil War

A solo female figure stands in front of a blazing city. Her body and hair are black, putting her pink-yellow face into sharp relief.[45] Her eyes are closed. Perhaps she is imagining the scene behind her; perhaps she is fleeing it. The foreground and the background, both a deep, burning burgundy-plum, blend together, suspending this figure alone amid the chaos. Ash falls around her, and impaled bodies puncture the background. Twelve-year-old Ibtissam Zein's image (figure 3.1), along with others like it in *Lebanese Children and the War*, might reflect a scene the child witnessed but more likely captures the child's feelings about the war: the confusion, the chaos, the fear of being left alone. Some children painted happier scenes, but most children depicted the conflict itself and its victims or represented their inner pain and trauma through their somber olor palette or their chosen subject matter, which foregrounded conflict and suffering.

43. Drolma, interview.

44. In Darsalia, *Mother Sela*.

45. All images referenced in this section come from S. Manoukian, *Lebanese Children and the War.*

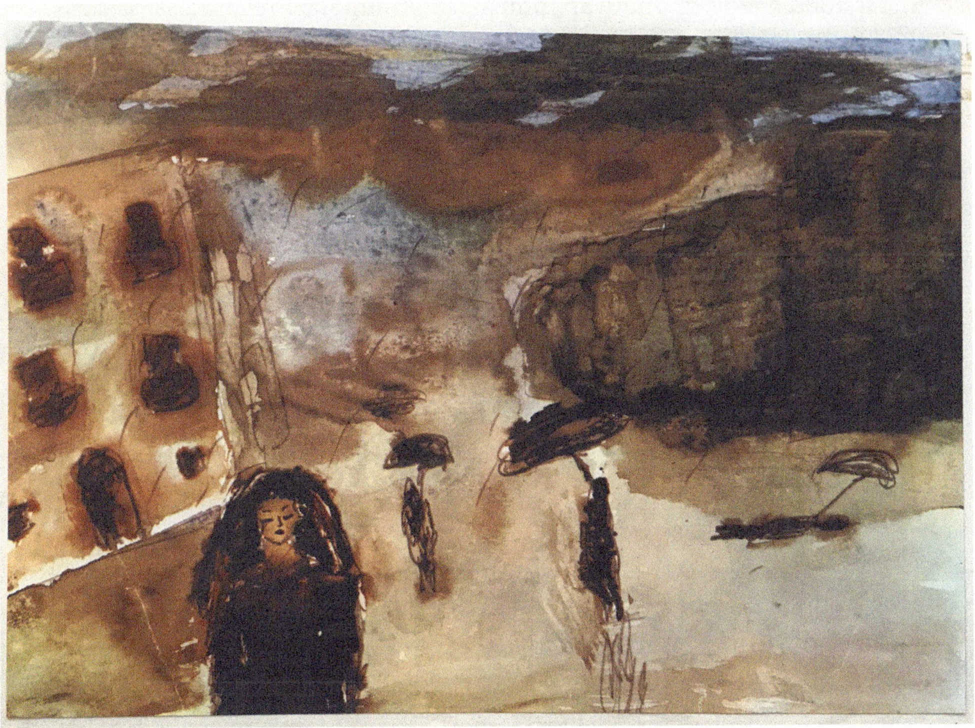

3.1. Photo reproduction of Ibtissam Zein's watercolor, originally published in Zeta Manoukian, *Lebanese Children and the War* (Beirut: Technopress Moderne/Dar al-Farabi, 1977), 14.

The images in *Lebanese Children and the War* feature the artwork of three groups of children: two from the Lycée Fakhreddine and the Lycée Abdulkader, lower-middle-class schools in West Beirut, and one from Chiah, a socioeconomically depressed neighborhood to the southwest of the city that was home to a large Palestinian community.[46] The visual tropes and patterns that pervade their images reveal how children from across the socioeconomic spectrum in Lebanon experienced and

46. All my efforts to locate a full copy of Manoukian's second text, *Traces rouges et bleues: Exprimées par les enfants durant l'occupation* were unsuccessful. I thank Mary Dib of the League for Lebanese Women's Rights for sharing a few images from the text with me.

understood the war. The war influenced childhoods regardless of class, though it compounded and complicated the material realities of poorer children more than of their wealthier peers, who often had the resources to escape into the countryside when the fighting in the city escalated. The children from Lycée Fakhreddine and Lycée Abdulkader had more artistic training than their counterparts in Chiah, but, overall, the images produced by all three groups provide similar visual testimonies to the children's emotional experiences during the conflict, dominated by confusion and fear. Their images blend the real and the imagined. The power of each image lies in the uncertainty about whether it depicts something the child witnessed or something conjured from the child's imagination. In blending lived experiences of the war with imagined hellscapes, the images provide a hitorical record of the emotional duress experienced by Lebanese children during the war.

Black, graduated black, and deep gray dominate the foregrounds and backgrounds of many images. The child artists also frequently dipped their paintbrushes in red paint to depict blood and flames. The dark color choices reveal that preoccupied, worried, and fearful children painted the images selected for inclusion in the book. Eleven-year-old Sabah Dimechkie painted one especially arresting image of a masklike face, more demon than human (figure 3.2). Two blood-red eyes with green pupils stare back at the viewer. A thick, off-white outline sets off the black, angular face—like two diamonds stacked on top of one another—from the blood-red backdrop. White horns protrude from the figure's helmet. An elongated nose and a square mouth complete the frightening face. This nightmarish face captures the menace Sabah felt during the war. Not all children rendered their unnamed fears in such a precise manner. Hussein Ibrahim, a nine-year-old from Chiah, drew a single home and a small shrub in pencil and then painted over it in drippy, thick watercolors that blended black, fuchsia, vermillion, aubergine, burnt umber, and marigold (figure 3.3). The effect is as if light is coming out of darkness, only to be consumed by darkness again: a window into the child's turbulent inner world during the war. Hussein was not the only child to paint over a happier image with dark colors; when asked if any images children painted stayed with her, Manoukian recalled the work done by a young

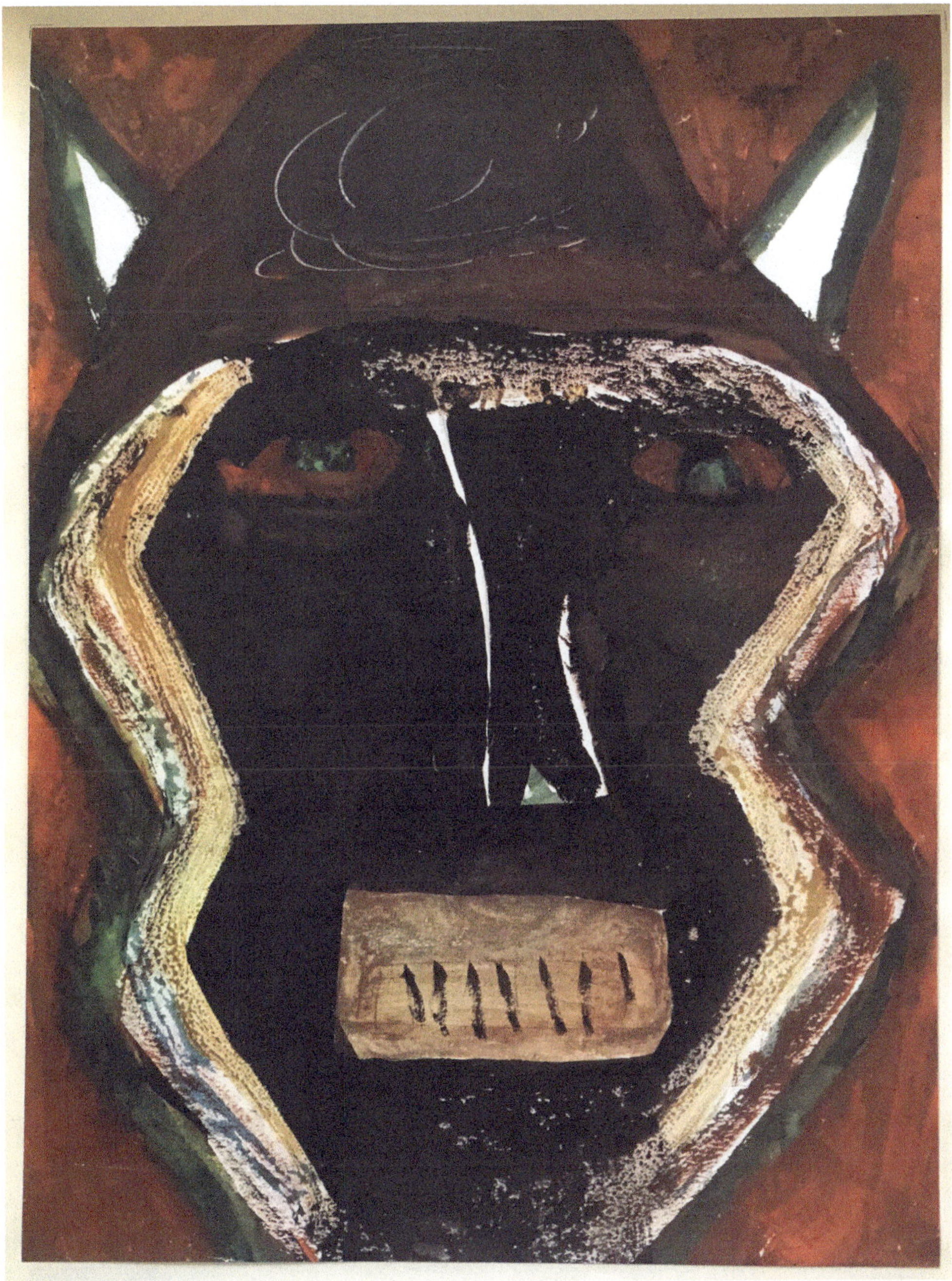

3.2. Photo reproduction of Sabah Dimechkie's watercolor, originally published in Seta Manoukian, *Lebanese Children and the War* (Beirut: Technopress Moderne/ Dar al-Farabi, 1977), 24.

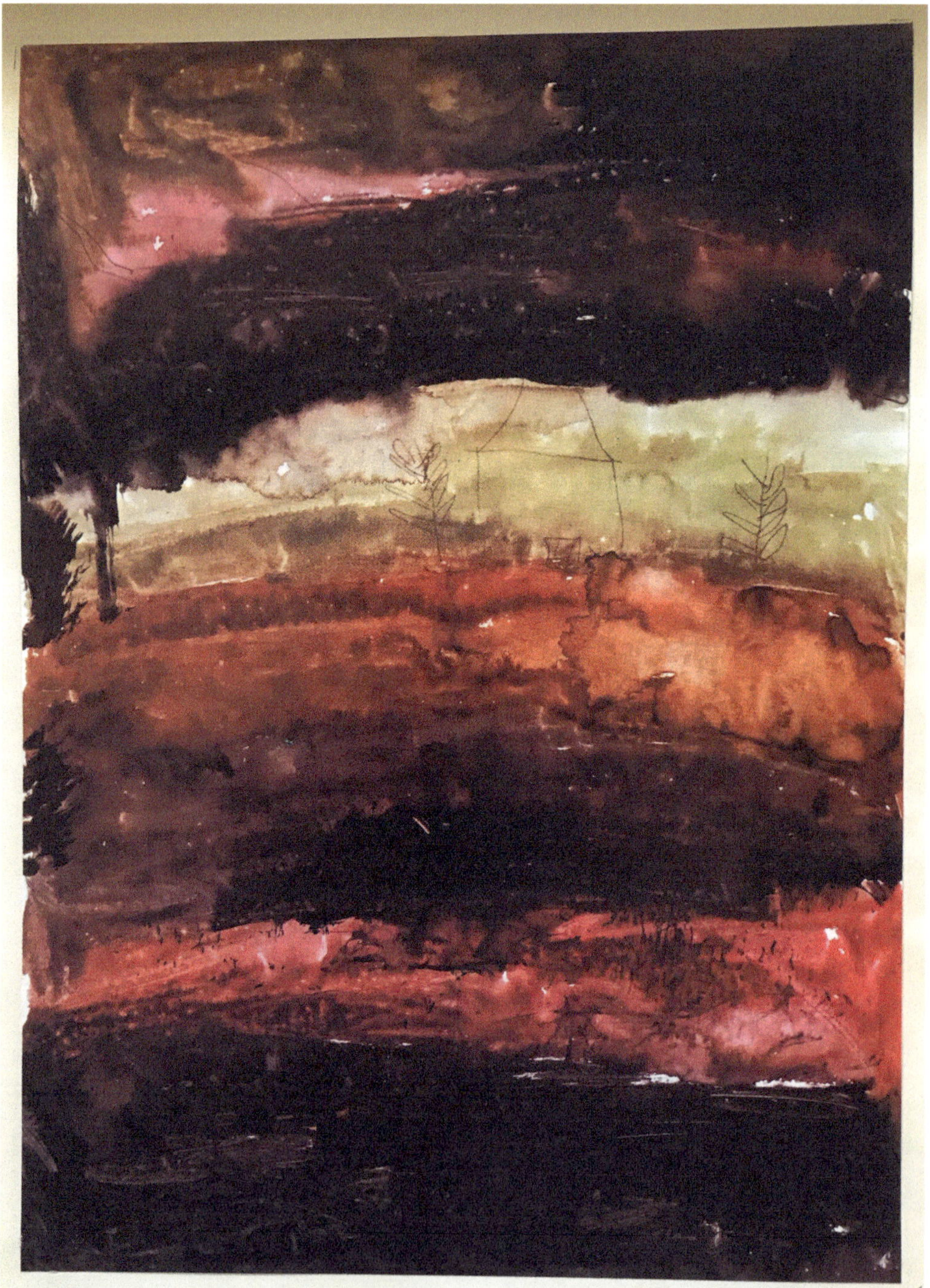

3.3. Photo reproduction of Hussein Ibrahim's watercolor, originally published in Seta Manoukian, *Lebanese Children and the War* (Beirut: Technopress Moderne/ Dar al-Farabi, 1977), 26.

boy named Nabil, who painted a "nice home with trees and then painted black on top of everything."[47] Sabah's detailed depiction of a monster, Hussein's impressionistic image, and Nabil's black canvas reveal the way the war buried hope and fueled nightmares. These images and the other ones featured in the book depict the undeniable reality of children's angst and fear during the war.

The images shed light not only on the children's emotional experiences but also on the history of the war. In particular, they depict the way war engulfed Beirut. The Beirut painted or drawn by the children was not a living, vibrant city but rather a deserted urban scene devoid of life. In some images, an abstract city smolders, and generic streets feature dead or bleeding bodies. In others, the city is sandbagged, divided, and patrolled by well-armed militias. In others still, very specific elements of the child's neighborhood are destroyed: the Librairie Antoine burned, and the *forn al-sha'ab* (people's bakery) boarded up, its walls pocked by bullet holes. Bodies of victims line the front of the bakery. Manoukian recalled that this particular painting was a record of a dark day when "a bomb fell outside a bakery. I lost a friend that day too."[48] The children understood that their city was under siege and that they were powerless to do anything other than bear witness to the violence and destruction of human life and property. Adults such as Manoukian felt powerless, too.

As the children painted with Manoukian in 1975 and 1976, militias affiliated with the major factions in the war fought for control of Beirut, most famously in the Battle of the Hotels, which lasted from October 1975 to April 1976. The young boys in particular captured the wider militarization of society. Hussein Hazime, who was seven, painted bombs falling from the sky. Mouhammed Wazneh, a ten-year-old, drew a detailed image of a tank. Girls drew tanks, too. Ibtisam Tayani, an eleven-year-old, painted a tank, but in her picture the tank's gun is blocked, perhaps conveying a hope that the fighting would end. Were the young children drawing tanks to express a mechanical fascination or fear or some combination of the two?

47. Drolma, interview.
48. In Darsalia, *Mother Sela*.

As a general rule, the older the child, the more detailed their depictions of war matériel were, which aligns with the general expectation that older children would be more aware of a conflict and have more advanced fine-motor skills. Twelve- and thirteen-year-old Nabil Srougi and Fouad Bekdache painted extremely detailed images of fighting scenes. But in their images and in those by other children, it is not clear who is fighting whom, which perhaps reflects the artists' confusion about the nuances of the militias' allegiances. Fouad painted foreign journalists taking photos of the war, perhaps revealing he was basing his images on photos he had seen. Nabil titled one of his paintings *Qawa Nabil* (Nabil's Forces), which conveys that some children saw themselves in the conflict unfolding around them. Did Nabil's older brothers or father bring home stories about the war? Did Nabil feel left behind because he was too young to fight? Given the duration of the conflict, Fouad and Nabil could have joined the fighting as early as 1982 or 1983.

Girls painted battles, too. Yet one of the major differences between girls' depictions and boys' depictions of the fighting is that the boys focused exclusively on the fighters and what weapons they were using. The twelve- and thirteen-year-old girls Rania Dada, Samira Ismail, Hiba Karout, Bania Kebbeh, and Hala Medawar painted militias brandishing weapons in front of bullet-filled building facades, but they also painted suffering and death, especially that of women. Women and children make up the majority of war victims worldwide. The wartime victimization of women is manifold, including but not limited to increased domestic violence, rape as a weapon of war, food and housing insecurity, displacement, and psychological trauma.[49] The Lebanese Civil War was no exception;

49. Efforts in the late 1990s to raise awareness about women's roles in war, conflict, and peace led to the passage of UN Resolution 1325, "Women, Peace, Security," in 2000. The Balkan Wars in the 1990s brought increased attention to the ways women were differently and disproportionally affected during and after periods of prolonged civil conflict. Research in the past twenty years has pushed back against the notion that women are only victims in war. See, for example, the International Committee of the Red Cross project "Women and War" at https://www.icrc.org/en/document/women-war. There still remains comparatively little emphasis on women's experiences during the Lebanese Civil War, however, which this volume seeks to correct.

women were victimized in many ways during the fifteen-year-long conflict that killed an estimated 120,000 people and wounded a further 300,000.

Women also participated in the conflict as combatants and formed coalitions to resist their victimization and to end the war. Even so, the soldiers in the children's images are exclusively male, and most of the corpses wear dresses, indicating the children likely wanted to convey the victims as female. In Samira's painting, three women's bodies lie abandoned on the street, blood coming out of their mouths. In Hiba's painting, two women flee toward the viewer, away from an armed soldier. In Rania's image, a mother flees the frame with a baby in one arm and her hand leading another young child. It is one of the few images of a young child in the entire volume; the children avoided painting their age contemporaries in the images, and when they did include them, they generally painted them by themselves.

We do not know whether the battle images were scenes the children witnessed, figments of their war-soaked imaginations, or depictions of stories they heard at home. Regardless, such images provide a window into how the children absorbed and understood the war around them. The children feared how the war might affect them, and the paintings present an affective record of those fears. Wadad Ramadan, a thirteen-year-old girl, painted a young girl seated on a cot, all alone in a shelter. Manoukian recalled the children were afraid of the war, but they were especially fearful of being left alone. She also observed, "The children who went through bombardments always painted themselves alone, not with their parents. Frightened and alone. When bombs come, children know instinctively that they are alone."[50]

In the introduction to *Lebanese Children and the War*, Walid Saffi thanks Manoukian for "training these young buds with loving care and for bringing their beautiful works to light. Let it be known that spring is coming / For I have seen the flowers bloom."[51] Indeed, the children's images of war also contain glimmers of hope and playfulness. Many children painted suns rising out of the sea, spilling orange-yellow rays across

50. Drolma, interview.

51. Saffi, introduction to Manoukian, *Lebanese Children and the War*, 9.

the surface of the water. Yet even these happier images could not escape the specter of the war. Hala Ayoub, a twelve-year-old, painted a sun caught between black clouds. She wanted the future to be bright, but the reality of the war trapped her hope and tried to obscure its rays. Some children painted alternative, imaginative futures: a brief escape from thinking about the war. Nergess Masri painted a Santa Claus dancing in the snow, and Zeinab Hachem painted an elaborate stage full of clowns dancing in front of a rapt audience; both artists were eleven. Overall, the visual consensus of the children's images selected for the volume is that despite hopes for peace in the future, the present was bleak.

Many of the children in the refugee camps and neighborhoods surrounding them were Sunni Muslim, and they knew that Manoukian was an Orthodox Christian, but they used their paintings to show that they rejected the politicized differences that contributed to the war unfolding around them. Mouhammad Wazneh, a ten-year-old boy who also painted images of tanks and guns, painted six rounded Orthodox church steeples, with a cross prominently displayed at the top of each one. He gave the drawing to Manoukian. She interpreted the image as the child choosing to paint peace rather than war.[52] Recent scholarship on art therapy projects with displaced Iraqi children reveals that "children's understanding of war precedes their understanding of peace."[53] The images in *Lebanese Children and the War* support this finding. Of the fifty images in the volume, few directly relate to peace, though some hint at it in images of flowers, birds, and dancing figures. The war—battles, bodies, injured victims, burning buildings, and displacement—features in twenty-nine of the paintings. Twelve-year-old Wadad Kebbeh's image on displacement shows two fighters fighting on top of an image of Lebanon with individuals and families fleeing in every direction. Thirteen of the children's paintings are "war adjacent," a category that comprises images of Lebanese history, solo homes, and general free-form angst. The remaining images depict the sun and the sea.

52. Saffi, introduction to Manoukian, *Lebanese Children and the War*, 9.

53. Jabbar and Betawi, "Children Express," 1.

The images published in *Lebanese Children and the War* represent a small fraction of the images produced by Lebanese children in Manoukian's peripatetic art room. A more comprehensive exhibit of the images was displayed in an abandoned exhibition space in downtown Beirut in 1976. Manoukian recalls that many people attended the event. After the exhibit, her friends approached her with the idea of turning the images into a book. Leftist women's organizations in Beirut, such as the League for Lebanese Women's Rights, had been trying to raise awareness about the humanitarian toll of the war, but their internationally oriented activism had not secured much response.[54] In using children's wartime artwork, women's organizations hoped to gain greater recognition of the civilian suffering that accompanied the war. It is impossible to measure the impact of *Lebanese Children and the War* and *Traces rouges et bleues: Exprimées par les enfants durant l'occupation* on viewers and on international solidarity for the victims of the war, but the books provide an enduring record of how children experienced the war. Many of the children who painted with Manoukian between 1975 and 1983 had transitioned into adulthood by war's end.

Manoukian's Wartime Paintings: Art as Personal Therapy

Manoukian was one of the few painters who painted the Lebanese Civil War as it unfolded rather than in hindsight.[55] As a consequence, her paintings, like those of the students to whom she gave art supplies, provide a visual record of the war. Manoukian asserts that the paintings were not meant to "be a documentary of the war" but rather were "trying to capture the moment, like the children's [work]."[56] Several themes surface in Manoukian's impressionistic, fragmented depictions of Beirut's streets during the war, but none more so than alienation. Isolation and fear were apparent in many of the paintings children made under her guidance. Manoukian's paintings were clearly more sophisticated than those

54. Village Welfare Society's correspondence with the Women's International League for Peace and Freedom, Village Welfare Society Archive, Beirut, Lebanon.

55. Drolma, interview.

56. Drolma, interview.

produced by the children, but the thematic resonance between her and their images is striking and reveals that Lebanese of all ages felt alienated, alone, and powerless as the war tore their city and country asunder.

The first pictures Manoukian painted during the war depict Beirut's streets. "I started painting the streets of Beirut, and I started to feel that the whole country was experiencing the same trauma as me."[57] She painted men whose faces were formless or distorted to appear like masks, not unlike in Pablo Picasso's *Les demoiselles d'Avignon* (1907). In *Before the Events* (1975; figure 3.4), five male figures mill about in short-sleeved button-down shirts and slacks. The face of the figure closest to the viewer is enlarged and distorted, looking more like a Dogon mask than a man's face. The next figure has no mouth and bulging eyes that convey suspicion. Two of the figures are faceless. The final figure wears square-rimmed glasses; concern consumes his face. The images capture the distrust and anxiety that comes with social conflict: Who is that person really? What is he or she hiding? A later image, *On the Sidewalk* (1980), turns four women's faces into empty canvases or distorted, discolored visages. The figures share the same frame, but they do not come into contact with one another. Indeed, throughout all of Manoukian's wartime images, all human figures are represented in isolation: moving through the frame alongside others but not with them. These wartime figures are thoroughly alone, "each person going in a different direction."[58] Beirutis were fragmented, and so too was their city.

Manoukian's skill as a painter comes through in her depictions of Beirut's deserted or nearly empty streets, in which figures uneasily share space. She uses scale and color to convey the emptiness of the city. Many images feature exaggerated monochromatic facades—deep yellow, purple, teal—etched with deep shadows. The representations of fear and foreboding that surfaced in her "Inside the Room" series now extended to the city as a whole. The nonnatural building colors capture a sense of disorientation in the public sphere, a break with normalcy. Manoukian later reflected that her images of the city conveyed a "cold fear," which was "very much

57. In Darsalia, *Mother Sela*.

58. In Darsalia, *Mother Sela*.

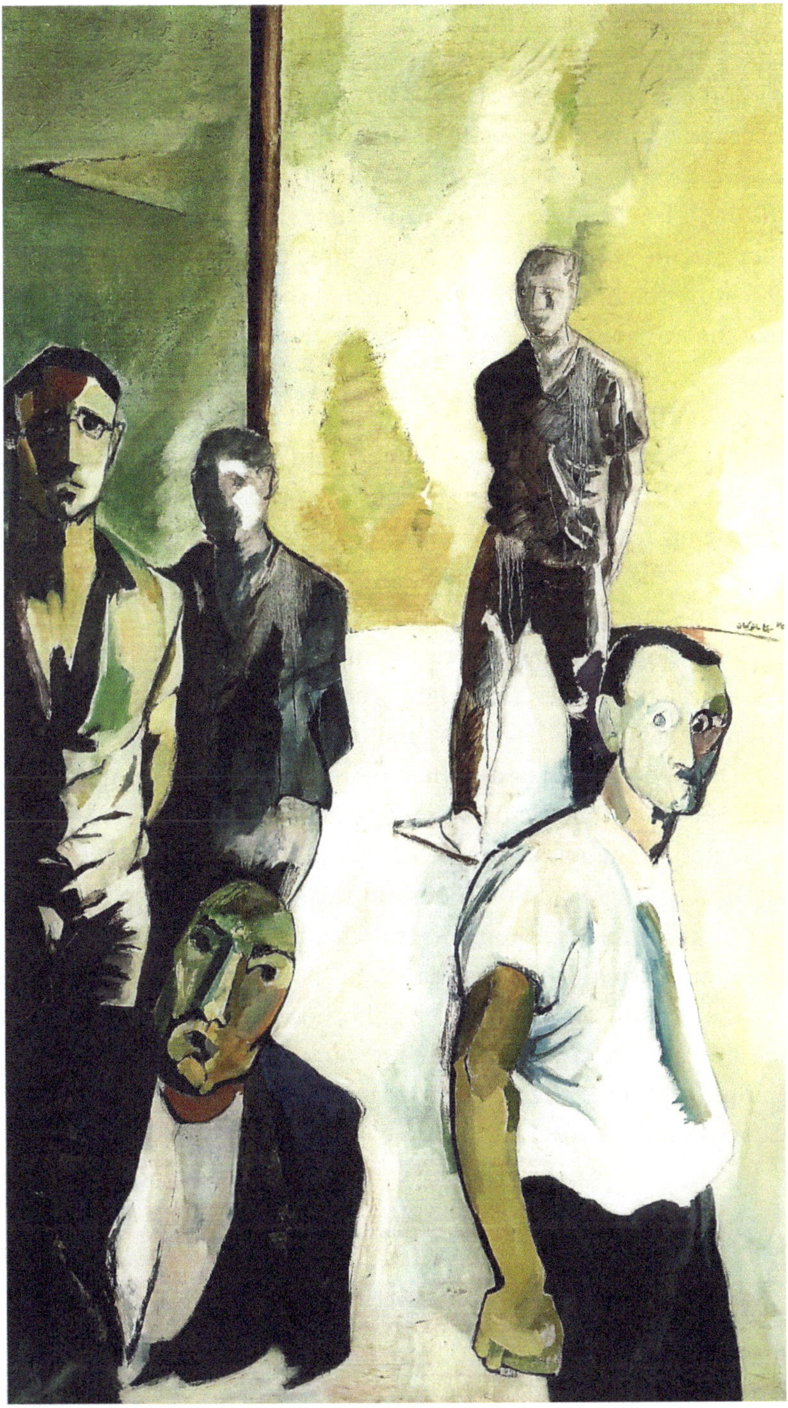

3.4. Seta Manoukian, *Before the Events*, 1975, acrylic and sand on board, 220 × 121 centimeters, private collection, Beirut, Lebanon.

what people felt in the streets of Beirut during that time of civil war."[59] In describing *Crossroads 2* (1985), she observed, "The pavement is sliding down, there is no wall, it is space, and in that space is a flashback of a building, like a movie. Again, people appear to be detached from one another, but in reality it is not so, all [are] connected."[60] Her paintings never feature the militias that so fascinated the children but instead focus on how the war shaped the city and its citizens' orientation toward public space and each other.

The destruction of the city felt personal for Manoukian. In *La fête rose* (1981), she coveys how she suffered with her city. The city grows out of her flesh. She asserted, "The street is my own skin under a microscope, expressing my feeling of pain and my identification with Beirut under the bombs."[61] In reflecting on the image after the war, she said, "I was Beirut."[62] Manoukian's and the child artists' emphasis on the city's emptiness and destruction captures how difficult it must have been to watch familiar spaces—the local theater, the neighborhood church—be destroyed.

Manoukian wanted her wartime paintings to "express what people feel."[63] The people depicted in her paintings felt alienated, alone, and fearful, but what they really wanted to feel was normal. In the face of the destruction, people attempted to persevere and preserve normalcy. In addition to the alienation found on the streets of Beirut, Manoukian also painted her relatives going to church and friends gathering and talking. She participated in these attempts to "be normal" when she provided traumatized children in poor neighborhoods with an artistic outlet. As she notes, "Life continued during war," and there was "life between bombings."[64] Despite these attempts to live a normal life, the bombs fell, which she depicted, too.

59. Quoted in *Seta Manoukian*, 78.

60. Quoted in *Seta Manoukian*, 78.

61. Quoted in *Seta Manoukian*, 62.

62. In Darsalia, *Mother Sela*.

63. In Darsalia, *Mother Sela*.

64. Drolma, interview.

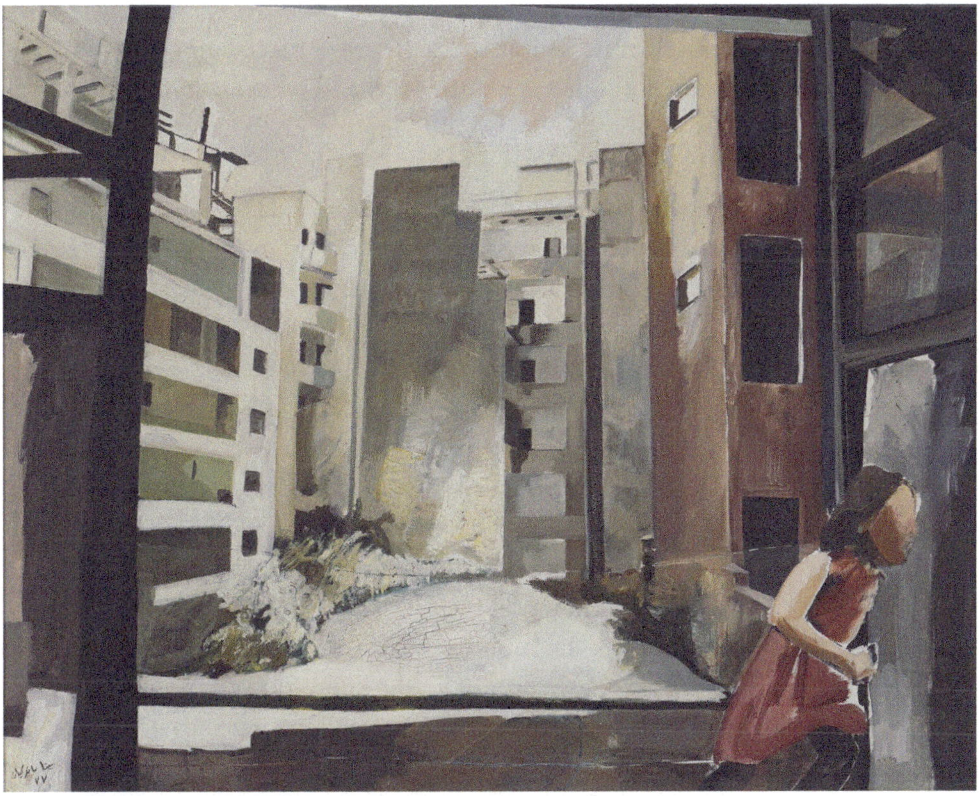

3.5. Seta Manoukian, *After the Bombing*, 1977, acrylic on canvas, 150 × 180 centimeters, private collection, Byblos, Lebanon.

In *After the Bombing* (1977), a young faceless girl in a red dress flees the frame (figure 3.5). She is alone yet is running to seek shelter. But where is safe? Was this composition featuring a child all alone shaped by Manoukian's encounter with the paintings children made in her classroom? Manoukian's art therapy lessons with children gave her a window into the children's deepest fears, which aligned with the deepest fears of many Lebanese adults: not being able to protect their children from the war. The courtyard behind the child in Manoukian's painting is not an abstract representation of space but a real space she knew well. It was the courtyard behind her sister's house in Sanayeh, where Manoukian spent most of the war (her sister had moved to California in 1967).[65] Is this a scene that Manoukian witnessed or a nightmare: a niece being left alone as bombs fell? As in the children's paintings, the line between reality and the imagined is blrred, and it is in that blurring that the images gain their potency as a record of war.

Manoukian lived in Beirut until 1985, when militias started kidnapping educators. She fled the city and joined her family in California. Even though she left the war behind, she carried its memories with her, and vestiges of the conflict continued to surface in her work. The Lebanese Civil War ended in 1990 with the Ta'if Accord, but Manoukian's work from the 1990s reveals that the psychological wounds of the war lived on well after the signing of the peace deal. Her postwar art reveals her continued spiritual anguish. Shortly after moving to the United States, she started to explore feelings of alienation and displacement in installation art and performance pieces that, for instance, featured a horse in an empty gallery or a bed in the street or a father in a tree.

In *Absurd* (1994), part of the "Boules" series, three commanding, elongated, commalike, black shapes dominate the center of the triptych. The side panels are filled with amateurish line drawings produced by one of her students. In the right frame, roughly drawn bodies—two stacked circles, a smaller one for a head and a bigger one for the body, sit atop stick legs—kick one another. In the left panel, a police officer grabs a victim by the hair; an absurdist chicken-headed body lies on the ground and a man in a flame costume throws a woman outside the frame. At the top of the right and left frames, small national flags are planted in a row. The juxtaposition of the refined black shapes in the center of the frame and the children's art is purposefully jarring. The title of the piece reflects the absurdity of violence, not just in the image but in society overall, especially violence in the name of the nation.

Manoukian's wartime and postwar art reveals an artist trying to process and record both her anguish and that of others caught up in the war.

65. Compare the courtyard in the painting with the courtyard in a photograph of Seta on her sister's balcony in *Seta Manoukian*, 8.

Art was a healing outlet for her, and she shared it with vulnerable children whose perspectives on the conflict would otherwise have been forgotten or altered by the passage of time. When Manoukian's wartime paintings are viewed alongside the images children produced in her art room, one cannot help but see the parallels in the emotions the artists of all ages were trying to convey: fear and alienation. These visual records remind us of the ways in which war affects civilians and how its imprint lives on long after the end of war.

Conclusion

Throughout Manoukian's life, art has been her vehicle for exploring and experiencing the spiritual world. Yet in the aftermath of the Lebanese Civil War, putting the brush to the canvas was not enough of a spiritual salve, and she started seeking additional avenues for spiritual exploration. In the early 2000s, she had a fateful meeting with a Buddhist monk, who attuned her to the Buddhist tradition. In 2005, she went on a year-long Buddhist retreat in Sri Lanka. After weeks in silent contemplation, she took the vows to become a Buddhist nun and took a new name, Mother Sela. The documentary *Mother Sela: Artist and Buddhist Nun* (2012) chronicles her conversion.[66] In 2007, she encountered the Nyingma branch of Buddhism and started following its teachings under her new name, "Ani Pema Tsultrim Drolma," which she continues to go by today. Her father observed that "changing religion is foreign to us [Armenians]," but he was supportive of her choice to follow her own path toward deeper spiritual understanding.[67] Drolma's lifelong spiritual quest and evolution remind us that healing after trauma is an ongoing, active process.

Drolma returned to painting in 2016 after a ten-year hiatus. Her spiritual quest continues. She describes her recent work as reflecting her inner state of mind as a Buddhist.[68] *Ah 2* (2017) features a small red-yellow rose in full bloom on a large, empty, white canvas. The stem is cut short, so the

66. The documentary was filmed in 2004 and 2005 and released in 2012.

67. In Darsalia, *Mother Sela*.

68. Ani Pema Tsultrim Drolma to Nova Robinson, July 7, 2020.

flower features prominently. It is an invitation to focus on beauty. Drolma asserts she has found peace and meaning through her art.[69] The most remarkable thing about Drolma is that she shared her healing practice with others during the war and continues to do so today.

The students Drolma worked with in Beirut in 1976 and 1982 are likely now in their fifties and sixties. Some of the children may have been kidnapped or killed in later stages of the war; some may be among the twelve thousand Lebanese who are still missing. Like their former teacher, those who survived the war carry their war memories with them, reexperiencing the conflict through flashbacks. During the war, their paintings of tanks, bombs, and victims provided a vivid account of their experiences at the front lines. Today, their paintings serve as a record of the war's violence and its impact on civilians, something that lives on in memory but is rarely addressed. Indeed, Sabah, Nabil, Mouhammad, and Ibtissam's images of violence and anguish are sites of cultural memory. Their pictures serve as a reminder that even though the fighting has ended, the emotional and psychological wounds left by the war have not fully healed. From her perspective as a Buddhist nun, Drolma believes that "Lebanon needs to heal on many levels."[70]

Many of the public efforts to remember the Lebanese Civil War are deeply politicized and sometimes even blocked by individuals who were able to translate their power in militias into postwar political power. The lack of public reconciliation and memory projects leaves individuals to process the war trauma on their own, which exacerbates the feelings of alienation and isolation prevalent in both the children's drawings and Drolma's artwork. As Ani Drolma's postwar art reveals, war trauma lives on in civilians long after the cessation of fighting. The children's war images from *Lebanese Children and the War* are a reminder of the impact of the war on children and are simultaneously a call to begin the process of remembering. Remembering is the foundation of personal and national healing.

69. Drolma to Robinson, July 7, 2020.

70. Drolma, interview.

4

Disaster Seen by Three Female Contemporary Lebanese Artists

YASMINE NACHABE TAAN

"Many stories about the Lebanese Civil War have yet to be told, discussed, or described," Samar Mogharbel expressed to me during an interview in Beirut.[1] Mogharbel uses the medium of clay to reproduce the recurring car-bomb explosions that took place in Beirut following the assassination of Lebanon's prime minister Rafic al-Hariri in 2005. Other Lebanese artists, such as Walid Raad, fictionalize events of the war because they were too violent to remember.[2] Unlike Raad, Mogharbel confronts violent scenes of war by reproducing tragic moments for the purpose of remembering them, hoping that they will not be repeated in the future. This chapter examines the artwork of three generations of Arab female artists who bring the history of conflict, war, and disaster into conversation with art history in Lebanon and the broader region. It demonstrates how art practices that deal with conflict—directly and indirectly—allow for an aesthetic appropriation of the codes of war, a critique of risks and contexts, ideological positioning, and the rewriting of history. Tagreed Dargouth, Samar Mogharbel, and Ginane Makki Bacho represent three generations of Lebanese artists and their engagements with the Civil War. All three artists are based in Beirut, where they have participated in

1. Samar Mogharbel, interviewed by Yasmine Nachabe Taan, Aug. 30, 2018, Beirut, Lebanon; all quotations from Mogharbel in this chapter come from this interview. All translations are mine.

2. Cotter, *Out of Beirut*, 30.

collective exhibitions at home and abroad, and all have won prestigious awards in recognition of their distinguished artistic achievements.[3]

Reflecting on the postwar art scene in Lebanon, the art historian Hanan Toukan explains, "Lebanon's persistent grappling with numerous identities and multiple narratives means that cultural production and representation, whether for a local or global audience, inevitably become domains of contestation."[4] As artists who are engaged in human-rights-related concerns including but not limited to Palestinian rights and women's rights, Dargouth, Mogharbel, and Makki Bacho often use their artwork to make sense of horrific lived experiences and traumatic memories of war. This is what marks their transition from artists to activists, positioning their art as indispensable to how they understand war. In this sense, their works—like the works of a large number of contemporary Lebanese artists that address the Civil War—can help us to understand disaster, violence, memory, and trauma. Moreover, their creations and their discussions of those creations provide ways of thinking about how we look at and archive images of war.[5]

This chapter focuses on the contemporary postwar artistic production of these three female artists based in Beirut. In particular, it examines each work of art as political and subversive in its reasoning as well as the process of its production. It explores the following key questions: How does war influence art production? How does the mediatization of war in real time affect contemporary art practices? What discourses emerge from artistic practices and works that deal with war and conflict?

3. All three artists are represented by Saleh Barakat Gallery in Beirut, which was founded in 2016 and specializes in modern and contemporary art from the Arab world.

4. Toukan, "On Being the Other in Post–Civil War Lebanon," 125.

5. The configuration of war as a culturally regenerative force is not unique to art or art history in general. Famous examples include Goya's *The Execution* (1814) and Picasso's *Guernica* (1937). The former is a depiction of the execution of patriots from Madrid by a firing squad from Napoleon's army in reprisal for their uprising against the French occupation. The latter was completed in June 1937 as a reaction to the Nazi bombing of the Basque town Guernica during the Spanish Civil War. It stands as Picasso's powerful political statement against violence and disaster inflicted on innocent civilians.

Are there particular ways of conveying stories through paintings, collages, and sculptures when attempting to go beyond narrating conflicts to criticizing and analyzing them? According to Michel Foucault, "words and things" were reconnected through modern science;[6] in this case, however, it is through art that war and the viewer are reconnected. I explore how Dargouth, Mogharbel, and Makki Bacho represent war and disaster through a logic of signification and meaning and respectively through layers of paint, three-dimensional reproductions of scenes of crimes, and anachronic collages of pre- and postwar Beirut.

Whether through images circulated in the press or through images recorded in their minds as traumatic memories, Dargouth, Mogharbel, and Makki Bacho grapple with their relationships to and experiences of war to produce their art. To understand these images of war, I employ social, political, cultural, and historical analyses to examine the three artists' intentions and continuous attempts to use alternative perspectives as a way to engage with their public. Toukan identifies Arab artists whose major concern is to engage the public in a critical discourse on society and politics from the burgeoning market for Arab art, epitomized by the United Arab Emirates' growing role as one of the major artistic centers in the Arab region.[7] The artwork discussed in this chapter falls into the former category. In this sense, they can be understood as alternative artistic productions and read as countercultural, subversive, and dissident in the face of established orders that resist discourses of war memory. It aims at disrupting established agendas that are focused on erasing traces of the war, ignoring its repercussions, frictions, and complexities within the regional political context, and hence avoiding a confrontation with the consequences of war.

This chapter demonstrates in detail how Dargouth, Mogharbel, and Makki Bacho's artistic production resists Lebanon's official policy of memory erasure and postwar amnesia. I am interested in how these three artists bring together archival documents—printed photographs, screen

6. Foucault, *The Order of Things*, 46.

7. Toukan, "On Being the Other in Post–Civil War Lebanon," 121.

images, and mental images—about the Civil War as well as other conflicts in the region to recount their stories and lived experience while blurring the boundaries between fact and fiction. Using interdisciplinary theoretical methods drawn from history, art history, and memory studies, and based on my analysis of selected works of art produced by Dargouth, Mogharbel, and Makki Bacho as well as on a series of interviews with them, this chapter puts Dargouth, Mogharbel, and Makki Bacho's artwork in conversation with each other in relation to disaster and war.

Art Makes Speaking of War Possible: Tagreed Dargouth

The difficulty of speaking about the war while it continues to haunt us is a feeling shared by all three artists. "It is hard to speak about the war and even harder to draw it," said Dargouth in an interview, referring to her exhibition at the Saleh Barakat gallery in Beirut in 2018.[8] In an attempt to forget, Dargouth tried to put aside memories of disastrous events of the war. For example, she drew the Palestinian olive trees that were destroyed by the Israeli army to make space for additional Israelis to settle in the Occupied Territories. While in the process of painting the trees, however, she found herself painting skulls, Merkava battle tanks, and Israeli Thunder aircraft (figure 4.1).[9] In her exhibition *Analogy to Human Life*, Dargouth mourned the dead, the loss of the olive trees, and the loss of land.

When I first asked her about the theme of her exhibition, Dargouth remarked, "My work is inspired by Van Gogh's trees; he drew them when he was thirty-six; he was observing the harvest. . . . My understanding is that when we harvest, we become closer to God." She continued speaking about everything but the war in describing her work. Yet in the series of large paintings exhibited at the gallery, we see the skeletons, Merkavas, and other war machinery used by the Israelis during the Lebanese Civil War that she referred to in the interview. What sets this work apart is

8. Tagreed Dargouth, interviewed by Yasmine Nachabe Taan, Oct. 3, 2018, Beirut; all quotations from Dargouth in this chapter are from this interview.

9. The Merkava is a main battle tank used by the Israel Defense Forces. It was first used extensively in their invasion of Lebanon in 1982.

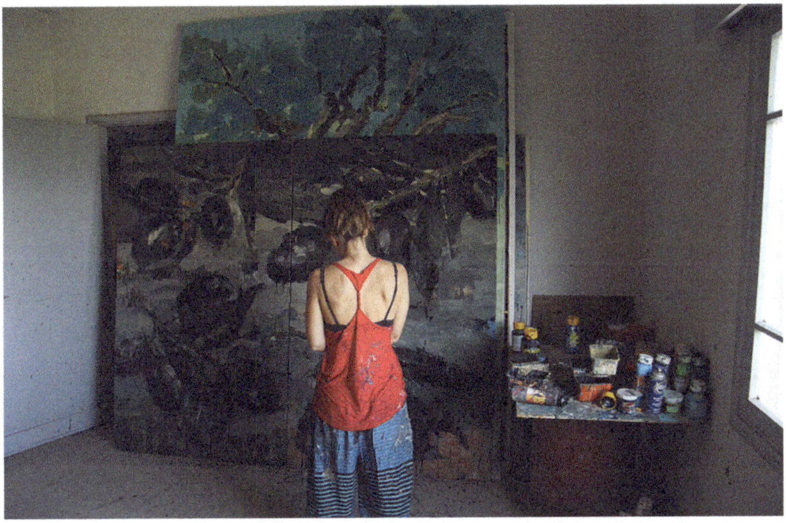

4.1. Tagreed Dargouth in her studio, Beirut, 2018. Photograph by André Smits.

that elements commonly seen in Dargouth's work—and not just in the works exhibited in *Analogy*—are camouflaged within the olive trees. In Dargouth's artwork, we can see how difficult it is for her to tell stories about the war. This prompts us to acknowledge the role of art in facilitating the telling of such stories and in creating narratives about the war. This is what she had in mind when she painted her olive trees: to document injustice and to display the massacre of the olive trees as metaphorically expressing the loss of a people and their land. Hence, it becomes clear through Dargouth's work that documenting loss is an analogy to human life, as in her exhibition's title. The Palestinian cause is not just a Palestinian concern but rather a universal one. Dargouth's drawings of the Caterpillars snatching tree branches and destroying olive trees that were once carefully harvested by young Palestinian men and women are part of her larger artistic oeuvre. Her artistic production is notorious for being a critical voice against state authority, so her work has at times been under state surveillance. In short, both her activist and artistic work convey the reality that surveillance cameras, nuclear bombs, and explosives deny all forms of humanity.

Dargouth's work can be read as an artistic expression of the concept of cultural memoricide, explored by the historian Ilan Pappé in *The Ethnic Cleansing of Palestine* (2016).[10] Pappé's work highlights the diversity of Zionist methods—scholarly, political, and military strategies—used to dispossess the Palestinian people of their land. They are deprived not only of their olive groves and their villages but also of their heritage and history. Dargouth's large paintings of cut-down olive trees imply a metaphorical palimpsest at work and point to the erasure of a people's history to make space for another people's history. The reduction of many layers of history to a single layer is what Mahmoud Darwish, the Palestinian poet, describes as "the plan to expel us from history" in the poem "Mural."[11]

Dargouth explained to me that while preparing for her exhibition, she painted all over her canvases with blood; depictions of flesh, meat, and dismembered bodies appeared everywhere on the walls of her studio. She stopped and looked at them, then realized that no one could confront these images, no one would be able to look at her paintings. She decided to cover the layers of blood with olive trees and leave only a few traces of blood in between the tree branches. Dargouth prefers to paint rather than draw because "it is different to work on paper and on canvas. Ink on paper cannot be erased, while paint on canvas can always be covered by another layer." Paper is sensitive, but the sturdy structure of the canvas is a better support for Dargouth's often-violent strokes. Using paint allows her to produce layers and to cover or add to the initial image drawn on her canvas.

This technique gives Dargouth the opportunity to weave different ideas and emotions into the layers of paint.[12] She uses these layers to metaphorically express the layers of mental images and condensed memories of wartime experiences, such as her memory of her sister. Dargouth remembers the sharp fear of loss she felt for the first time when her sister

10. Pappé, *The Ethnic Cleansing of Palestine*, 225–34.

11. Darwish, *Unfortunately, It Was Paradise*, 122.

12. Dargouth learned this technique from her mentor Marwan Kassab Bachi, and like other prolific young artists who were trained by Kassab Bachi, such as Ayman Baalbaki, she is a master of it.

disappeared during the Israeli bombing of Palestinian camps located on the outskirts of Beirut, right near Dargouth's home. "Death is not something that we can confront easily," she said as she recalled the desperate expression on her mother's frightened face and the images of death and atrocities imprinted on her mind, never to be forgotten. Echoing the words of Jalal Toufic, who claimed, "In Beirut some features of 'the real' must be fictionalized to be thought,"[13] Dargouth also fictionalizes some elements of "the real" to draw them. The Caterpillar bulldozer in earlier stages of Dargouth's paintings had pieces of meat, body parts, and shredded flesh dangling from it and was painted with violent strokes and dripping paint. She said that she had to soften this bloody scene for people to be able to confront it. Some scenes are simply too bloody and repel the viewers' eyes: "If I leave them the way they are, people will cover their eyes when they visit my exhibition." At one point, she herself could not look at the Caterpillar painting and decided to "erase" these bloody parts to tame the image. These modifications resulted in the replacement of dismembered body parts with olive trees.

Through her artistic production, Dargouth tries to make death visible by transforming disaster into a historical event. For example, she works with the Nakba—when more than seven hundred thousand Palestinian Arabs were expelled from their homeland in 1948. Dargouth uses a rich color palette in her thick layers of paint. In her series of olive trees, layers of combined green and gray splashes of paint reveal the previous layers of bloody carmen red. She leaves traces of blood-red color uncovered under the dense paint top layers to reveal the precarious Palestinian olive trees being snatched from the earth, destroyed by Israeli Caterpillar machinery. Every living entity—trees, plants, and humans—is collapsing or dead as the Caterpillars advance through the land, smashing and uprooting everything standing in their way.

Most of Dargouth's paintings in *Analogy of Human Life* depict such disasters. Yet on a number of canvases we see an olive tree centered in her composition, standing still, its branches spread with pride. Dargouth is

13. Toufic, "Ruins," 28.

referencing previous generations of Arab artists who often used the olive tree as a symbol of pride and resistance. Hilmi al-Tuni, for example, is an Egyptian artist and illustrator who painted the picture-story *Qissat hayat shagara* (The Life Story of a Tree) in 1982.[14] The book begins with the image of a blooming tree centered on its cover, and it ends with the same tree. On the pages of the book, the tree gradually disintegrates; its branches are broken down; it loses strength and gradually decomposes. As the story continues, though, one of its seeds grows into a new tree. Al-Tuni's story is about the persistence of life and rebirth. Like Dargouth, he drew this story when he was in Beirut during the Israeli invasion of 1982.

Al-Tuni's tree and Dargouth's trees invoke the same ideas—the uprooting of trees as a metaphor for the uprooting of the Palestinian people. Both artists here strive to convey the same message: the icon of the tree turns into an icon of defiance refusing to be uprooted and persisting in life. Like al-Tuni, Dargouth turns the uprooted olive trees into living, blooming trees. In her paintings, the Israeli Caterpillars keep uprooting the trees, but the trees continue to grow. The trees, like the Palestinian people, refuse to surrender. As Dargouth explained to me, "In another life, I would have liked to paint other things, more joyful events, but, unfortunately, war is very present in my daily life and thus in my art. The theme of war is not intentional; it is imposed upon me. . . . I try to change and draw other things, but I keep returning to the skulls and the bloody scenes."

When describing her artistic practices and process, Dargouth said that she is never satisfied with the end results: "I have what we call in Arabic *qalaqel*—a combination of anxiety and fear. . . . When I paint, I overcome my fear." She is constantly haunted by doubt and uncertainty: "All my work is open ended. Fear makes me hesitant and worried, so I repeat the layers again and again; my paintings are never complete. Adding a layer is always a possibility, depending on my emotional investment. For me, each work is a path, an unknown path, a coincidence, followed by another one and another one. There is always an element of surprise within the

14. A children's story in the form of a picture book published by Dar al-Fata al-'Arabi in Beirut in 1982.

path, an accidental dripping bit of paint or a brush stroke that happened to remain on the canvas for some unknown reason."

Dargouth expressed that she now suffers from panic attacks and other fears when she hears news announcing another war. She seems to embody her mother's fears from 1982. The Civil War has officially ended, but it persists in Dargouth's subconscious, which is made visible in the art she creates. War, indeed, constitutes an eternal part of her subconscious. Through her artistic practice, she attempts to confront this persistence by developing an aesthetic of war.

Samar Mogharbel's Forensic Installations

"The understanding of war among people who have not experienced war is [now] chiefly a product of the impact of these images," notes Susan Sontag in her well-known work *Regarding the Pain of Others* (2003).[15] War is a geopolitical phenomenon marked by traumatic events that are personally experienced by some and transmitted to others far from the conflict zone through images and accounts. Unlike Dargouth, Samar Mogharbel did not rely on her memory of lived experience when she produced her art depicting car bombings and explosions. She used dramatic photos assembled from the local and international press to create her images. According to Mogharbel, these photos were very difficult to look at. Uncensored, widely circulating images of dead bodies, severed body parts, and flesh protruding from a series of exploded cars appeared in the press on a daily basis in Beirut during a period of heightened violence and conflict. Haunted by the fear of being in or near a car that might explode at any moment, Mogharbel worked on reproducing the moment of the explosion in her art to commemorate these tragic incidents.

Like Dargouth in claiming that it was only Van Gogh who first influenced her painting of the olive tree harvest, Mogharbel at first dismissed the impact of war on her as an artist when I interviewed her. "I like cars in general. . . . My work is not about making a political statement about the Civil War in Lebanon. . . . I did not live the war—I was not in Lebanon

15. Sontag, *Regarding the Pain of Others*, 21.

during this time. I came back to Beirut in 1987." Yet a closer look at her artistic production likewise reveals that it has everything to do with making a political statement about the war. She continued, "My work reflects my everyday living, reality, and the daily news. . . . I therefore cannot draw flowers. An artist who lives under these circumstances cannot paint or produce flower sculptures. The car-explosions project symbolizes the condition of our daily lives threatened everyday by random car explosions around the streets of Beirut. While traveling around the city, we didn't know when and where a car would explode in front of our eyes again."

In 2005, six major political figures in Lebanon—Walid Eido, Marwan Hamadeh, Rafic al-Hariri, Georges Hawi, Samir Kassir, and Gebran Tueni—were either injured or killed in booby-trapped cars. Some of the victims survived, but others burned to death, along with their drivers and bodyguards. Mogharbel reproduced these cars without the corpses in fifty-by-seventy-centimeter clay sculptures, which were exhibited at the twenty-seventh Salon d'Automne at the Sursock Museum in Beirut. Her installation won the first prize at this exhibition (figure 4.2). The exploded cars were later cast in bronze and exhibited in London in 2011. The display of her powerful and evocative sculptures in a museum setting raised many questions about ethics and artistic practice. Mogharbel was concerned with how appropriate it was to turn a disaster into sculptures that were later cast in bronze and sold for thousands of dollars. She posited the following questions: "I am working with a sensitive topic, one that deals with the tragic deaths of humans. How can this be considered art? And how ethical is it to commodify these objects that represent disaster?" She reflected on the absurdity of the art market and failed to make sense of the transition of her work from devastating images of disaster to ceramic sculptures depicting the scenes of he horrific events in three dimensions and then to valuable art objects cast in bronze.

According to the artist and critic Lucy Lippard, artists interested in war stand not only in relation to a conflict but also in relation to the media that records it.[16] An important part of Mogharbel's process in developing

16. Lippard, *A Different War.*

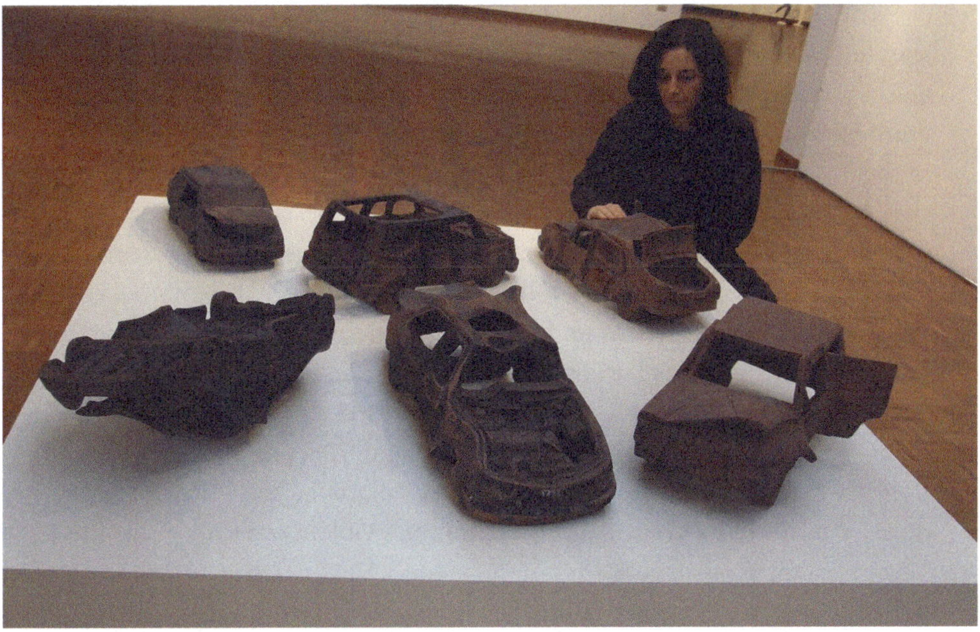

4.2. Samar Mogharbel, *Booby-Trapped Car Sculptures*, July 28, 2006, ceramics, 50 × 70 centimeters. Photograph by Faisal Sultan.

her concept was thorough visual research. She gathered a collection of disturbing photos of car bombs and explosions, often with body parts and burned bodies protruding from the cars. The photographs were troubling to look at, but Mogharbel used her art to reconfigure each barbaric crime scene. The car that exploded with Gebran Tueni inside it, for example, had no interesting shape for her to reproduce, so she turned it upside down. The challenging part for Mogharbel was to empty the car, casting out the clay as if she were removing the debris of dead bodies from inside the car. The carving, welding, and burning of the clay into ceramic were a repetition or a reenactment of each violent event itself. Each car was distorted in different ways. Mogharbel went in search of clues—like a forensic detective or an archaeologist digging at an excavation site. She studied how each explosion was carefully conceived by the person who executed it, the amount of dynamite trapped in the car, and the amount of destruction the bomb inflicted.

The artist and critic Jalal Toufic writes that the Lebanese Civil War should be thought of as a rupture: a break that disrupts history and alienates not only the generation who lived through it but also the future generations who have little or no access to the heritage, traditions, and history of the time before the war.[17] As Mogharbel put it to me, many stories about the Lebanese war have not been told, discussed, or described. Unlike other Lebanese artists, such as Walid Raad or Lamia Joreige, who choose to fictionalize events of war that are too violent to remember,[18] Mogharbel confronts actual violent scenes and reproduces these traumatic moments to remember them. Gilles Deleuze, the French philosopher and scholar, has written on the problematic question of representation in the context of being haunted with death and war. According to Deleuze, the image offers us a way to go around and to negotiate the catastrophic experience and the disaster of war. The artistic reproduction of a violent wartime event then becomes a form of survival.[19]

In reproducing the car explosions in clay, Mogharbel was able to transcend her fear. As soon as she finished one piece, another explosion would take place in Beirut, creating another scene for her to struggle with. What stands out in her forensic scenes is how she used the medium of clay in an unconventional way to express anger and distress. Contrary to how ceramists typically use clay as a smooth, soft, and tender medium, Mogharbel is rough in her manipulation of the clay. She uses heavy-duty tools and machinery to create rough edges and angular shapes. Her ceramic sculptures serve as a nodal point around which other elements happen. The production of the artwork is based on photographs taken immediately after the explosions, in which we can still see the flesh of the unrecognizable burning bodies. Thinking about how Mogharbel produced "art" from the disasters seen in these images is disturbing; it causes schizophrenic feelings of being unable to understand reality, she told me.

17. Toufic, "Ruins," 31.

18. For more on Walid Raad and Lamia Joreige's artistic production and memory, see Cotter, *Out of Beirut*.

19. Deleuze and Guattari, *Image and Text*.

Just as Dargouth's work recalls al-Tuni's, Mogharbel's work is in conversation with other works by Arab artists that use cars. For example, Mahmoud Obaidi's *Fragments* (2016) is now placed on the rooftop of the recently inaugurated Nabu Museum in North Lebanon.[20] Obaidi's sculptured car, a 1971 Ford, represents a US military vehicle reconstructed in rusted steel and carrying a Mesopotamian bust, columns, and other valuable objects. *Fragments* depicts the looting of heritage collections from national museums in Iraq by the American army during the US invasion of the country. Its message is that it is not only organizations such as ISIS that are looting and destroying cultural heritage but also US troops in Iraq long before ISIS began its campaign of cultural destruction.

This installation by the Iraqi artist is a political commentary on the American occupation, including the destruction of Iraq's history and heritage.[21] The installation echoes the Nabu Museum's mission to reappropriate and protect lost or looted Arab heritage. Although both Obaidi's and Mogharbel's car sculptures are about rethinking events of war, Mogharbel's works represent a different concern through different geographical and temporal contexts. Her sculptures' message is not about looting but rather about remembering tragic events such as the assassinations of several major political figures in Lebanon since 2005. Mogharbel explained the survival instinct to turn traumatic events into art in order to make sense of the disaster. She questioned her role as an artist and as a ceramist in particular during the time she was creating the car sculptures: "In honor of the dead humans inside these cars, regardless of their political affiliations, I made these installations." These forensic installations play a prominent role in mediating among the unknown killers, the victims, and the population. Indeed, her work has raised many questions about the intention and the details of the crimes that remain unanswered to this day.

20. The Nabu Museum was founded by Jawad Adra, Badr el-Hage, and Fida Jdeed. It houses a large collection of antiquities from the Levant and Mesopotamia alongside local and regional modern art. See Kadi, "Nabu Museum Offers New Attraction in Northern Lebanon."

21. See Khoury, *Bab al-Shams*, translated as *Gate of the Sun*.

The media had become the narrator of these images and the stories they tell. Mogharbel wanted to take over this role by materializing each event in a forensic effort to re-create the crime scene.

Ginane Makki Bacho: Turning Shrapnel into Art

"The shrapnel came to me. I didn't choose to work on the war; the war came to me. The shrapnel invaded my home, destroyed my furniture, my walls, my life," said Ginane Makki Bacho in an interview when discussing her cedar sculptures made out of welded shrapnel gathered from the rubble of her apartment after it was hit by a bomb during the Israeli invasion in 1982.[22] She used and continues to use shrapnel as a medium for her catharsis, in the process releasing and thereby providing relief from strong or repressed emotions. She has made art out of the symbol of war—shrapnel, a sharp and invasive object of killing that eventually became her obsession. In her artistic practice, the sharp and aggressive shapes of the shrapnel are transformed into figurative forms that represent the war. Her goal is to assemble shrapnel and turn it into artwork for contemplation. For instance, she transformed these angular shapes into 101 cedar trees—the national symbol of Lebanese pride and the nation. "The cedar tree is my identity; it represents my relationship with my identity," she remarked in the interview. Her identity is based on dichotomies: love and hate, displacement and stability, war and peace. She uses the shrapnel that she claims was "sent [here] by the enemy [as a medium] to produce art and fight [through that art]." To express these dichotomies, she uses a symbol of war to produce the Lebanese symbol of life. In its transformation from shrapnel to cedar tree, the invasive tool of the enemy is "tamed" and made an object of healing. As in Dargouth and al-Tuni's work, trees are a symbol of resistance against the Israeli forces as well as a symbol of hope.

Even today, Makki Bacho continues to gather leftover pieces of war. In 2006, during the Israeli war on Lebanon, she amassed thousands of new pieces of shrapnel for her new artwork. She recounted in my interview of

22. Ginane Makki Bacho, interviewed by Yasmine Nachabe Taan, Oct. 8, 2018, Beirut; all quotations from Makki Bacho in this chapter come from this interview.

her: "I am impulsive, and I tend to leave things to take shape while I am playing. I try not to think much when I work and let the piece take shape while I am enjoying the process of making it. I was welding the metal pieces together, and while doing so, I kept a few openings. I look at the finished piece, and I see the iconic Murr Tower." The Murr Tower in Beirut is another haunting relic of the Lebanese Civil War. Built in the 1970s and later acting as a key hideout for snipers, it was abandoned after the war. The tower is so present in the artist's subconscious that it appeared as a piece she was letting "take shape." While working, she discovered that her art had taken the shape of an object related to one of her mental images of war—the deserted Murr Tower. Through her art, she calls for reclaiming her rights, and she strives to denounce injustice. She seeks to heal her deeply wounded identity as Arab and Lebanese in a world mired in the sectarianism and incomprehensive hate that infiltrates humanity. During the war, all of her artwork was destroyed or lost, but this did not discourage her; rather, it encouraged her to produce more work to articulate her anger and despair.

She recalls not being able to reach her family during the war. For more than seven months, she did not know if they were dead or alive. Living in the unknown was the most disturbing thing for Makki Bacho. She recalls rushing with her children in the car to flee the danger zone and speeding on the highway through dead bodies. She covered her son's eyes so as not to expose him to the images of such atrocities during the war. It is the image that is imprinted in our brains and that we are unable to remove that prompts us to produce art. Art is a way to make the image in our brains visible again and to share it with our compatriots—to ease the pain, face it, confront it, and participate in the production of collective memory.

I HAVE SEEN WAR

I HAVE SEEN WAR ON LAND AND SEA
I HAVE SEEN BLOOD RUNNING FROM THE WOUNDED
I HAVE SEEN THE DEAD IN THE MUD
I HAVE SEEN CITIES DESTROYED . . . CHILDREN STARVING
I HAVE SEEN THE AGONY OF MOTHERS AND WIVES

I HATE WAR

Makki Bacho hand-wrote these words in *I Hate War*, a painting that was part of the *Afterimage* exhibition in 2013.

For *Afterimage*, Makki Bacho combined images of pre- and postwar Beirut.[23] She painted herself in a series of works torn between past and present, rubble and flowers. Makki Bacho appears as if pasted on an unconnected background—an image with no referent. Disoriented, she is situated in time and space that do not exist anymore. The connective tissue to access the past is now missing. Unpacking monstrosity in her work, Makki Bacho represents the images in her head, fleeting memories of war in Lebanon as remembered by the artist. She attempts to express the paradoxes between her life in Beirut before the war and her life after the war. *Afterimage* presents a series of paintings that Makki Bacho refers to as her "memoirs." Showing personal photos collaged together to create "flashes" of her past that overlap and merge, the paintings allow the viewer glimpses into Makki Bacho's history set against a wider narrative of the changing face of Lebanon. The viewer shares not only her intimate memories but also the pain of a country torn apart.

War and its subsequent displacement trigger emotions and questions about politics, religion, the killing of innocent people, identity, nationalism, fear, and loss. Makki Bacho remembered, "I used to live very close to the Palestinian camps. I ended up in New York, after I graduated in 1982 from the Lebanese American University. On the day of my graduation, Israel invaded Beirut." Being far from home and her own culture prompted her to produce new images with a fresh new lens. In *Afterimage*, she tells stories in which she recounts events in Beirut before the war, when she studied alongside renowned figures in the Lebanese art scene, such as Mohammad el-Rawwas and Seta Manoukian.[24] In *Horseshoe* (2013; figure 4.3), she recalls going to the cherished meeting place of artists in the 1950s and 1960s, the infamous Horseshoe Café on Hamra Street, and studying

23. *Afterimage* was a solo exhibition at Ayyam Gallery in Beirut from April 11 to June 15, 2013. See Makki Bacho, *Afterimage Catalog*.

24. Nova Robinson focuses on Seta Manoukian in chapter 3 of this volume.

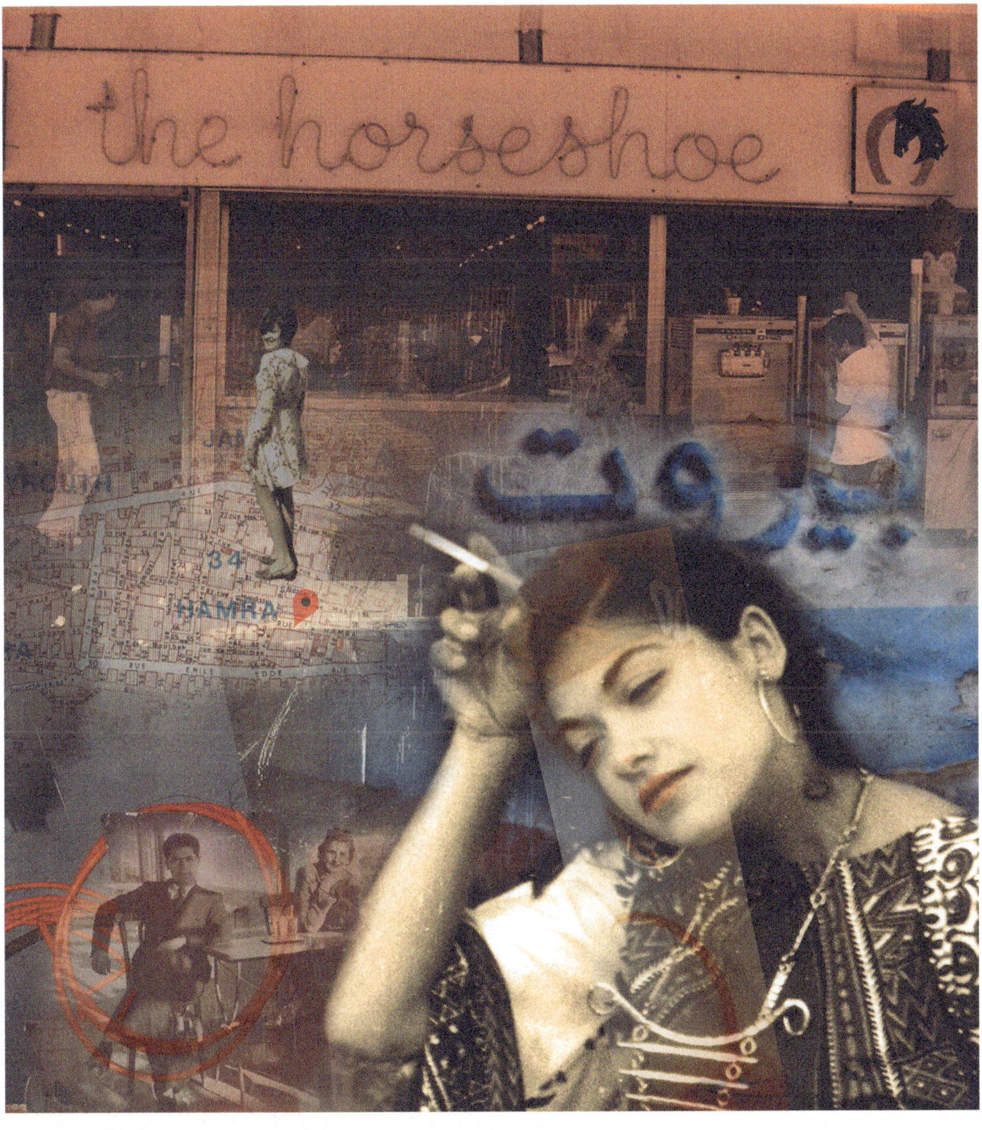

4.3. Ginane Makki Bacho, *The Horseshoe*, 2013, mixed media, 150 × 120 centimeters. Image courtesy of Ginane Makki Bacho.

under the mentorship of Rafic Charaf, Aref al-Rayess, and Paul Guiragossian in her youth. The muted pastel palete of that painting is evocative of scenes of rubble and destruction in postwar Beirut.

In the foreground of *Horseshoe*, Makki Bacho appears, eyes closed as if unable to face the future, smoking a cigarette and wearing tribal ornaments and fabric. In the background hangs the sign of the infamous Horseshoe Café, where artists and art critics of the intellectual milieu used to meet before the war. She depicts a young couple dancing on a map of Hamra Street and below that another couple sitting in a café in Raouché. All this is woven together into a tale of the artist's life in her painting. Unlike Mogharbel, Makki Bacho does not rely on shocking imagery to engage with her viewer on the subject of war. She juxtaposes prewar photos with present-day photos. She seems to "look away" or "look the other way," as the title of one of her *Afterimage* pieces indicates. Makki Bacho's artwork is about reconciliation with the past and her national identity. This theme is reflected in the many self-portraits integrated in her paintings as well as in her cedar sculptures.

Conclusion

Confronting violence, conflict, and war is crucial to the creative production of these three women artists who lived through the Lebanese Civil War and its aftermath. They deploy different strategies in their artistic practices—all of which allow representation to overtake reality, putting the disciplinary uncertainties that haunt the process of historical narration at the forefront. The artists thus confront the conflicting task of the visual: both to capture and to question history. They thus archive the aftermath of the war, assuming the role of the critical historian. In this sense, Dargouth, Mogharbel, and Makki Bacho's aesthetics carry a political agenda. Whether in the repurposing of fragments of Israeli weapons in Makki Bacho's cedar trees installation or in the reduction of layers of history to a single layer in Dargouth's paintings of the Palestinian olive trees or in the meticulous reproduction of crime scenes in Mogharbel's car-explosion installations, the three artists continue to engage the wider public in an ongoing discourse about the unresolved conflicts in the region through their art. Neither their lives nor their displacement could ever totally prepare them to confront war. Their artwork is a result of the intensity of their feelings, to which they give artistic expression.

Each artist developed a strategy to confront images of disaster. Although Dargouth attempts to move away from disaster, it nevertheless haunts her and sometimes erupts from her. She therefore creates images of disaster to negotiate her experiences of disaster. Although at first trying not to, she painted bloody scenes that she herself could not face or erase from her memory, but the canvas as a medium offered her the option to erase them. Mogharbel expressed her fear by physically reproducing forensic scenes of car explosions in three-dimensional sculptures, while omitting the disturbing images of dead bodies inside her cars. She forced herself to look at the details in the press photos that were taken immediately after the car explosions. Looking at the images and reproducing the scenes in clay were exhausting for her, but she felt she had to do these things to surmount her fear and tell this story. Makki Bacho attempts in her *Afterimage* series to reconcile events of war and displacement by creating collages in which time and space collapse.

Consisting of paintings and sculpture installations, the artwork of these three women successfully constructs an emotionally complex perspective of significant, tragic events. Each artist had an impulse to reconstitute a disastrous moment that occurred during or in relation to the Lebanese Civil War. The narratives behind these artistic productions speak about the physical and psychological damage of war, whether locally or universally understood. Putting the artwork of three different women artists who explore disaster and war in conversation with each other offers us a way to understand lived experiences of the Lebanese war and its aftermath.

In this chapter, I have demonstrated how Tagreed Dargouth, Samar Mogharbel, and Ginane Makki Bacho express their deeply felt, lived experiences of the Lebanese Civil War through their art. Traumatic memories, tragic life events, and the images of atrocities circulating in the media have affected their psyches and consequently their artistic productions. The attempt to reimagine sites of disaster and retell war stories in a visceral, physical way can be understood as a survival impulse: for Dargouth, the attempt focuses on the Israeli uprooting and destruction of olive trees in the Occupied Territories from 1948 on; for Mogharbel, it centers on the recurring car explosions in Beirut in 2005; and for Makki Bacho, it comes from her own personal experience of forced displacement and the longing for prewar Beirut. All three refuse to ignore what they have witnessed. Each artist has chosen to confront images of war through her own artistic practice despite the fact that the images she has produced might be distasteful or even repulsive to her viewers. "If people just want to see something to please the eye, that's not art, for me," contends Makki Bacho. This chapter has told the story of how Dargouth, Mogharbel, and Makki Bacho have conceptually and formally recounted untold stories of the Lebanese Civil War. Their artistic productions tell stories that would perhaps not be found in official histories. In this way, they are filling a gap, remembering events that have not or cannot be told and doing so through media that can tell those stories differently. Art can do much more than written history in recounting events of war.

5

Warring Body

Art and Life in Lina Majdalanie's Appendice

ZÉNA MESKAOUI

This chapter analyzes Lina Majdalanie's performance piece *Appendice* as personal and intimate war story. Majdalanie's war, like any war, is fought in the name of liberty and autonomy. Conceiving of her body as inherently hers but seeing that her right to dispose of her dead body has been taken away from her, she turns her own body—the field to conquer—into a weapon and a battlefield. She then deliberately transforms it into ruins because, she feels, the more she ruins her body, the more territory she conquers. Yet, unlike nations' wars, her war is for individual sovereignty, and the territory to conquer is her own female body. Majdalanie's personal and intimate war story is a story of destruction, ruins, and violence. Her story "acts like a topos, in which aesthetic as well as mnemonic and therapeutic stakes are in play,"[1] and it "raise[s] questions on life, politics, and art," as do many of the collaborative works by Majdalanie and her partner, Rabih Mroué.[2]

Analyzing the content of both the text and acting of *Appendice*, I explore how the performance tells a personal story that raises historical, social, political, and cultural issues and produces challenging constructs.

1. Nayla Tamraz, *Littérature, art, et monde contemporain*, 5; all translations into English are mine unless otherwise noted.

2. Fertat, "Rabih Mroué et Lina Saneh," 15; the page numbers cited for this source refer to the electronic version.

It takes up "key notions and fundamental concepts" that Majdalanie and Mroué deal with in their work, summed up by the theater researcher Omar Fertat as "war, memory, and the body."[3] In *Appendice*, the body is the pivotal site where the concepts of ruins—relating to memory—sovereignty, violence, and war are conflated, together with other notions such as absence, presence, and representation. The experience of war in the performance is revisited, and the concepts at stake during the war are redefined to produce a complex web of relations that challenge and undermine their workings. The narrative, although grounded in the Lebanese cultural, social, and political context, transcends the specificity of place and time.

Majdalanie and Mroué, a Break in Lebanese Theater

The early 1990s in Lebanon witnessed the rise of performance art, the incorporation of various media in theater, and a diversification of the visual arts. Performance art in Lebanon is derived in part from theater and can be considered the critical response to the artistic production of the so-called "sixties generation" by what became known as the "war generation" of artists, actors, directors, and playwrights. The war generation is often tagged as "the postwar generation" in the discourses produced by the "international art world's investment in postwar Beirut."[4] This apparent inconsistency is explained by the fact that the term *postwar generation* refers to the period of this generation's artistic activity; its members became active after the war. The term *war generation*, in contrast—used by Lina Majdalanie, for example—refers to the "chronological" place of a generation that was born in the 1960s and early 1970s and grew up during the Lebanese Civil War.[5] The tag *international* was given to a loose group of cultural producers whose "mixed-media practices converge on a critical interest in the war, its histories and memories."[6] This is the internationally

3. Fertat, "Rabih Mroué et Lina Saneh," 15–16.
4. Rogers, "Out of History," 11.
5. Fertat, "Rabih Mroué et Lina Saneh," 2, 3.
6. Rogers, "Out of History," 9.

recognized group to which Lina Majdalanie and Rabih Mroué belong. Yet Majdalanie and Mroué are also perceived as very anchored in the local scene and at the same time in dialogue with the previous generation of Lebanese artists.

The actress and playwright Hanane El Hajj Ali, a major actor of the preceding generation, describes the play *Come in, Sir, We Are Waiting for You Outside* (1998), written by Rabih Mroué in collaboration with Toni Chakar, as "a manifesto for a radical break with previous plays' practices."[7] She thus considers the play as embodying the changes in the theater that were gradually instated in the 1990s by the war generation. The play not only broke from traditional forms but also stood out in its language and content. Performed within a program to commemorate the fiftieth anniversary of the Nakba, it challenged the sacralization and rarefication of traditional discourses and issues—for example, in relation to the Palestinian cause.[8] As Mroué explains, "I wanted to say that the memory of the Palestine you revive and that you celebrate is a Palestine that exists only in images, in media, in our memories. . . . I decided to work with images, with videos[,] . . . [to] create an illusion—how different montages of the same sentence and of the same shot could change the meaning upside down."[9] Lina Majdalanie similarly confirms a "double rupture" "both in the theatrical language and the customary discourse that surrounds the Nakba."[10] The incorporation of various visual media in *Come in, Sir* confirmed this "radical break" from traditional theater and celebratory discourses and underlined the already blurred boundaries between theater, performance art, and other visual artistic practices in postwar Lebanon.

7. El Hajj Ali, *Theatre Beyrouth*, 120.

8. The volume *Theatre Beyrouth* (2010) by Hanane El Hajj Ali played a major role in the promotion and evolution of theater and other contemporary arts.

9. Quoted in El Hajj Ali, *Theatre Beyrouth*, 120.

10. Fertat, "Rabih Mroué et Lina Saneh," 4. Majdalanie's play *Ovrira* (1997) was a statement to highlight the importance of language and signify her rejection of a theater dominated by bodily expressions. The burlesque performance was a demonstration of how extreme gestural and corporeal expressions silence words and language.

Both graduates from Lebanese University, Majdalanie and Mroué began their collaboration with their stage adaptation of the novel *The Journey of the Little Gandhi* by Elias Khoury in 1991. Since then, they have worked together both "formally and informally,"[11] making it very difficult to distinguish each contributor's input. But they stand out, according to Kaelen Wilson-Goldie, because they "are to Beirut what the Wooster Group is to New York, a blend of avant-garde innovation, conceptual complexity and political urgency all grounded in earthy humor."[12] In their work, they project an "extreme" vision of playacting that is either minimalist or burlesque and that rejects all half measures. They are "unwilling[] to tell stories because a story does not tell the truth. And what they hope for is an audience that shares with them their questions on life, death, politics, and art."[13]

Power Play: Body, Silence, and Language

Grounded in a postmodern philosophy critical of certain assumptions pertaining to the notion of humanity, the performance of *Appendice* raises questions rather than gives answers in the realms of both art practice and life.[14] The performance continuously produces statements that contradict each other. Every stage of the analysis weakens or undermines the previous one, delivering inconstant and sometimes conflicting results. This ambivalence makes analysis of the performance an uneasy task because the performance resists a linear reading. To overcome this complexity, I address the topics as they appear in the play, identifying key elements that produce meanings. "These elements, images, documents, and real facts [ses éléments, ses images, ses documents et des faits réels]"[15] pertaining to the text, the acting, the context, and the strategies employed help unravel the netting that entangles the different concepts mentioned earlier as these elements reproduce or modify how those concepts work.

11. Wilson-Goldie, "Lebanon Bans Tale of Fighters in Militias."
12. Wilson-Goldie, "Lebanon Bans Tale of Fighters in Militias."
13. Fertat, "Rabih Mroué et Lina Saneh," 15.
14. Fertat, "Rabih Mroué et Lina Saneh," 8.
15. Fertat, "Rabih Mroué et Lina Saneh," 11.

The Set-Up

Spoken in the vernacular Lebanese dialect, *Appendice* opens with the following lines:

> I have a problem.
> I've always wanted to be cremated after my death
> But incineration is prohibited in Lebanon
> on account of religious reasons.[16]

Facing the audience behind a wooden lectern, Mroué speaks these lines as though delivering a public lecture. Next to him, Majdalanie sits, silent and immobile, her back straight, looking away with a placid facial expression. She will remain silent throughout the performance, but to remind the audience of her presence, she changes her position about three or four times. Each change is nearly imperceptible, though, as she moves only her head.

Mroué's opening sentences set an impersonal tone, with minimal playacting. The only perplexing note is the presence of Majdalanie, who sits next to him silently. A Lebanese audience can immediately understand the story framework. The obstacle that prohibits Mroué from disposing freely of his own body relates to the Personal Status Laws grounded in the Lebanese Constitution. Article 9 of the Constitution "guarantees that personal status and religious interest of the population, to whatever religious sect they belong, [are] respected,"[17] so "Lebanon does not have a civil code regulating personal status matters."[18] Instead, there are fifteen separate Personal Status Laws for the country's eighteen different recognized religious communities. The amalgam created by "the respect" of religious communities has led to a system of governance based on confessionalism

16. Lina Saneh [Lina Majdalanie], *Appendice*, 1, paginated script in the author's files; subsequent citations to Saneh's play are given parenthetically by page number in the text. This piece, like all of the work done by Majdalanie and Mroué, is performed in spoken Arabic, but the written script that Lina Majdalanie gave me is written in French. Here, I have translated from the French into English and provided the translation, giving the original French at times only when it clarifies the meaning.

17. *Arab Law Quarterly*, 226–27.

18. Human Rights Watch, "Unequal and Unprotected."

and defined as "the blending of religion and politics through apportioning government positions based on individual identification with a religion or a confession."[19] Thus, one *must* register under one of the eighteen religious sects for Personal Status Laws to apply. Otherwise, in the absence of civil laws, one is simply outside the law, an outlaw.

The speaker's reference to "religious reasons" as the obstacle to cremating his body, albeit vague, points clearly to the absence of civil laws. It reopens the issue of the separation of the state from religion, which dates back to the founding of Lebanon as a modern nation-state based on a confessional system of governance. This system continues to be contested by generations of activists consistently pushing for a change, but it remains intact.[20] The performance allows all of these ideas to stir the audience's minds when Mroué corrects himself and states,

> in reality these are Lina's words,
> maybe I should read them in a different way.
> I repeat: (1)

The rectification makes the audience glance at "Lina" and understand her presence. The speaker is in fact not Mroué but "Lina." This change in context affects the reading of the content since, as the audience suddenly becomes aware, the words uttered by Mroué, a man, are actually that of a woman. Mroué *speaks in the name* of Majdalanie. This feature in the casting is a fundamental but quiet element that affects the outcome of the analysis of the piece in particular situations. Another element I highlight is the use of language. It begins with Mroué's change of subject from "I" to "she."

19. Kisthardt, "Confessionalism in Lebanon."

20. To change the confessional system without recourse to force or politics, some activists try to breach the legal system by creating legal precedent based on existing laws. In 2013, a couple was able to have a civil marriage "without leaving the country" by using "a legal loophole" (Hamadi and Farhat, "Civil Marriage in Lebanon"). The marriage opened a breach in the system: making a legal precedent, it reenforced existing civil laws and allowed for the revision of current law and the making of new laws. The organization Legal Agenda works in this manner; see its website at http://legal-agenda.com/en/mannahnou.php.

Mroué reiterates the same words, replacing "I" with "Lina" and "she" (the third-person feminine pronoun): "Lina has a problem. She has a problem // she always wanted to be cremated" (1). The change of the subject from "I" to "she" is at first confusing. The correction allows the audience to understand that the words uttered by the standing speaker, Mroué, are not his own. They are Lina Majdalanie's. Mroué is speaking in her name. The indications of the speaking subject as the silent one and the deliberate change in pronoun at the beginning of the performance expose a complex web of power relations between the two actors on stage, on the one hand, and Majdalanie and Mroué, the actors' doubles in life, on the other. The result resembles a mise en abime of an infinite mirroring of characters because the figures the actors embody in the story are both themselves and their doubles: they are artistic partners *and* husband and wife. The complex relations between the "actual" entities and those "represented" involve at least three elements—language, the body, and silence—in a web of power.

Language and Words

The question of who is speaking intertwines with silence to blur the boundaries between the person who utters words and the one who has formulated the utterance and is thus "speaking." Speaking in the name of Majdalanie at the beginning of the performance, Mroué accidentally overtakes the mute voice of Majdalanie. The audience confusion as to who is speaking is normal since the immediate understanding of the subject of "I" is the person who utters it. Mroué's first faux pas, though rapidly corrected, reveals the inescapable interference of the speaker's voice. His neutrality is challenged a second time when he reveals his personal interests and emotions. The two cases betray the impossibility for a spokesperson to remain neutral when speaking in the name of another person, an institution, a state, or God.

Shortly after introducing Majdalanie's will and the "problem" standing in the way of its fulfillment, Mroué struggles to control his emotions. He first restates Majdalanie's strong commitment to getting cremated despite all barriers: "Nevertheless Lina wants absolutely to be cremated / 'I insist, I will not give up,' she says ['J'y tiens, je n'en démordrai pas,' dit-elle]" (2).[21] But he hesitates while pronouncing the following sentence that involves him: "she bothers the life of her . . . of her husband [Elle enquiquine la vie à son . . . mari]" (2). His voice betrays surprise when he adds, almost despite himself, "it's me her husband" (2). This sudden awareness doubles Mroué's presence; he becomes both the performer and the husband as he realizes that he is annoyed by her "incessant repetitions" of "wanting absolutely to be cremated" (2). He loses his placid, official tone to speak in an exasperated tone and in the first person, thus "kidnapping" the "I" to speak for himself: "She wants to be cremated / she wants . . . shit! What can I do?!" (2). He then rapidly corrects himself, replacing the "I," the sovereign "I" of the exasperated husband, with a noun beginning with the possessive pronoun *her*, as if surrendering to Majdalanie: "What could her husband do?" (2). He finally manages to control his exasperation and regains his role as actor, speaking calmly while describing *his* irritated state of mind. He thus refers to himself in the third person, as "her husband," the *other*

> who is already annoyed by the idea that he should attempt
> to discuss, negotiate, convince,
> to have her incinerated when she dies. (2)

After those initial losses of control, Mroué's neutral tone throughout the performance confirms that he is speaking "in the name of" Majdalanie. He even reintroduces the "I" that speaks for Majdalanie and alternates between "I" and "she" throughout the performance, keeping a dispassionate tone, as if truly lending his voice (and the "I") to Majdalanie. This switching back and forth from speaking subjects to objects of speech ("I" and "she") adds a layer to the interplay of power. It produces alternative readings of an "I" whereby either Majdalanie's power takes over the "I" that Mroué utters or produces an "I" in which Mroué fully identifies with Majdalanie. The former interpretation posits a silently dominant Majdalanie. The latter can be clarified through a concept articulated by

21. The French verb for "not giving up" is *démordre*, which contains the verb *mordre*, "to bite." The term vividly evokes the notion of bestiality.

Emilie Berteau, whereby "the 'I' loses itself in social codifications and even within the couple. Individuality and singularity become myths."[22]

This subtle switching of the pronoun points to the ambivalence of the commanding voice in relation to the speaker: Who is really speaking? This question is raised in the performance, but no definitive answers are given. This ambivalence leads to an open-endedness typical of Majdalanie and Mroué's work that serves their purpose because what "they hope for," as noted earlier, "is an audience that shares with them their questions on life, death, politics, and art."[23] The fact that Majdalanie chose to remain silent and chose Mroué to speak on her behalf adds another layer of inquiry to the performance: Why him? Is her voice "kidnapped," as suggested by her stillness? Is it because her husband's or a male's voice is more powerful than hers, so that he has to speak *for* her? Or is it because they identify with each other as a married couple and/or as artistic partners?[24] The performance gives no clues to what the right answer is. The ambivalence created by the choice of male and female roles points to gender rights without explicitly naming the issues involved.

Bodies and Words

On stage, Mroué's natural acting juxtaposed with the immobile and mute Majdalanie minimizes the attention given to the actors' bodily presences and heightens the power of speech. The emphasis on speech happens on at least two levels. The first concerns how the audience, in the absence of staging, is thus forced to concentrate on the spoken words. As Mroué has put it elsewhere, "It is through speech [*paroles*] that images arise in the spectators' imagination; words liberate their imagination."[25] The second level of emphasis is how the authority and legitimacy of the *actual* speaker are put into question: even if the uttered words are Majdalanie's, Mroué is the one who moves and speaks, while she remains still and silent. The contrast between Majdalanie's immobility and silence, one the one hand,

22. Berteau, "Du refus d'être recyclé."

23. Fertat, "Rabih Mroué et Lina Saneh," 15.

24. Berteau, "Du refus d'être recyclé."

25. Quoted in Fertat, "Rabih Mroué et Lina Saneh," 13.

and the increasing violence of her words, ventriloquized by Mroué, on the other, is disconcerting. As the performance continues, her loud silence heightens the power of her ghostly presence because of her determination to continue to fight a war despite the violent impact of the battles.

Soon, layers of images of Majdalanie's dissected body fill the audience's imagination. During the first performance on April 21, 2007, which I attended, some people soon walked out, clearly showing their disapproval and disgust: as if the violence of words sufficed to make the spectators forget they were experiencing only a staged performance based on a fictitious story, as if the words transformed in the audience's imagination into the acts they represent. The impact of the imaged construct increases as the performance continues, changing the listener-viewer's perception of Majdalanie. The initial image of an apparently passive person because silent and immobile gradually transforms into the image of an aggressive and almost beastly person. The transformation happens because of the power of *her* words uttered by someone else. The contrast between the mute and withdrawn figure of Majdalanie and her sharp and precise words nurtures the impact of her mute voice. As the performance continues, her silence grows louder and transforms from that of a subaltern into that of a sovereign.

Eloquent and Dominant Silence

Reading Majdalanie's silence through this lens allows the audience to understand that when Mroué speaks in the name of Majdalanie, he confirms her authority rather than undermines it. Typically, people speak in the name of a state, a sovereign, or even God. Rather than disempowering her, Mroué's speaking for Majdalanie transforms her from being a subaltern into being a sovereign. The power to remain silent, in this context, proves to be stronger than the power of speech, as Jacques Derrida argues: "The sovereign has the right not to respond, he has the right to the silence . . . he needs not to speak, he almost must not-speak."[26] Majdalanie's sovereign silence indicates that she has chosen not to speak and has chosen who is allowed to speak on her behalf. Her silence and her immobile body nurture the

26. Derrida, *The Beast and the Sovereign*, 51.

images created by the words. Her spectral presence grows as images of her warring body replace the sight of her immobile body. The effect is similar to the omnipresent image of a sovereign or of political figures and martyrs, such as those found in governmental offices or on street posters. The latter comparison is particularly powerful in the Lebanese context, where such street images are omnipresent and reflect how political parties mark and delineate territories and spheres of influence in their struggles.[27]

Majdalanie's sovereign silence offers an alternative to the silence of both war and postwar contexts, and her female body disrupts the masculine image attached to sovereignty. In war, silence is often imposed, and speaking might get you killed.[28] Similarly, the silence of postwar Lebanon was also imposed. The General Amnesty Law, issued by the Lebanese government on August 26, 1991, retrospectively exempted Lebanese war protagonists from being charged with war crimes and "for abuses committed . . . throughout all the years of the civil war."[29] The law and those who enacted it thus silenced the dead and the sufferers. The political elite, consisting mostly of male warlords, enforced and imposed silence, wiping out all traces of violence by erasing the past. Majdalanie's sovereign silence parodies the silence of this political elite that decided it needed neither to justify nor to apologize for its crimes.

Majdalanie attempts to intertwine sovereignty, violence, and silence in complex representations whereby each one is an unavoidable condition for the others. Moreover, the inversion of the male sovereign figure into a female one raises the question of the interplay of silence, sovereignty, and violence in relation to gender. It opens up the question of the inevitability of violence not only as mimicking men's hunger for power but also as challenging human sovereignty, liberty, and autonomy for men and women alike. As the performance continues, the motif of ruins adds a new layer to the representations fostering the concepts of sovereignty, war, violence, and the body, forming new sets of relations and raising further questions.

27. See also Becherer, "A Matter of Life and Debt," and Maasri, "The Aesthetics of Belonging."

28. Beydoun, *Le Liban*, 8.

29. Amnesty International, *Lebanon*, 7.

Body, Ruins, War / An Act of War

Majdalanie decides on a radical solution to her problem, dismissing everything she had previously considered as "too hypothetical, / uncertain" (5). Her final re-solution is to excise her body parts one by one, "though without endangering her life" (6). The process would allow her to achieve cremation "bit by bit . . . to win the most part / of herself" (7):

> One day, Lina heard that in hospitals
> excised members and organs of some of the patients are burned
>
> It put a buzz in her ear.
> She said to herself there may be
> a way to solve her problem.
>
> That is, she could, for example,
> undergo operations, in several steps,
> removing, one by one,
>
> members and organs of her body,
> from the least necessary to the most vital ones,
> though without endangering her life.
>
> Her organs and limbs removed during the operations
> will then be burned;
>
> she would thus try to gain the most "terrain"
> possible of her own body possibly
> to what will remain from it to be buried upon her death.
>
> She would burn herself bit by bit,
>
> slowly [literally: over a gentle heat], to win the most part
> of herself over her enemies,
>
> until perhaps they surrender? (5–7)

Majdalanie's clear description of her re-solution is a declaration of war, both logical and absurd. Its coherence lies in the fact that the process "of burning herself bit by bit" would logically allow her to reach her wish of cremation after death. The process is absurd if not "stupid," to use Majdalanie's word for the appendix, because dismembering herself would harm her. Why would one dismember one's own body and hurt one's self? Majdalanie's answer is clear: she will dismember her body to assert her autonomy and liberty. Majdalanie's war is for sovereignty. Her war directed against herself questions common understandings of war, violence, and their absurdity if not stupidity. Majdalanie's war supports the idea that violence and absurdity are inherent to a sovereign act.

Majdalanie's words represent and personify a war in which she through her body—simultaneously the site of struggle, the field to conquer, and the weapon—battles the obstacles preventing her from cremating her body after her death. Unlike in the many wars she has witnessed, she takes responsibility for this war instead of being subjected to it and erases the distinctions between the self and the enemy by embodying both. Her aim for sovereignty takes her very close to a death—she willingly flirts with the promise that her necessary self-destruction will not "endanger her life." War is redefined on her own terms: it is an inevitable process for autonomy, dignity, and liberty—for sovereignty—to be fulfilled. If sovereignty is indeed an undeniable human right, then there is no escape from war; one may as well initiate and take control of it.

Deliberate Ruining

Keeping his neutral tone despite the violence and crudeness of the words, Mroué continues detailing the slow process of self-destruction that will transform Lina's immobile and silent body into desolation and ruins. The use of the conditional voice imparts a hypothetical undertone that slightly tempers the violence of the words and delays the fulfillment of the represented acts. Yet the detailed description of the dissection and mutilation renders vivid and painful images of a ruined body without organs.[30]

30. This recalls Antonin Artaud's use of the metaphor "body without organs" to refer to liberty: "When you will have made him a body without organs, then you will have delivered him from all his automatic reactions / and restored him to his true freedom" (Artaud, *To Have Done with the Judgment of God*).

The incising and dismembering of limbs, fingers, hands, and legs follow the extraction of the appendix, uterus, breasts, and then one kidney. Each part's uselessness is justified, fulfilling the condition that removing it will affect neither Majdalanie's life nor her artistic practice. For the ablation of some organs, a (potentially) positive outcome is highlighted; the removal of the breasts, for example, prevents cancer. The black humor is obvious when Mroué in an impassive tone states: "She could also play around by combining and alternating" the body parts to be removed; "the possibilities are infinite" (17).

The violence of the repeated acts of dismantling and ruining the body produces layers of images of destruction. They recall Sarah Rogers's description of the city of Beirut during the war: "The image of the city was transformed from one of cosmopolitanism to one of uncontrollable instability, creating a breeding ground for snipers, kidnappings, suicide bombers, and a general, unbridled chaos."[31] Majdalanie transposes the image of a city at war onto her own body. Unlike the city's state of instability and chaos, her gesture, a claim for sovereignty, is supposedly a thoughtful act in which ruining the body is a necessary part of making that claim. The images of her ruined body thus transform into a sign of victory. The analogy to images of a city in ruins reflects ironically, reversing the image of a desolated city into the image of a victorious one.[32] The outcomes of war—ruined inhabitants and ruined cities—become signs of triumph. Her triumphal ruined body parodying the outcome of war makes her claim to sovereignty seem to be different from the various claims made by the protagonists who sparked the war.

Excising her body parts one by one, Majdalanie reenacts the violence of the war yet without endangering anyone except those body parts, her many selves but paradoxically not her self. This assertion raises fundamental questions regarding the "members" of a body and, by analogy, the members of a community and a state. Is harming a single body part

31. Rogers, "A Short History of Postwar Art in Lebanon," 137.

32. The rhetoric of a victory despite defeat is commonly used by Lebanese political parties and even Arab states. The "Divine Victory" of Hizbullah in 2006 sparked many controversies (Higgins, "Divine Victory").

isolated from harming the self, the whole? Are the members of a body, a community, a political body or the citizens of a state an inseparable part of it? According to Thomas Hobbes's account of the Leviathan, the answer prioritizes the sovereignty of the state: if the sovereignty of the state is at stake, excising body parts is necessary to preserving that sovereignty. Majdalanie's absurd (if not stupid) dismemberment of her body is thus logically justified: her individual body parts comply to the sovereign "self," just as the citizens of a state do.

Majdalanie reproduces the image of a self-state in which her body parts "perform their duty."[33] Alongside the image of a state within a state, she also reproduces a self-state within the state. Her proclaimed self-state exemplifies the reclaiming of individual sovereignty over state sovereignty. The simultaneous staging of the two different sovereignties is ambivalent because sovereignty is by definition indivisible. This ambivalence recalls the conflicting consequences of human sovereignty, highlighted in Derrida's statement, "If sovereignty is, indeed, defined as the proper of man . . . it is nonetheless also in the name of man, the humanity of man, the dignity of man, therefore a certain proper of man, that a certain modernity has begun to question, to undermine, to put into crisis nation-state sovereignty."[34] In the staging of her self as a divisible entity like a state, Majdalanie's claim for sovereignty questions and undermines the very absolute sovereignty it reclaims.

Humanism Reappropriated

Lebanese visual artists explored the concept of memory through the motif of ruins in their work during the war to confront the realities of war and after the war "to confront the legacies of the war."[35] The motif of ruins, according to Ken Seigneurie, has common ground with a humanist tradition as much as with the Arab traditional "literary topos" of "stopping by the ruins" (*wuquf 'ala al-atlal*)—or "standing by the ruins"—that makes them "speak" memories. Humanism bridges the gap between prewar and

33. Hobbes, *Leviathan*, 7.

34. Derrida, *The Beast and the Sovereign*, 70, 106.

35. Rogers, "A Short History of Postwar Art in Lebanon," 136.

postwar periods through a shared lived experience of war, despite the differences in tactics and underlying principles practiced by the artists. Making ruins "speak," an approach traditionally used to "expand the object of longing and imaginative identification from the absent beloved," was developed "to include consciousness of justice and self-responsibility." This change, according to Seigneurie, was triggered when the war provided for individual explorations of related notions such as "justice" and "responsibility."[36]

In *Appendice*, the motif of ruins suggests a reappropriation that deviates from investigating "the consciousness of justice and self-responsibility" to challenging and undermining those notions through the performance's staged singular war.[37] Ruins in *Appendice* are not a natural outcome of war or a subject for longing. Mroué clarifies that the dismemberment, this ruining of the body he describes, is not a punishment but a deliberate process, even if it resembles "those old and far away practices [of punishment] that still exist" (19). "For example, they cut the hand of the thief, // the tongue of the one who lies" (19). Therefore, the repetitive act of dismemberment Majdalanie undergoes resembles a punishment but is *not* one. Her dismemberment, Mroué explains, is not

> for the redemption of this stubborn body
> [a] social, communitarian, confessional, tribal, clan-based body
>
> No! her dismemberment is for her
> and for her alone. (20)

Majdalanie's dismemberment is done for the sake of nothing and no one else but her—a way for her to attain sovereignty over her body and her self (20). Dismissing the process as a punishment and insisting that her dismemberment is only a means to sovereignty amplify the absurd and foolish aspects of this process of ruination. The process reconfigures war and sovereignty as intimately linked and raises doubts about the rationality of both.

36. Seigneurie, *Standing by the Ruins*, 32, 143.
37. Seigneurie, *Standing by the Ruins*, 143.

Logically Absurd, Imminently Violent

For Majdalanie, removing her body parts and leaving her body and thus her self in ruins constitute a process toward something more valuable, the most valuable for Lina: the liberty and autonomy to be herself. Majdalanie's act of dismemberment resembles an implosion in slow motion. The images of her ruined body recall vividly the horrifying results of suicide bombers and protesters who deliberately kill themselves. The anthropologist Ghassan Hage humanizes these bombers and, although seeing the condemnable violence of their actions, explains that the act of blowing up oneself stems from a "lack of concern with the humanity of the people murdered in the course of the conflicts." Instead of blindly condemning suicide bombers, Hage reveals the dehumanizing acts that trigger the human bomb. Suicide bombers and protesters blow themselves up to reach a "higher" goal: "care for the actual material being-ness."[38]

Majdalanie's dismemberment and burning of her body parts recall self-immolation without its ultimate form of protest: death. Her body is the means "to accumulate personal status and self-esteem."[39] Like the suicide bombers, Majdalanie uses her body as a weapon, a battlefield, and the territory to conquer in order to prohibit the "colonizers" from dominating her. If for the suicide bomber death "disrupt[s] the ability of the colonizer to consolidate 'a normal peaceful life' inside the colonial settler state" (68), for Majdalanie her dismemberment stops at the limit where life is separated from death. In death, she would lose the war, for her success lies in recuperating "the most parts of her body" so that she can cremate it. Majdalanie's conditions are for a self-directed war that doesn't "excessively damage / the quality of her life and endanger her life" (12). Her conditions leave in suspense the defining terms for a worthy life because the "quality of life" she aspires to protect is extensively jeopardized by the state of her ruined body. Blurring the line between life and death, her dismemberment questions the extent to which her war for sovereignty forces her to abandon both a life worthy of the name and, to an extent, her humanity.

38. Hage, "'Comes a Time We Are All Enthusiasm,'" 65, 66.

39. Hage, "'Comes a Time We Are All Enthusiasm,'" 76.

The ambivalence of Majdalanie's formulated terms subtly questions the success the suicide bomber and protester achieve for themselves in a process whereby they abandon their humanity along with that of others.

Majdalanie stages a "violence of last resort"[40] in a war where her enemies are represented as disembodied "colonizers." Her enemies are dematerialized very much like "the dehumanizing gaze" that unifies protagonists by reducing "them to undifferentiated entities" (66). Majdalanie's war resembles both no war and any war in which "them" can stand for everybody and nobody—Israeli and Palestinian (as in Hage's case), Christian and Muslim, Left and Right, Arab and European, Black and white. Both Hage and Majdalanie base their analyses on experiences of the Lebanese Civil War, the former as a protagonist, "a participant and a student," and the latter as a civilian and a student. Their mutual conclusion is "that when the logic of communal war prevails, neither of the warring sides really cares for the actual material human being-ness of the situation. More 'important' things like 'community' and 'nations' are at stake."[41] Community and nations are the very institutional traps—political and religious systems—that Majdalanie is fighting.

Majdalanie's performance blurs the boundaries between peace and war. It also normalizes violence, a normalization that can be considered a form of extreme violence.[42] Parodying this extreme form of violence, the performance recalls the consequences of war in which the normalization of violence helps civilians survive as much as it holds them hostage and dehumanizes them as well as sometimes others. It may also be a provocative gesture to reverse the state of acceptance and feelings of powerlessness and helplessness that overwhelm civilians. Further, the performance revives the memory of the uprising in Beirut in 2005, reacting against the explosion that killed Prime Minister Rafic al-Hariri, Minister Bassil Fuleihan, Hariri's bodyguards, and many civilians. According to the journalist Samir Kassir, the Beirut uprising anticipated the so-called Arab Spring

40. Hage, "'Comes a Time We Are All Enthusiasm,'" 73.

41. Hage, "'Comes a Time We Are All Enthusiasm,'" 66.

42. Hage, "'Comes a Time We Are All Enthusiasm,'" 72.

that erupted in 2011, spurred by a suicide protester in Tunisia[43]—a suicide that rightly and sadly falls within an "accumulation of death as a mode of seeking a meaningful life" in a region with predominately authoritarian regimes.[44]

Given the regional context, Majdalanie's performance can be read as a parody of suicide bombers and suicide protests that both emphasizes and undermines their legitimacy.[45] As she underscores, even in death the ultimate goal of sovereignty is endangered because in death one is subjected to institutional codification. The dead can be turned into martyrs and reclaimed by political or religious institutions, as suicide bombers and protesters often are. So even with this solution of last resort, a new obstacle emerges. The setback seems systematic and inevitable. The performance draws on this inevitability, as "with each attempt at liberation, she [Majdalanie] is drawn backwards. There is always a person or an institution who wants to vouch for her body and its future."[46] Yet with each setback, she comes up with a solution and a new place that guarantees liberty and autonomy until a new obstacle rises. She takes up each new fight and keeps battling by means of her warring body in a way that goes far beyond the war and is always already in a war, crystalized in her body, a terrain that is both possessed and dispossessed in a state of constant reconquering. Her body grounds her continual struggle and underlines the process of war as a key element for attaining autonomy and liberty.

Art as the Final Recourse

Majdalanie finds a new place for her warring body—art. Managing to escape religious and civil institutions by mutilating her body—dissecting it to better conquer it—she confronts the medical institution in which

43. "Suicide Protester Mohammed Bouazizi Dies in Tunisia." Samir Kassir's reading of the Beirut uprising is summed up in his article's title, "Beirut Is the Spring of Arabs," predicting the Arab revolts that would erupt across the region six years later.

44. Pierre Bourdieu, quoted in Hage, "'Comes a Time We Are All Enthusiasm,'" 80.

45. See Kraidy, "The Revolutionary Body Politic," which proposes that we theorize the human body as a vital medium in the Arab uprisings.

46. Berteau, "Du refus d'être recyclé."

mutilating a healthy body is illegal (36). She thus decides to turn her warring body into a workshop and transform her body parts into works of art and "sell" them (42). Escaping social, religious, and medical institutions, Majdalanie's body falls into yet another institutional space and the last mentioned in the performance—art. She then extends her warring body into the virtual realm: the "physical" performance took place in 2007 in Beirut, but the virtual one in the form of a website is ongoing. Her online art gallery, more of an auction house, is a virtual place where one can "buy" and "sell" her body parts.[47] The art gallery obstructs the force of the market because the "selling" of her priceless body parts is achieved for a mere signature from the buyer.

Majdalanie's war for freedom and autonomy prompts her to shelter her warring body in the space provided by art. Yet even art raises a fundamental question: Is art really a place for freedom? Cultural institutions, Majdalanie posits, can restrain liberty, too. In her talk titled "De l'acte théâtrale: Une affaire de parole et de distance," she clearly denounces "the fascist and impossible injunction ordered by the official, liberal, and global culture [la moderne, fasciste et impossible injocntion de performance qui lui est intimé par la culture officielle libérale et mondiale]."[48] Majdalanie "fights" on these fronts, too: "[For] me," she says, "the theatre of the body where we dance, express ourselves, and drool, I don't give a damn about it" (20). Her warring body doesn't give up. She challenges the injunction "ordered by the official and liberal institutions" by offering minimal bodily expressions and gestures in her performance because "her tongue is sufficient to do theatre / and to have sex too" (21).

Using the tongue, Majdalanie crosses the lines between art and life, being provocative in both realms. In theater, she underlines the importance of a single body part, the tongue that represents language—especially in French where the same word, *langue*, is used for both "tongue" and "language." Through her tongue, she also challenges conventional social norms because the tongue is linked to a social taboo, oral sex. And,

47. Majdalanie's online art gallery can be found at http://www.linasaneh-body-p-arts.com.

48. Quoted in Berteau, "Du refus d'être recyclé."

once again, her dismembered warring body extends into virtual reality, defying bodily perfection in the same provocative manner: she offers her "amputated" body to the sex market—pornography. As Mroué narrates,

> She then decided to open a porno site
> on the Internet www.kinkylina.blogspot.com
>
> On this site, she presents herself
> as an amputated person [une personne amputée]. (22)

Antonym for an Epilogue: The Warring Body

In art as in life, Majdalanie's war is interminable. Through and with her warring body, she posits situations in which the same body then challenges and undermines them. Her body constantly transforms and simultaneously enacts a dwelling, a weapon, and a battlefield. Its absence and presence as well as representations of its appearance and disappearance are pivotal in moving between fiction and reality, practice and life. The body is in a continuous battle fueled by re-presentations and constantly navigating between the realm of art and the realm of life. The body spreads out and multiplies in the very act of dismemberment, offering a sense of her being simultaneously possessed and dispossessed. The body's multiplicity paradoxically both preserves and jeopardizes her sovereignty as the body's dismemberment multiplies her selves. The multiplicity of the body in analogy to the self is represented in the way Majdalanie describes her skin. "But the skin . . . the skin . . . / is all that holds me [together], all that keeps me from falling [apart]" (31–32). Yet her skin, like her body, has paradoxical attributes. "Unified and continuous" yet "improperly closed," her troubled skin is what holds her together, preventing "her body parts" from breaking free and "err[ing] all around the world." Her skin, like her, is

> this aching shield, this unified and continuous surface. . . .
> This surface not enough unified and discontinued,
> improperly closed, that doesn't prevent me enough,
> alas, to flee, to break free. (32–33)

The paradoxical attributes of the skin, like those of the body, allow Majdalanie's troubled self to be simultaneously unique and multiple.

Majdalanie's body is a paradox through which ambivalence turns into a strategy to counter ideologies. It is "a form of skepticism toward any partisan engagements" that the war generation has in common. Majdalanie's position is one where "personal commitment is privileged over all ideological demands."[49] Her closing statement in *Appendice* reflects her personal commitment to calling for absolute sovereignty and to rejecting any compromise. It represents a last situation that creates the same ambivalence encountered throughout the performance, simultaneously nurturing and undermining the very sovereignty it cries out for.

> I don't want to participate in the recycling of the world
> I don't want to feed the soil that nourished me
> I don't want to continue to prosper in something else than myself
>
> If I have to burn in hell,
> I would begin by burning at the entrance,
> or I would immortalize my body.
>
> I would have been the one who started the fires of hell down here
> instead of in a hell in the hereafter. (44)

In the final statement, Mroué reuses "I" as if to amplify the stubborn and indefatigable reclaiming of the sovereign "I." The opening sentence of this statement reiterates the unsettled notions of self and sovereignty in which both are already compromised: "I don't want to participate in recycling the world." The "I" is ambiguous regarding *who* is really speaking: Mroué who utters the "I," Mroué the husband, or Mroué the artistic partner? Or the silent Majdalanie? Sovereignty, in turn, is represented as an impossible situation whereby the "I" should never "prosper in something else than myself" and totally "disappear" from the world or be absolutely independent from it. The paradoxes inherent in the proclamation of such an autonomous and independent "I" undermine the validity and the possibility of absolute sovereignty. But the insistence and the stubbornness of the inevitably lost battle turn the impossible quest into a call for a lucid critical

49. Chabrol, "La fabrique artistique de la mémoire," 492.

thinking of one's engagement with the surrounding world and highlight the possible contained in the impossible. Majdalanie's stubborn quest for the impossible transforms the performance into the promise of an autonomous and free self because it is grounded in her warring body: *hope* is what she projects, maybe despite her self.

The various possible interpretations of *Appendice* make the performance a groundbreaking piece. The "I" that Mroué utters on behalf of Majdalanie represents any-I-body and every-I-body who battles or wishes to resist being constrained by a "we"—a confession, a tribe, or a clan that "still reject[s] and always will / to let go of its members" (20). This is especially true when the "we" represent dominating social, religious, political, and cultural ideologies and norms. Through the playacting, Majdalanie's loud yet silent voice incarnates silenced voices that struggle to speak and exercise freedom. Her warring body is a challenging call for a never-ending war because the objective can never be definitively attained. The systematic failures of this warring process are an appeal for critical awareness about the ambiguity and difficulty of exercising liberty and autonomy. Despite the negativity produced by failures, what the performance *Appendice* achieves is a *promise*—the promise embodied in this stubborn warring body that keeps the struggle going despite its heavy cost; the promise of getting as close as possible to autonomy and liberty, always "halfway."

Warring Self

The quest *Appendice* embodies does not end with the end of the performance. Majdalanie's quest for sovereignty, underlined in the performance, is an ongoing quest in both her art and her life. It resurfaces in the form of her name. In 2015, Lina, who then went by the name "Lina Saneh," sent me an email announcing that she would be using "Lina Majdalanie" as her new name. I was surprised to receive this message, especially because she gave no explanation for this change. At the end of the email, following her new email address, was a courteous command followed by an apology, asking people to take note of the change, which she admitted was a little bit confusing, and saying sorry for that. The name change was indeed confusing, but it can be seen as yet a new step in Majdalanie's quest for sovereignty. Giving up the name she was given at birth and acquiring a new one resembles cutting off her body parts to maintain control over her body and her self. Giving up on her birth name is another way to assert her self. In the process, her name, like her body, multiplies the transformation of Majdalanie's self into multiple selves—body parts and names—that elude one fixed identity.

The meanings of her two names relate directly to sovereignty and to art. The name "Saneh" recalls the Arabic word *san'*, "maker." With the feminine ending *ah*, *saani'ah* is the common word for "maid." The verb *sa-na-'a* (from the root *S-N-'*) refers to the act of manufacturing, making, or producing. In contrast, the name "Majdalanie" comes from the root *M-J-D*, which invokes "glory." The verb *ma-jja-da* means to "glorify" or "canonize." Majdalanie's name change thus can be read as an elevation in social status or her transformation into a glorified person if not a divinity. It once again raises the question of sovereignty. The name change transformed her from a maker, a laborer, to a sovereign. The same parallel can be made regarding a number of art historical subjects: the question of the artist as maker or constructor versus the artist as creator and the ongoing debate of material/form versus concept in art. The difference is the degree of autonomy and liberty each represents, the main goals in the performance *Appendice*. The same aim appears in Majdalanie's personal reasons for her appropriation of that name.

It seems that she deliberately chose her mother's family name, "Majdalanie," over that her father's, "Saneh." Her renaming acts like a weapon, as her body does, to confront her father and simultaneously to raise and undermine certain decrees in the Lebanese Birth Registration Law that discriminate against gender equality. Only a father can pass a surname and Lebanese nationality to a child.[50] If the father is unknown, the child is registered under his mother's name with the identification "bastard" clearly written on his identity card. Lately, that term was changed to "illegitimate"[51] and omitted in the identity card, but it is not clear whether

50. *Birth Registration Procedures in Lebanon*, 69.

51. For the relevant laws, see *Birth Registration Procedures in Lebanon*, 70; for more on registering "illegitimate" children, see pages 56–59.

it is also deleted from official papers. This discriminatory law increases the number of stateless children and subjects mothers to difficult procedures to renew identity papers and other documents for their children. If the name "Majdalanie" is Lina's mother's name, then the act of giving up "Saneh," her father's name, deliberately draws attention to discriminating laws and refuses to abide by them.

The strategy of giving up her surname and naming herself anew is similar to giving up her body to better conquer it. Her name and her body are like her skin, uniform and discontinued. They "hold her together" but do not sufficiently prevent her from wanting, "alas, to flee, to break free." They are necessary but not essential components to her self, a self that keeps battling for autonomy and liberty over her body and her name, creating a multitude of selves. In a performative manner, her many selves undermine the idea of fixed, immutable self-identity. The ability to divide and multiply her self into many selves, names, and body parts is the very attribute that allow hers to keep the fight going for a sovereign self-I in which "I" is already compromised and compromises the claim for an absolute sovereignty. Yet Majdalanie's renaming, like her reclaiming of her body, exemplifies a stubborn warring self that works like a promise for an impossible essential, autonomous, and free self.

6

Truth, Fiction, and Leaving the Page Blank

Women and the Sabra and Shatila Massacre

MICHELLE HARTMAN

Asked again and again to recount the story of her life by her son Hassan, an oral historian documenting the Nakba and Palestinian global dispersal, Ruqayya refuses. She has talked enough about herself, she claims. But at points she does relent and tells him about a number of events in her life, including the massacre in and depopulation of her hometown, Tantoura. This fictional protagonist named in the title of the novel by Radwa Ashour—*The Woman from Tantoura*—flatly refuses to discuss one event she lived through: the massacre at the Sabra and Shatila refugee camps. This event appears in the text differently than any other. It is placed almost exactly at the center of the work, but no details or facts are provided about what happened. The novel alludes only indirectly to the extreme violence that ensued. This very brief chapter contrasts with the rest of the long novel and is written in short, staccato sentences, conjuring up quick flashes of thought. The chapter closes with the protagonist ruminating to herself, "Leave the page blank[,] Ruqayya."[1] Accordingly, the pages following this last line—in both the original Arabic text and its English translation—are

1. Ashour, *The Woman from Tantoura / Al-Tanturiyya*, 150/189. In quoting Ashour's, Elhassan's, and Shibli's novels, I use the published English translations, and in note citations I give the page numbers of the English and Arabic publications in that order.

left empty; the reader is confronted with blank white pages that they must turn to continue reading the story.

When Ruqayya tells herself to leave the page blank, she signals to the reader that she will not narrate this massacre. This opens a space for the reader to question why this woman does and does not tell stories about the massacre and war. Ruqayya's reticence and refusal to narrate echo strongly the words of another traumatized and powerful fictional protagonist, Toni Morrison's Sethe. Morrison's now-classic novel *Beloved* (1987) is a story of slavery in the United States, and Sethe is read as the embodiment of both its horrors and resistance to it. Sethe refuses to tell her traumatic and traumatizing story to her daughter because, as she repeats in an echo throughout the book, "This is not a story to pass on."[2] Repeated throughout, this line haunts the novel, which is itself a story and the refusal of a story. The double meaning of this line is one of the novel's hallmarks. Scholars of *Beloved* have engaged in depth with Morrison's brilliant use of the ambiguity: Sethe literally refuses to pass the story on to her daughter and will not narrate it, but she also cannot simply let people "pass on" it and ignore the brutality and traumas of slavery.[3] Moreover, the phrase "pass on" also invokes death and what happens when the body transitions to another way of being—layering meaning in a novel filled with living people and ghostly apparitions.

Like Sethe's story, Ruqayya's story is also being passed on, as she has or has not advocated; the novel itself tells her story. But also like Sethe, Ruqayya refuses to narrate her trauma, the story of the massacre at Sabra and Shatila, to her child. In her case, her older son Hassan is an oral historian collecting the stories of the war. These two novels have more in common than these few details, however. Both works are literary expressions of events too horrible to speak of or narrate: African American slavery and the massacre of Palestinians and displaced Lebanese at the Sabra and Shatila refugee camps during the Israeli invasion of Beirut in 1982. These

2. Morrison discusses this recurring line in *What Moves at the Margin*, 324.

3. See Holloway, "*Beloved*"; Horvitz, "Nameless Ghosts"; and Hostettler, "Telling the Past—Doing the Truth."

novels are two of many artistic and literary expressions that seek to access and express something larger than a dry, historical narrative, retelling of facts, or detailing of horror. They search for ways to craft such histories and events into artistic expression.

To think more deeply about how women write such war stories, I build on Toni Morrison's intellectual work in relation to her fictional projects. In *What Moves at the Margin* (2008), for example, Morrison has written about the stillness and quiet that come to a writer when she is working on difficult and traumatic issues such as slavery, infanticide, and histories of oppression. Morrison delves into her own writing process in creating Sethe's refusal to tell her story of enslavement to her daughter and discusses *Beloved*'s overall exploration of how to write/tell or not write/tell about things too horrible to say—the traumas of slavery, for example. Wrestling with this profound question is what leads directly to Morrison's important claim about her writing: "The crucial distinction for me is not the distinction between fact and fiction, but the distinction between fact and truth."[4] The claim that fact and truth may not be the same thing is a crucial entry point into understanding stories that deal directly with trauma and violence. The sum of facts, when recounted, may not encompass a person's or a community's truth. For Morrison, therefore, fiction becomes a location where we can dispense with the notion that we must seek facts or "what really happened."

I use Morrison's formulation as a point of entry into thinking through how to read four literary works that shape war stories to narrate such truths about the Sabra and Shatila massacre. They seek out truths in how they do and do not tell their stories. I argue that these novels build and accumulate their powerful truths by narrating stories of war in a dialectical relationship with history. They intervene in the present by looking to the past to shape futures. I read Ruqayya's conscious silence in Radwa Ashour's *The Woman from Tantoura* (*Al-Tanturiyya*, translated into English in 2014); Susan Abulhawa's grand narration of Palestinian history,

4. Morrison, *What Moves at the Margin*, 72.

Mornings in Jenin (2010); Jana Elhassan's psychological portrait of a child survivor of the massacre, *The 99th Floor* (*Tabiq 99*, translated into English in 2014); and the short and sensual *Touch* (*Masas*, translated into English in 2010) by Adania Shibli through the questions of how and why we tell stories, which stories we tell, and who gets to tell them. A related set of questions informs this inquiry in that I also discuss how novels don't tell certain stories, resist particular kinds of narratives even as they are told, and/or simply refuse to tell a story. In different ways, all four works tightly control which "facts" are narrated in their stories about the Sabra and Shatila massacre, as seen through the eyes of people who experienced or witnessed extreme violence as Palestinian children. They also use a combination of telling their stories and refusing to tell them in order to convey their truths about stories not to pass on.

Fiction and Art on the Sabra and Shatila Massacre

To further contextualize how we read women's narrations of war, these four novelistic engagements with the massacre at Sabra and Shatila can be set against the backdrop of other literary and artistic works that depict the Israeli invasion of 1982 and this specific massacre. The larger project of this collected volume, *Women's War Stories*, is to recover the overlooked narratives of women and to use them to think differently and more deeply about women's experiences and analyses of war and violence. Art, fiction, and literary scholarship on the Lebanese Civil War and on this massacre in particular reveal a lack of attention to women, women's experiences and lives, as well as women's analyses of these experiences, with a few notable exceptions, which I discuss later.

If women's experiences and analyses of the massacre at Sabra and Shatila are underrepresented, it must be noted that this particular massacre is rather overrepresented—and even overresearched—in scholarship within the context of the Lebanese Civil War. Indeed, scholars have even claimed that the invasion of 1982 and this massacre more specifically have become an iconic moment emblematic of Palestinian suffering, thus leading to a lack of attention to other equally horrifying and violent massacres and acts of war, including, for example, the massacres at Tal al-Za'tar, Miyeh Miyeh, and so on.[5] Mayssoun Sukarieh and Stuart Tannock have documented the issue of research saturation in "On the Problem of Over-Researched Communities: The Case of the Shatila Palestinian Refugee Camp in Lebanon" (2013). This article shows how the camp is a good example of what is called "research fatigue" in populations where large numbers of researchers are continually working and discusses the specific problems the researchers' continual presence has engendered in Shatila. I reflect here upon how we as historians, literary critics, and activists promote the telling of certain stories and what our roles are in reproducing these stories within our scholarship and writing.

Similar dynamics are reproduced in literary and artistic expressions of the Sabra and Shatila massacre specifically and of the Israeli invasion of 1982 more generally. Lebanese and Palestinians as well as other Arabs and non-Arabs have produced a relatively large amount of art, fiction, and poetry on these topics. Works of literature about this massacre have become world renowned and, indeed, have made the story of violence against the refugees in the camps known to broader audiences—the most iconic of these works being Jean Genet's "Quatre heures à Chatila" (1982), translated as "Four Hours in Shatila" (1983), which Genet wrote after a visit to the camp following the massacre. Other works by Arab authors, such as Elias Khoury's *Gate of the Sun* (English translation, 2007), Mahmoud Darwish's *Memory for Forgetfulness* (English translation, 1995), and Rawi Hage's *De Niro's Game* (written in English, 2008) have become well known outside the rarefied circles of Arab literary critics, both in their original Arabic versions and in translation.

Despite this relatively large literary production, there is little scholarship or criticism of artistic, poetic, and literary representations of the invasion and massacre.[6] Moreover, what is written almost exclusively focuses on works by four male authors: Darwish, Genet, Hage, and Khoury. There are exceptions, of course—for example, Zahra Ali's interesting article

5. Karmi, "Recording Memory," 176–77; Sukarieh and Tannock, "On the Problem of Over-Researched Communities," 498–99.

6. This is discussed in Rooney and Sakr, *Representations.*

"Aesthetics of Memorialization: The Sabra and Shatila Genocide in the Work of Sami Mohammad, Jean Genet, and June Jordan" (2010), which takes up the work of two important artists—a Kuwaiti sculptor and an African American poet—who are less visible or noted for their work related to the Lebanese Civil War. With the exception of June Jordan, therefore, the vast majority of works of criticism deal with men and men's experiences of the war.[7] Two further crucial exceptions are important books written by women that underline women's experiences in the Civil War and the invasion of 1982: Jean Said Makdisi's memoir *Beirut Fragments* (1990) and Bayan Nuwayhed al-Hout's *Sabra and Shatila, September 1982* (2004), which remains the lone extensive oral history of the massacre.[8]

The sidelining of women's art and poetry within criticism and scholarship means that Arab women in general and Palestinian women in particular are all but ignored, with a few exceptions. We know that experiences of war and violence are gendered and disproportionally affect women.[9] Women's analyses of gendered violence are crucial to understanding their experiences and often highlight and center these dynamics. Women have also produced some of the most important representations and expressions of the gendered nature of war in their artistic and literary productions. This chapter refocuses the discussion of the literary production of the Sabra and Shatila massacre by exploring the works of four Arab women authors who have taken up this story and written it as a gendered experience by children. I begin with the two longer epic narratives of Palestinian families told through the lives and experiences of women—Radwa

7. June Jordan's contribution to creative expressions of this war has been recognized, particularly by Arab Americans who have admired her poetic, scholarly, and activist commitments that date to this period, in particular her poem in homage to the victims of the Sabra and Shatila massacre. See Harb, "Naming Oppressions, Representing Empowerment"; Hartman, *Breaking Broken English*; and Saliba, "June Jordan's Songs of Palestine."

8. It is relevant here that Radwa Ashour extensively invokes Nuwayhed al-Hout's book; see *Woman from Tantoura*, 183, 187, 190, 192.

9. Abu-Nasr, "The Effects of War on Women in Lebanon"; Maksoud, "The Case of Lebanon"; Schulze, Stokes, and Campbell, "Communal Violence, Civil War, and Foreign Occupation"; and Shehadeh, *Women and War in Lebanon*.

Ashour's *The Woman from Tantoura* and Susan Abulhawa's *Mornings in Jenin*. Both novels center on women's stories of 1982, while also calling into question if we should narrate a massacre at all. I then discuss two novels that focus on Shatila more obliquely: Jana Elhassan's *The 99th Floor* and Adania Shibli's *Touch*. The former is narrated by a man living in New York, literarily and figuratively scarred by the massacre as a boy when his mother was murdered. The latter is an evocative nonlinear short novel told through the senses of a girl.

From Tantoura to Shatila: Ruqayya's Blank Pages

The words "leave the page blank," spoken by the woman from Tantoura, Radwa Ashour's narrator Ruqayya, overcode my chapter because all of the fictional works I explore here deal with its central concept. I invoke it so strongly to home in on how we can read and think about the notion of not telling a story even as it is being told. I uncover here the idea implicit in Ashour's novel that we can resist the narratives imposed on us as well as the imperative to narrate ourselves to others. We can decide what to pass on, as Morrison would put it. Even as Radwa Ashour's text does tell us what happened to Ruqayya—in Tantoura, in Shatila, and so on—she also powerfully expresses a Palestinian woman's refusal to make herself, her stories, and her pain legible to others—particularly to those identified as outsiders. She even denies the stories to her beloved son, who is begging for her story for the good of her people. Eventually, we gain access to parts of Ruqayya's life through her son's voice. Thus, the story that she insists is not meant to be passed on is passed on—all of the contradictions and complications invoked by Morrison's *Beloved* are at play in *The Woman from Tantoura*.

The complexities of how Ashour engages the idea of both narrating and refusing narration are crucial to understanding this epic story of Palestine told through the eyes of Ruqayya from her childhood in Tantoura through her golden years in diaspora. *The Woman from Tantoura* assembles her life story through her first-person narration, letters to and from friends and family members, and clippings from newspapers and magazines, among other techniques. This creative assemblage style of writing thus narrates even as it questions straightforward, linear narration; it tells a history of

Palestine even as it questions what such a single history might be. The novel is a metafictional intervention that follows the massacre, depopulation, and destruction of Tantoura in May 1948, its peoples' forced migration to Lebanon, and their lives in refugee camps in Beirut through the Israeli siege in 1982, the Sabra and Shatila massacre, and beyond.

Metafictional tension is created through the character of Ruqayya's older son, Hassan, who records people's memories of their lives in Palestine as well as their experiences of diaspora. One of his major projects is to document Tantoura, the ancestral village he has never seen but where Ruqayya grew up. As she expresses it, "Hassan was collecting the statements of the residents of the villages along the Palestinian coast about their forced emigration in 1948."[10] Ashour uses this character to provide a historical narration about Tantoura and the story of its massacre, which is far less known and documented than the one at Sabra and Shatila. Her Arabic-language novel—like others that do similar fictional/historical work[11]—includes a bibliography of works about the village, suggesting further readings and giving supplemental information about other villages and sites of massacres in Palestine.[12] In the English translation, this bibliography is reduced to a short note about the historicity of the massacres and destruction of villages.[13]

Ruqayya remembers and recounts her life in Palestine, including fleeing Tantoura, but cannot talk about Shatila, September 1982, in the same way. Hassan's imprecations to Ruqayya to share the story of her experiences of the Israeli invasion and massacre in the camp cause her to fall ill. Her methods of refusal shift—she puts him off, she insists he speak to others. She tries to convince him to speak to officials, to men, to the people whose stories are traditionally more valued. Hassan continually rejects her logic, insisting that he wants to hear and record the stories of

10. Ashour, *The Woman from Tantoura / Al-Tanturiyya*, 67/78.

11. See, for example, Khoury, *Bab al-Shams*, translated as *Gate of the Sun*.

12. See *Al-Tanturiyya*, 460.

13. See *Woman from Tantoura*, 363. Elias Khoury's similar intervention in *Gate of the Sun / Bab al-Shams* is also different in the Arabic original version and the English-language translation.

ordinary people. In these passages, Ashour's text works on multiple levels. At the same time that Ruqayya maintains her control over her own stories and narrative through her refusal to tell them, the importance of official stories and men's stories is also undermined. Ashour uses both Hassan and Ruqayya implicitly to emphasize the value of the "real-life" stories of everyday people, especially women. To find truth in stories, such official histories, politician's statements, the stories of men alone will not suffice.

Ashour's narration of what Ruqayya refuses to narrate is itself complex. The chapter in which the Shatila massacre is explicitly told—where Ruqayya tells herself to leave the page blank[14]—is crucial to understanding how this works. The novel unfolds chronologically in a more or less linear fashion for its first half. The first time the massacre is referred to directly, however, is about halfway through the 362-page novel (450 pages in the Arabic original). Up to this point, Ruqayya has narrated her life's events in detail, but she hesitates when it comes to Sabra and Shatila. Most chapters in the work are long and full of description, but this one is uncharacteristically short, consisting of only thirty-two lines in the English translation (a mere twenty-nine in the original Arabic). It has the one-word title "Flies" ("Dhubab"). No details about the violence of the massacre are given in these lines. The entire brief chapter consists of short, evocative lines about flies. The sense of tragedy and horror is present but not explicit or graphic. Thus, that this massacre is de-emphasized in some ways, with details appearing sporadically, is a noticeable absence and thus a powerful reminder that it is only one of many horrible events that Palestinians have endured. This point is recalled in *Mornings in Jenin*, the next novel discussed here.

Following this short chapter, chapter 28 provides another discussion about Ruqayya's refusal to tell her story. This time we learn how she had declined earlier to give her testimony about what happened at the massacre to the real-life, nonfictional, oral historian Bayan Nuwayhed al-Hout, though she'd been pressed by the historian to do so.[15] As mentioned

14. Ashour, *The Woman from Tantoura / Al-Tanturiyya*, 149–51/189.

15. Ashour, *The Woman from Tantoura / Al-Tanturiyya*, 183/231.

earlier, Nuwayhed al-Hout's book *Sabra and Shatila, September 1982* is until today the only detailed oral history of the massacre. In a letter to Hassan, Ruqayya recounts her refusal to talk to "Sitt Bayan." Giving Ruqayya's account through Hassan's voice allows Ashour to pass on the story that Ruqayya insists not be passed on. It is also a way to address and critique the issue of being a member of an "overresearched community" and how insiders and outsiders consume stories differently.

As noted earlier, this particular story is told through an assemblage of literary techniques, making it necessarily fragmented and multiple. Ashour sets the stage for this fragmentation through a long interior monologue by Ruqayya earlier in the novel that lays out her thoughts about the notion of what it means to tell a life story and about the mechanisms by which one might do this:

> Am I really telling the story of my life or am I leaping away? Can a person tell the story of his life, can he summon up all its details? It might be more like descending into a mine in the belly of the earth, a mine that must be dug first before anyone can go down in it. Is any individual, however strong or energetic, capable of digging a mine with their own two hands? It's an arduous task requiring many hands and minds, many hoists, bulldozers, and pickaxes, lumber, and iron and elevators descending to the depths beneath and bringing those they took down back to the surface of the earth. A wonderfully strange mine into which you have to descend alone, because it does not belong to anyone else, even if you find things belonging to someone else in it. Then it might suddenly collapse on your head, cracking it open and burying you completely under the debris.[16]

The imagery of the mine is evocative of the English expression "mining the sources" used in some histories, which Ruqayya is not completely comfortable with. She lets us know that this discomfort stems not only from the strength needed to excavate a mine but also from the extractive process involved. Her second metaphor is a "bundle":

16. Ashour, *The Woman from Tantoura / Al-Tanturiyya*, 66/84.

> Perhaps it's more like a bundle than a mine; but can a person tie up his story in a kerchief and then hold it out to others in his hand, saying, "This is my story, my lot in life"? And then, how can you transport a bundle the size of a hand, or a large bundle like those women carry on their heads as they flee east over the bridge, the story of a whole life, a life that's naturally intertwined with the lives of others.[17]

Bundling replaces the destructive and extractive digging into the ground with a feminized image of women carrying their possessions. The woman with her possessions in a bundle is evocative of refugee women and in this case Palestinian women, underlined "as they flee east over the bridge," a reference to leaving Palestine and crossing the Jordan River. The bundle image also underlines the collective experience of women and refugees, making it explicit by stating that this life being told is "naturally intertwined" with others.

Radwa Ashour's novel constructs the character of Ruqayya in giving her the power both to narrate and not to narrate. We hear her story of this massacre along with stories of many other episodes in her life and life story. Ashour documents history through Ruqayya in this way. It is not a straightforward or linear narration or even an interior monologue. Rather, Ashour employs a series of narrative techniques, including replaying the recording of the voice testimony given to Ruqayya by her younger son Abed; Abed's own recollection of her stories in a letter he wrote to his older brother, Hassan; Hassan's telling of the story while begging his mother to tell her own story; and her declining to do so in a letter. The novel ensures that Ruqayya's story is in her own hands, and Ashour allows it to be told throughout the novel in a variety of ways. She also thus challenges us as readers to grapple with the fact that we are reading a story even as its central figure is refusing to tell it. The ethical questions about what is represented, who is representing it, and to whom it is being represented are thus intricately woven into the textual fabric. *The Woman from Tantoura* fills its pages while at the same time leaving them blank, questioning the power structure of who owns stories and whose they are to tell.

17. Ashour, *The Woman from Tantoura / Al-Tanturiyya*, 66–67/84–85.

The novel suggests to us that we can retain the power to narrate as much as we can wield a different kind of power when we elect to do the opposite.

Keeping It Inside: Palestinian Women and Intergenerational Trauma

Susan Abulhawa's *Mornings in Jenin* has much in common with *The Woman from Tantoura*, including its large historical sweep as an epic story of Palestine over time. It also is focused on women through its complexly drawn female characters. The novel begins before the Nakba and follows the Abulheja family's travails, casting important political, literary, and cultural figures in supporting roles. Though the focus of the plot is the Abulheja family, their lives are also woven through important and famous events in Palestinian history, especially moments of world recognition. The novel pays intertextual tribute to one of the most important Palestinian novelists, Ghassan Kanafani, by narrating the story of a child stolen by a settler family and raised as Jewish after they become refugees in 1984 and eventually move to Jenin. This retelling of Kanafani's novella *Returning to Haifa* (translated in 1984)[18] has a feminist bent; unlike that novella, Abulhawa's version deeply explores the emotions and reactions of the stolen child's mother and sister,[19] which sets up the narration in general as a work concerned with amplifying the voices of women and with focusing on women's and girls' experiences of war, occupation, colonization, and resistance.

The major difference between *Mornings in Jenin* and Ashour's text—as well as those by Elhassan and Shibli discussed later—is that it is written in English. This is important in the analysis of how Abulhawa writes the story of the massacres at Sabra and Shatila. Though the novel is comparable to *The Woman from Tantoura* in plot and scope, it also belongs to a more specific subgenre: the American coming-of-age immigrant story, suitable for English-language book clubs and discussion groups in the United States. It does some of the same kinds of work that Ashour's novel does by

18. *Returning to Haifa* is included in Kanafani, *Palestine's Children.*

19. Hartman, *Breaking Broken English*, 121–24.

providing a bibliography of further reading—this time in English—and narrating a history of Palestine.[20] In this bibliography, the novel shows the mechanisms of the occupation and colonization of Palestine by Zionists from before 1948 up to 2002—when the novel comes to a tragic ending with Amal's death in Jenin. Abulhawa's text thus has a pedagogical intent similar to that of Ashour's work, albeit designed for Abulhawa's audience. The intertextual framing of the Sabra and Shatila massacre, for example, invokes the book by the British journalist—and massacre witness—Robert Fisk with the chapter title "Pity the Nation."[21] This can be contrasted to the equivalent intertextual framing of the massacre in Ashour's text with Nuwayhed al-Hout's book. By drawing upon the intertextual weight of a famous British man's moving account of the massacre, Abulhawa inserts her Palestinian historical novel within a firmly Western context.

The story of the massacre at Sabra and Shatila and the larger story of the Israeli invasion of 1982 play a similarly central role in *Mornings in Jenin* as they do in *The Woman from Tantoura*. These stories are even more closely tied to the Abulheja family's story because some are murdered in the massacre. Two chapters of the novel are devoted to the Israeli invasion of 1982: chapter 32, "A Story of Forever, Forever Untold," and chapter 33, "Pity the Nation," located about two-thirds of the way through the 332-page novel. As noted earlier, the latter chapter title is directly linked to Robert Fisk's book about the massacre, which is cited in the text, as well as to the intertextual reference that book is making—also cited here—to the famous poem by the Lebanese American Gibran Kahlil Gibran. The references to Gibran and Fisk reflect the more journalistic style in which this chapter is written and are reworked to fit into the overall flow of the novel.[22]

20. See *Woman from Tantoura*, 338. Susan Abulhawa also provides a list of references in *Mornings in Jenin*, 331, and an author's note, 323–25, in which she discusses some of these issues.

21. See Fisk, *Pity the Nation*.

22. Zahra Ali's insightful essay on literature and art during the war, "Aesthetics of Memorialization," treats the question of how journalistic style is repurposed in artistic texts.

The protagonist of *Mornings in Jenin* is Amal. When she is a child, she is told that her name's doubled vowel sound (Amaal) signifies more than just "hope" but in fact is the plural; she embodies "the hopes, dreams, lots of them," of her father, her entire family, and her community.[23] The novel opens when Amal is a young child, and it follows her family in general and her in particular as she takes up her mother's legacy in Palestine and later comes of age as a woman in diaspora. It traces her life through marriage in Lebanon, her immigration to the United States, her husband's death, and the life she builds for herself and her daughter in Philadelphia before returning to Palestine in 2002.

The Sabra and Shatila massacre represents a crucial moment in the narration of the novel. It is depicted as one in a series of injustices that Amal, her family, and Palestinians endure; it is also emblematic of these injustices because it completely changes Amal's life. In her narration, for example, she recalls, "That week in September, starting with Yousef's telephone call, is the mantelpiece of my life. It is my center of gravity. It is the point on which all of my life's turning points hinge at once. It is the deafening crescendo of a two-thousand-year-old lineage. It is the seat of a demonic God."[24] The telephone call she receives from her brother Yousef informs her that his wife, Fatima, their young daughter, Falasteen, and their unborn baby have been murdered. This scene is told in graphic detail in the novel, contrasting to Ashour's more oblique telling. The impact of this news on the pregnant Amal—who has been looking forward to her child growing up with cousins of the same age—is instantaneous. She immediately goes into labor and wanders outside of her house disorientated and confused. She is soon found and taken to a hospital, where she gives birth.

Amal deals with the impact and aftermath of the horror of the massacre by internalizing her own suffering and trauma. This reaction echoes her own mother's coping strategies in response to her dispossession in the Nakba and the kidnapping of her son: Dalia simply goes silent and

23. Abulhawa, *Mornings in Jenin*, 72.

24. Abulhawa, *Mornings in Jenin*, 223.

refuses to care for her other children. Amal struggles with how to process emotionally the extreme traumas of her life, and because of her childhood experience, she resists the impulse to dissociate completely from the people around her. As she puts it, she was taught and can find no other way to deal with life than to tell herself again and again, "*Whatever you feel, keep it inside.*"[25] Amal finds it impossible not to pass on her own gendered, intergenerational trauma(s) to her daughter, despite her efforts to stay connected and be emotionally present.

Bringing how Amal keeps everything inside into conversation with how Ruqayya leaves the page blank is a powerful testament to the role of stories and narrations. On the one hand, both novels demonstrate ways to narrate out of trauma. They simultaneously focus on and marginalize telling the story of the massacre at Sabra and Shatila by means of multiple narrative techniques. Despite the use of graphic details in *Mornings in Jenin* at some points, at others Amal cannot narrate or even think about such details. Abulhawa's narrative walks a carefully balanced line between giving enough details to make the story plausible and powerful and teaching her reader about events, on the one hand, and granting Amal some "privacy" in not having to tell her story—as her mother, Dalia, refused to do before her.

The parallels drawn between these two generations of Palestinian women is a powerful narrative technique and message in the novel. Their lives look extremely different on the surface—a "traditional" Bedouin woman and a "modern" Palestinian American—but the two women are shaped by similar traumas and experience them in similar ways. These traumas are not the only tragedies of the book. Part of what gives this novel such power is that it shows the reader how these women should not have to tell their stories to outsiders. Abulhawa demonstrates why they should be left some private moments, though they often suffer greatly from not telling. Abulhawa thereby offers her characters the dignity of making their own choices to refuse. Amal desperately wishes that she could have

25. Abulhawa, *Mornings in Jenin*, 228, italics in the original.

told her daughter more of her story/stories before she dies—as perhaps her mother wished before her.

These two novels use different narrative techniques and structures in weighing the balances of fact and fiction, though both weave substantial historical and political "evidence" and materials into their works. The target audiences and subgenres of these works are also different, with one written in Arabic and the other in English for a mainstream "outsider" audience. What is and what is not told, therefore, must also be read in relation to these dynamics, in particular the investment of the reading audiences in the characters' lives and traumas. This is perhaps why *The Woman from Tantoura*'s refusal to narrate and resistance to certain scripts are somewhat bolder. Both texts focus on gendered experiences of war and probe the roles of women, but they also in different ways explore the inner dynamics of what it means to be a Palestinian—especially a Palestinian woman—in the face of such violence and trauma. They also trace this perspective through the women's points of view from when they are children to when they are adults and over the span of several generations. The third text analyzed here also looks at a Palestinian child. The story of Majd, scarred literally and metaphorically by the massacre, moves from the 1980s in Shatila to the 2000s in New York City, and the gendered perspective shifts to focus on the life of a boy.

Manipulation, Narration, and Childhood Scars

Told mostly from the perspective of Majd—an adult man who surveys New York City from the ninety-ninth floor of the skyscraper where he works, contemplating his childhood in the Shatila refugee camp—Jana Elhassan's novel shifts between childhood and adult perspectives to express the traumas of the Lebanese Civil War, the invasion of 1982, and the massacre at Sabra and Shatila specifically. Majd's mother and unborn brother are murdered in the massacre, and Majd is maimed by stepping on a bomb, leaving him with a prominent limp and facial scar. He grows up in the care of his father in a sort of inverse mirror of the mother-daughter relationships at the center of both *Mornings in Jenin* and *The Woman from Tantoura*. *The 99th Floor* is a complex exploration of the emotions and interpersonal dynamics experienced by deeply traumatized people. Like *The Woman from Tantoura* and *Mornings in Jenin*, this novel focuses on gendered experiences of war by telling them through the eyes of a male protagonist contemplating his childhood in the Shatila refugee camp and his adult life in New York, in particular his inability to have a successful relationship with a woman, his girlfriend, Hilda.

Written by a Lebanese woman author, the novel plays with gendered role reversals both inside and outside of wartime as well as with what happens when gendered roles are reinforced. One example of such a reversal is how the dynamic of care is shifted from the mother to the father owing to the mother's murder. A great deal of space in the novel is dedicated to the way in which Majd's father looks after his injured son not only immediately after Majd sustains his injuries but also throughout his life to adulthood. Indeed, Majd's father leaves his home and everything he has known, including his respected position in the camp as a teacher, to raise Majd alone in New York City, working in jobs such as an assistant in a flower shop in their Harlem neighborhood.

The parenting role reversal caused by Majd's mother's death is extended through how Elhassan writes the father's character to be the repository of national dreams and fantasies. Consonant with Amal's father in *Mornings in Jenin*, who tells her that her name is meant to symbolize the hopes of their community and the Palestinian nation, Majd's father keeps the memory of Palestine alive by constantly telling Majd stories about his mother. The novel thus activates the classic trope of the woman and mother as nation and therefore as a symbol of Palestine, and, indeed, Majd's mother is identified *as* Palestine in several points in the text.[26] The strategy for conveying these stories in the text, however, is concentrated in the male characters.

The Sabra and Shatila massacre is an even more crucial part of Elhassan's novel than it is of Ashour's and Abuhawa's works. Majd's experiences and traumas are centered around this tragedy, especially being maimed by a bomb and losing his mother. Like *Mornings in Jenin*, *The 99th Floor* uses

26. Elhassan, *The 99th Floor / Tabiq 99*, 106/97.

this event to work out how trauma is passed down through generations and what that trauma's enactment looks like. Whereas *Mornings in Jenin* and *The Woman from Tantoura* focus more on internal extended family dynamics, *The 99th Floor* explores in depth how intergenerational trauma, in particular living through extreme violence as a child, including losing a mother to war, prevents people from loving in committed romantic partnerships.

The 99th Floor focuses on Majd's personal story and particularly on his relationship with Hilda; it is thus narrated with an intimate urgency on a smaller scale than the epic sweep of *Mornings in Jenin* and *The Woman from Tantoura*. Like them, it narrates a balance between the experience of the trauma and resistance to victimization through telling stories and refusing to tell them, respectively. The narrative techniques used here are different, however. The novel is not told chronologically or as a history or extended family story. Elhassan narrates Majd's life by moving back and forth through time and space in different chapters from the 1980s in Shatila to the 2000s in New York and briefly to the 2000s in Lebanon at the end of the novel. We see what happens to Majd as a child through these narrations and through flashbacks; we also are privy to his contemplations of what might have happened differently and how he copes in different ways with his physical impairments and his Palestinian self in the challenging settings of Lebanon and New York. For much of the novel, especially in his interpersonal dynamic with his girlfriend, Hilda, Majd is not a sympathetic character. He manipulates Hilda and is cruel to her, acting out his trauma in various ways.

For example, he is resentful of people who can use their bodies, but he refuses surgery for his own impairments. Referring to his mentor in New York, who eventually helps him get a well-paid job in the technology industry, he remembers:

> He tried to persuade me to undergo medical treatment: plastic surgery on my face and a procedure to fix my leg. Perhaps my father also would have wanted me to heal the war's effects on my body, but no one understood what I needed inside myself, because I was still connected to the past. I could stay tied to memories without having to invite in

> the suffering that pained me every night. I used to know that life was ugly and not beautiful at all. I knew that making myself more attractive would feel to me like extracting the evil part of a story.[27]

Majd holds onto his suffering because he considers it a more authentic way to live. Everyone around him wants him to have surgery because they believe it will improve his life. What they do not understand, however, is that Majd feels that his injuries and suffering connect him to his past and thus to his mother and his homeland. Rather than forgetting the terrible things he has lived through and erasing the physical signs of them, he wishes to have the ugliness of this world present on his body as a reminder to him and to everyone who encounters him.

The complexity of Majd's character and how he relates to his suffering presents a challenge to the reader. It can be difficult to relate to Majd because he is not a sympathetic figure. He often lies about how he got his injuries and uses them for personal and financial gain. For example, as he recounts, "Sometimes visitors wouldn't ask what happened to me, but curious people wouldn't leave it alone. I would invent stories, including one that I fell off the balcony at my grandfather's house when I was young, and another that I fell off a motorbike and my face was cut on a broken glass bottle on the ground. I was well-versed in lying and I did it for fun."[28] He also uses his scars and limp as a way to manipulate his partner. One night after being particularly cruel to her and she has cried herself to sleep, Majd recounts, "I stood like a superhuman torturer contemplating the grooves of his victims' skin. When I was tired of being evil, and fed up with contemplating the torture I could cause her, I wished I could kneel down before those gray spots on her face and ask forgiveness. But when I tried to surrender, to bend my knees out of reverence to her tears, I found myself unable to adapt my body."[29] Reading Majd as an alternately sympathetic and unsympathetic character complicates a Palestinian narrative of resilience and resistance to victimhood. By showing how Majd changes

27. Elhassan, *The 99th Floor / Tabiq 99*, 190/173–74.
28. Elhassan, *The 99th Floor / Tabiq 99*, 87/80–81.
29. Elhassan, *The 99th Floor / Tabiq 99*, 50–51/48.

the ways he copes and deals with his trauma in different situations, Elhassan reveals the complexities of experiencing and surviving extreme childhood violence. In how Majd is both a hero and an antihero whom the reader may despise even while wanting to feel some kind of empathy for and connection with, his difficulties mirror the difficulties of telling one coherent Palestinian story.

The 99th Floor is different from the expansive epic fictional narratives of Palestine offered by Abulhawa and Ashour. It draws upon but moves away from the realism of a chronological, historical, family-based account into a psychological portrait of a disturbed man and how his trauma creates dysfunction in his emotional and intimate life despite his material success as a New York businessman. This way of expressing the truth of traumatic events lived as a child is recast in Adania Shibli's novel *Touch*, which focuses exclusively on life as depicted through the senses of the unnamed girl who is the novella's protagonist.

Missing Words and the Language of Senses

The most challenging work to understand of the four discussed in this chapter is Adania Shibli's short text *Touch* (*Masas*). Defined as a novel or novella, it plays with genre by incorporating a poetic style or an antinarrative prose, which pushes the reader into another realm of understanding what is and is not said/written in a text. As an experimental work, *Touch* has a different relationship to how it tells events and facts, writes its characters, and incorporates truth(s). This work is the only one of the four discussed here that is not "obviously" or overtly Palestinian. You can draw out and understand how it writes Palestine through small textual clues given in particular ways. It is at once a story that must be read as being about Palestine and a story that must be read as not clearly being "about" Palestine at all. The massacre at Sabra and Shatila is one of the key events it underlines as a textual moment in a particular way.

Touch is divided into five short sections, which are subdivided into even shorter vignettes, each of which is only a few pages long. Each section is named for and somehow filtered through one sense. The only section where there is a direct reference to a real place is in the third of eight short chapters in the fourth section of the work, "Language" ("Lugha").

The place mentioned is Shatila, and this reference is one of the only direct ways to understand that the story is taking place in Palestine. Moreover, you understand this only elliptically because in the rest of the text the reader is led through the young, unnamed protagonist's life as confused as she is about what is happening around her at various moments. In this specific section, the girl remembers one night of her life that was different from other nights because her mother sent her off to sleep on her own at a certain time. She was accustomed to being allowed simply to fall asleep when she was sleepy.

From her room, the protagonist listens to her parents' conversation through the wall: "From time to time, she would hear bits of words: 'imals,' 'ker,' 'Allah,' 'dren,' 'tards,' ratila,' through the door separating her room from the living room where the family had gathered. 'Ratila' was especially difficult. Then she heard the television set click on. Though the sound hardly made it through the door, but 'ratila' became 'abra and tila.' After more repetition, 'Sabra and Shatila.'"[30] Like the girl, we do not know what the parents are discussing and become aware of what it must be only with the final words here. But as readers of this book published in 2003 (and in translation in 2010), we are well aware of the massacre, and Shibli builds an increased sense of unease and even horror as the girl remains naively innocent while we understand why her parents have sent her away so they can have an adult conversation.

The way in which she then tries to understand what is happening then follows in her analysis of their conversation through language—the section's focus. She tries to make logical sense of the words she hears and opts for literal translations. "*Sabr* was cactus, and cactus plants, wherever they would be found, were always the same, never decreasing and never increasing. So she did not know if *sabr*: cactus had a *shatla*: a seedling form. She slept until the sound of honey being poured into her milk woke her. She followed it into the mother and the father's room."[31] Again, by the very absence of details, the girl's lack of understanding is used to underline

30. Shibli, *Touch* / *Masas*, 56/84.

31. Shibli, *Touch* / *Masas*, 56/84.

what has happened. The reader is expecting something about death and violence, something that links back to the kinds of details or even "facts" that they have read elsewhere. Here, Shibli refuses this expectation firmly and creatively by showing the logical thought processes of a young person who is experiencing an event from afar. Her inability to understand why the grownups are upset and speaking in hushed voices does not make sense. In a further contemplation, the narration recounts, "The color of the woman's dress in the picture was like the color of cactus. The girl tried to understand the meaning of the words *Sabra and Shatila*. Maybe they were one word. The word *Palestine* was unclear, except that its use was forbidden. The color of the green board resembled the color of cactus."[32] Her free associations lead her and the reader to mention Palestine, but, unlike us, she never receives the information to make sense of what is happening. She believes that she is stupid, and the other children in school curse her and cut her off from their community.

This way of writing about the trauma of the Sabra and Shatila massacre is significantly different from the way the other texts are written. Shibli invokes and insists on the color green being the cactus, *sabr*, and therefore connecting to the name "Sabra" as a location of the massacre. In a later passage, she is also able to link this color to one of the colors of the banned flag of Palestine, once again letting us know that the events are unfolding within historic Palestine, controlled by Zionist colonial forces. The girl in these passages is trying to figure out what everyone is talking about and what the words themselves mean because she can't make sense of them. Her inability to find the sense of the words—in terms of meaning but also experientially through feeling—mirrors our own inability to fully make sense of the horror and trauma that happened in September 1982 at Sabra and Shatila. It is important that these passages are located within the section on language specifically and that the massacre is explored in this way. Despite a very eloquent translation that conveys some of the play of the original Arabic, it merely hints at how the same passage in Arabic is so linguistically evocative. This chapter shows how language stands in the

32. Shibli, *Touch / Masas*, 58/86.

way of understanding even as it is the only thing able to give the massacre any meaning.

Adania Shibli's *Touch* does not leave the page blank but instead uses few words and incomplete language to advance her exploration of the kind of truth suggested by Toni Morrison. The truth of this massacre is told differently in each novel discussed here, with varying amounts of detail. All of the texts' characters somehow refuse to speak even as they speak: Ashour's Ruqayya leaves the page blank; Abulhawa's Amal learns to keep what she feels inside; and Elhassan's Majd won't talk about the massacre but insists on wearing its scars on his body. Shibli's unnamed protagonist finds her truth through language and in questioning what language might mean, which can be read as a different kind of writing history, one that is deeply connected to structures of sense and feeling and is feminist in a profound way. This way of writing indeed enacts the strong connection between words, histories, poetry, and feminism evoked by Sara Ahmed in *Living a Feminist Life*: "I think of feminism as poetry; we hear histories in words; we reassemble histories by putting them into words."[33] For Shibli, these words are a history as she assembles and reassembles the history of Palestine in general and of the Sabra and Shatila massacre in particular by exploring and investigating words. Ahmed suggests that this act of reassembling histories is intimately connected to the poetry of words, which in itself can be feminist and feminism.

Conclusion

Concluding this discussion with Adania Shibli's *Touch* allows us to think about how women's war stories about the same event can be different. How do these differences impact our reading of stories written by Arab women about Sabra and Shatila and the Lebanese Civil War? Sara Ahmed's *Living a Feminist Life* offers us a way to think about reading these kinds of war stories when she asserts, "A story always starts before it can be told."[34] Thinking through how women choose to write war stories, where they

33. Ahmed, *Living a Feminist Life*, 12.
34. Ahmed, *Living a Feminist Life*, 4.

begin them, and where they are located within them underlines Ahmed's crucial point about how a story "can be told." The notion that there is a power both in telling and in not telling a story, that you are in possession of your own stories, and that you can decide when to share or not share them comes through here.

These novels use different techniques to narrate their own stories and their own truths about the war. Abulhawa, for example, uses a reportage style in *Mornings in Jenin* that demonstrates what intergenerational trauma looks like and how women internalize and resist the idea that they should not talk about it. Ashour's *Woman from Tantoura* similarly narrates a chronology of women's lives over generations, also focusing on passing down trauma, while exploring the power of both telling stories and choosing not to tell them simultaneously. Elhassan flashes backward and forward through time to explore how Majd's truths are both authentic and traumatic but also troubling and the source of his abusive behavior when he is in a relationship.

Shibli explores truth and storytelling differently through a language closer to poetry. Her resistance to telling is written in a character who does not know the story. The horror and trauma in *Touch* are that the narrator senses something terrible but cannot tell it to us because no one has told it to her. By asking the reader to supply the story, Shibli thus in her own way resists the overtelling of the story, the overresearch of the community, and the exceptionalizing of this particular massacre. Ashour resists these things through metanarration. Shibli does almost the opposite in subtly assuming that we already know the story. The challenge of reading this passage about the massacre in *Touch* is not in understanding what is written on the page but rather that Shibli is activating something horrible that we already know. She does not have to tell the story; the truth of her story is that we can fill in the blanks while we witness a young girl who cannot. She plays on the emotions of readers who simultaneously want and do not want to narrate the story to the girl. All of these works suggest and Shibli's *Touch* underlines that you do not always have to recount every fact or event to write a history or tell a story. Sometimes in not telling, you indeed better tell the truth.

Bibliography

Contributor Biographies

Index

Bibliography

Abdallah, Hassan. "Ajmal al-umahat." N.d. At http://arabvoice.com/70746/%D8%A3%D8%AC%D9%85%D9%84-%D8%A7%D9%84%D8%A3%D9%85%D9%87%D8%A7%D8%AA-%D8%B4%D8%B9%D8%B1-%D8%AD%D8%B3%D9%86-%D8%B9%D8%A8%D8%AF-%D8%A7%D9%84%D9%84%D9%87/. Accessed Aug. 2, 2021.

Abisaab, Malek. *Militant Women of a Fragile Nation.* Syracuse, NY: Syracuse Univ. Press, 2010.

———. "'Unruly' Factory Women in Lebanon: Contesting French Colonialism and the National State, 1940–1946." *Journal of Women's History* 16, no. 3 (2004): 55–82.

Abisaab, Rula Jurdi, and Malek Abisaab. *The Shi'ites of Lebanon of Lebanon: Modernism, Communism, and Hizbullah's Islamists.* Syracuse, NY: Syracuse Univ. Press, 2014.

Abulhawa, Susan. *Mornings in Jenin.* New York: Bloomsbury, 2010.

Abu-Nasr, Julinda. "The Effects of War on Women in Lebanon." In *Arab Women between Defiance and Restraint*, edited by Suha Sabbagh, 95–99. New York: Olive Branch Press, 1996.

Achterberg, Jeanne. *Imagery in Healing: Shamanism and Modern Medicine.* Boulder, CO: Shambhala Press, 1985.

Ahmed, Sara. *Living a Feminist Life.* Durham, NC: Duke Univ. Press, 2016.

Ali, Zahra A. Hussein. "Aesthetics of Memorialization: The Sabra and Shatila Genocide in the Work of Sami Mohammad, Jean Genet, and June Jordan." *Criticism* 51, no. 4 (2010): 589–621.

American Art Therapy Association. "About Art Therapy." 2017. At https://arttherapy.org/about-art-therapy/.

Amnesty International. *Lebanon: Human Rights Developments and Violations.* London: Amnesty International, 1997. At https://www.amnesty.org/download/Documents/164000/mde180191997en.pdf.

Annahar.com النهار. ”أجمل الأمهات‘ مشهدٌ ’أيقونيّ“ جديد في انتفاضة تشرين“ (The most beautiful of mothers, a new “iconic” scene from the October Uprising). Nov. 19, 2019. At https://www.annahar.com/arabic/article/1071142%D8%A3%D8%AC%D9%85%D9%84-%D8%A7%D9%84%D8%A3%D9%85%D9%87%D8%A7%D8%AA%D9%85%D8%B4%D9%87%D8%AF-%D8%A3%D9%8A%D9%82%D9%88%D9%86%D9%8A%D8%AC%D8%AF%D9%8A%D8%AF-%D9%81%D9%8A%D8%A7%D9%86%D8%AA%D9%81%D8%A7%D8%B6%D8%A9%D8%AA%D8%B4%D8%B1%D9%8A%D9%86%D8%A8%D8%A7%D9%84%D9%81%D9%8A%D8%AF%D9%8A%D9%88?fbclid=IwAR17wAMZTbzLi2MxyrXb3xONKlKFfZtyFSCA41UIb7lw7vX4K-AvZFw5drE.

Arab Law Quarterly. “The Lebanese Constitution.” 12, no. 2 (1997): 224–61.

Artaud, Antonin. *To Have Done with the Judgment of God*. Radio play, 1947. At http://surrealism-plays.com/Artaud.html.

Ashour, Radwa. *Al-Tanturiyya*. Cairo: Dar al-Shuruq, 2010.

———. *The Woman from Tantoura: A Palestinian Novel*. Translated by Kay Heikkenan. Cairo: American Univ. in Cairo Press, 2014.

Baidoun, Nawal Qasim. *Memoirs of a Militant: Years in the Khiam Women's Prison*. Translated by Michelle Hartman and Caline Nasrallah. Edited and with an introduction by Malek Abisaab and Michelle Hartman. Northampton, MA: Interlink, 2021.

———. *Mudhakkirat al-munadila fi mu'taqal al-Khiyam*. Edited and with an introduction by Malek Abisaab and Michelle Hartman. Beirut: Dar Ab'ad, 2020.

Baker, Barbara Ann. “Art Speaks in Healing Survivors of War: The Use of Art Therapy in Treating Trauma Survivors.” *Journal of Aggression, Maltreatment, & Trauma* 12, nos. 1–2 (2006): 183–98.

Banerjee, Sikata. *Muscular Nationalism: Gender, Violence, and Empire in India and Ireland 1914–2004*. New York: New York Univ. Press, 2012.

Bannerji, Himani. “Projects of Hegemony: Towards a Critique of Subaltern Studies' ‘Resolution of the Women's Question.'” *Economic and Political Weekly* 35, no. 11 (2000): 902–20.

BBC News. “Suicide Protester Mohammed Bouazizi Dies in Tunisia.” Jan. 5, 2011. At http://www.bbc.co.uk/news/world-africa-12120228.

Becherer, Richard. “A Matter of Life and Debt: The Untold Costs of Rafiq Hariri's New Beirut.” *Journal of Architecture* 10, no. 1 (2005): 1–42.

Berger, John. Foreword to Kamal Boullata, *Faithful Witnesses: Palestinian Children Recreate Their World*, n.p. New York: Olive Branch Press, 1988.

———. *Ways of Seeing*. London: Penguin, 1972.

Berteau, Emilie. "Du refus d'être recyclé au droit de proclamer son corps en tant qu'oeuvre d'art: *Appendice* de Lina Saneh." *Edit Revue Recycling/ Recyclage* 6 (June 28, 2007). At https://docplayer.fr/194876968-Du-refus-d-etre-recycle-au-droit-de-proclamer-son-corps-en-tant-qu-oeuvre-d-art-appendice-de-lina-saneh.html.

Beydoun, Ahmad. *Le Liban: Itinéraires dans une guerre incivile*. Paris: Karthala/CERMOC, 1993.

Bhattacharya, Tithi. "Introduction: Mapping Social Reproduction Theory." In *Social Reproduction Theory: Remapping Class, Recentring Oppression*, edited by Tithi Bhattacharya, 1–20. London: Pluto Press, 2017.

Birth Registration Procedures in Lebanon: Practical Manual. Beirut: Frontiers Ruwad Association, Mar. 2015. At https://frontiersruwad.files.wordpress.com/2015/03/birth-registration-manual_english.pdf.

Byers, Julia Gentleman. "Children of the Stones: Art Therapy Interventions in the West Bank." *Art Therapy* 13, no. 4 (1996): 238–43.

Chabrol, Arnaud. "La fabrique artistique de la mémoire: Effet de génération et entreprises artistiques dans le Liban contemporain." In *Mémoire de guerres au Liban (1975–1990)*, edited by Franck Mermier and Christophe Varin, 485–509. Paris: Sindbad/ Actes Sud / IFPO, 2010.

Chebaro, Mona. "Cross-Cultural Inquiry in Art and Therapy." In *Tapestry of Cultural Issues in Art Therapy*, edited by Anna Hiscox and Abby Calisch, 229–40. London: Jessica Kingsley, 1998.

Cotter, Suzanne. *Out of Beirut*. Oxford: Modern Art Oxford, 2006.

Daher, Joseph. "Hezbollah's Military Apparatus." In *Hezbollah: The Political Economy of Lebanon's Party of God*, 153–68. London: Pluto Press, 2016.

Daou, Bernadette. "Feminisms in Lebanon: After Proving Loyalty to the 'Nation,' Will the 'Body' Rise within the 'Arab Spring'?" Civil Society Knowledge Center, Beirut, June 26, 2015. At https://www.academia.edu/30894505/Feminisms_in_Lebanon_after_proving_loyalty_to_the_Nation_will_the_Body_rise_within_the_Arab_Spring_.

Darwish, Mahmoud. *Memory for Forgetfulness*. Translated by Ibrahim Muhawi. Berkeley: Univ. of California Press, 1995.

———. *Unfortunately, It Was Paradise: Selected Poems*. Berkeley: Univ. of California Press, 2013.

Deleuze, Gilles, and Félix Guattari. *Image and Text*. Translated by Eugene W. Holland. London: Bloomsbury, 2009.

Derrida, Jacques. *The Beast and the Sovereign.* Translated by Geoffrey Bennington. Chicago: Univ. of Chicago Press, 2011.

Al-Durar al-Shamiyya. *Nar al-'Asha'r Tashta'il fi Lubnan.* N.d. At https://eldorar.com/node/63691. Accessed June 10, 2019.

Elhassan, Jana. *The 99th Floor.* Translated by Michelle Hartman. Northampton, MA: Interlink, 2014.

———. *Tabiq 99.* Beirut: Difdaf; Algiers: Itkhtilef, 2014.

Farine, Anais. "Imaginaire cinématographique du 'dialogue euro méditerranéen' (1995–2017): Formes festivalières, forms institutionnelles, formes alternatives." PhD diss., Paris III–Sorbonne Nouvelle, 2019.

Farrell-Kirk, Raquel. "Secrets, Symbols, Synthesis, and Safety: The Role of Boxes in Art Therapy." *American Journal of Art Therapy* 39, no. 3 (2001): 88–116.

Federici, Silvia. *Wages against Housework.* Bristol, UK: Falling Wall Press, 1975.

Fertat, Omar. "Rabih Mroué et Lina Saneh, comment ralentir l'occultation du corps/individu." In *Intermediality, Performance, and the Public Sphere: Selected Papers from Recent Meetings of the Tangier International Conferences,* edited by Khalid Amine and George F. Roberson, 80–89. Denver: Collaborative Media International, 2014. Copy of this paper downloaded from https://www.academia.edu/9736266/Rabih_Mrou%C3%A9_et_Lina_Saneh_Comment_ralentir_l_occultation_du_corps_individu.

Fisk, Robert. *Pity the Nation: Lebanon at War.* Oxford: Oxford Univ. Press, 1990.

Foucault, Michel. *The Order of Things: An Archaeology of the Human Sciences.* New York: Vintage, 1973.

Frangie, Samer. "The Anatomy of a Crisis: On Mahdi 'Amil's *Naqd al fikr al-yawmi.*" *Arab Studies Journal* 24, no. 1 (2016): 144–67.

Gago, Verónica. "WeStrike: Notes toward a Political Theory of the Feminist Strike." *South Atlantic Quarterly* 117, no. 3 (2018): 660–69.

Genet, Jean. "Four Hours in Shatila." Translated By Daniel R. Dupecher and Martha Perrigaud. *Journal of Palestine Studies* 12, no. 3 (1983): 3–22.

Georgis, Dina. *The Better Story: Queer Affects from the Middle East.* Albany: State Univ. of New York Press, 2013.

Global Women's Strike. "Global Women's Strike Demands." 2020. At globalwomenstrike.net.

Hage, Ghassan. "'Comes a Time We Are All Enthusiasm': Understanding Palestinian Suicide Bombers in Times of Exighophobia." *Public Culture* 15, no. 1 (2003): 65–89.

Hage, Rawi. *De Niro's Game*. Hanover, NH: Steerforth Press, 2008.

El Hajj Ali, Hanane. *Theatre Beyrouth*. Beirut: Amers Editions, 2010.

Hamadi, Ghadir, and Christina Farhat. "Civil Marriage in Lebanon: A Need and a Controversy." *An-Nahar*, Feb. 26, 2019. At https://en.annahar.com/article/941548-civil-marriage-in-lebanon-a-need-and-a-controversy.

Harb, Sirène. "Naming Oppressions, Representing Empowerment: June Jordan's and Suheir Hammad's Poetic Projects." *Feminist Formations* 26, no. 3 (2014): 71–99.

Hartman, Michelle. *Breaking Broken English: Black Arab Solidarity and the Politics of Language*. Syracuse, NY: Syracuse Univ. Press, 2019.

Higgins, Patrick Donovan. "Divine Victory: Uses of the 2006 War in Hezbollah Muqawama Rhetoric." MA thesis, Univ. of Texas at Austin, 2015.

Hirsch, Joshua. *Afterimage: Film, Trauma, and the Holocaust*. Philadelphia: Temple Univ. Press, 2004.

Hobbes, Thomas. *Leviathan* (1651). Project Gutenberg, 2002. At http://www.gutenberg.org/ebooks/3207.

Holloway, Karla F. C. "*Beloved*: A Spiritual." *Callaloo* 13, no. 3 (1990): 516–25.

Horvitz, Deborah. "Nameless Ghosts: Possession and Dispossession in *Beloved*." *Studies in American Fiction* 17, no. 2 (1989): 157–67.

Hostettler, Maya. "Telling the Past—Doing the Truth: Toni Morrison's *Beloved*." *Women's History Review* 5, no. 3 (1996): 401–16.

Hudson, Michael. *The Precarious Republic: Political Modernization in Lebanon*. New York: Random House, 1968.

Human Rights Watch. "Unequal and Unprotected: Women's Rights under Lebanese Personal Status Laws." Jan. 19, 2015. At https://www.hrw.org/report/2015/01/19/unequal-and-unprotected/womens-rights-under-lebanese-personal-status-laws.

Irth Lubnan mina al-ʿunf al-siyasi. Beirut: Al-Markaz al-Dawli lil ʿAdala al-Intiqaliyya, 2013.

Jabbar, Sinaria, and Amy Betawi. "Children Express: War and Peace Themes in the Drawings of Iraqi Refugee Children in Jordan." *International Journal of Adolescence and Youth* 24, no. 1 (2019): 1–18.

Jaber, Ali. "اجمل الأمهات" (The most beautiful of mothers). Twitter, Nov. 19, 2019. At https://twitter.com/alimouinjaber/status/1196765093628956672.

Jones, Sally Adnams. *Art-Making with Refugees and Survivors: Creative and Transformative Responses to Trauma after Natural Disasters, War, and Other Crises*. London: Jessica Kingsley, 2018.

Jung, C. J. *Practice of Psychotherapy*. Vol. 16 of *Collected Works of C. G. Jung*. Edited by Gerhard Adler. Princeton, NJ: Princeton Univ. Press, 2014.

Junge, Maxine Borowsky. *The Modern History of Art Therapy in the United States*. Springfield, IL: Charles C. Thomas, 2010.

Kadi, Samar. "Nabu Museum Offers New Attraction in Northern Lebanon." *Arab Weekly*, Nov. 11, 2018. At https://thearabweekly.com/nabu-museumoffers-new-attraction-northern-lebanon.

Kälin, Ana, and Julie Murphy, "'The Moment in and out of Time': Reflections on Context and Timing in Art Therapy in Kosovo." In *Art Therapy and Political Violence: With Art, without Illusion*, edited by Debra Kalmanowitz and Bobby Lloyd, 60–75. New York: Routledge, 2005.

Kalmanowitz, Debra, and Bobby Lloyd. "Art Therapy and Political Violence." In *Art Therapy and Political Violence: With Art, without Illusion*, edited by Debra Kalmanowitz and Bobby Lloyd, 14–34. New York: Routledge, 2005.

Kanafani, Ghassan. *Palestine's Children: Returning to Haifa and Other Stories*. 1984. Reprint. Boulder, CO: Lynne Reinner, 2000.

Karmi, Ghada. "Recording Memory: The Palestinian Experience." In *The Ethics of Representation in Literature, Art, and Journalism: Transnational Responses to the Siege of Beirut*, edited by Caroline Rooney and Rita Sakr, 176–81. New York: Routledge, 2013.

Kassir, Samir. "Beirut Is the Spring of Arabs." *An-Nahar*, Mar. 4, 2005. At http://www.atrissi.com/kassir/sub3.html.

Khalifa, Nabil. *Al-Shi'a fi Lubnan: Thawrat al-dimughrafiyya wa al hirman*. Beirut: Markaz Biblus lil-Dirasat wa al-Abhath, 1984.

Khalife, Marcel, and al-Mayadeen Ensemble. *Of All the Beautiful Mothers*. CD. 1978. Reissue. Houston, TX: Nagam Records, 1994.

Khatib, Lina. "The Voices of Taboos: Women in Lebanese War Cinema." *Women: A Cultural Review* 17, no. 1 (2006): 65–77.

Khoury, Elias. *Bab al-Shams*. Beirut: Al-Adab, 1998.

———. *Gate of the Sun*. Translated by Humphrey Davies. New York: Picador, 2007.

Kisthardt, Laura. "Confessionalism in Lebanon: Reflection and an Analysis of Issues." Senior Honors Projects, John Carroll Univ., 2013. At http://collected.jcu.edu/honorspapers/15.

Kraidy, Marwan M. "The Revolutionary Body Politic: Preliminary Thoughts on a Neglected Medium in the Arab Uprisings." *Middle East Journal of Culture and Communication* 5, no. 1 (2012): 66–74.

Lippard, Lucy R. *A Different War: Vietnam in Art*. Seattle: Real Comet Press, 1990.

Maasri, Zeina. "The Aesthetics of Belonging: Transformations in Hizbullah's Political Posters (1985–2006)." *Middle East Journal of Culture and Communication* 5, no. 2 (2012): 149–89.

Makdisi, Jean Said. *Beirut Fragments: A War Memoir*. New York: Persea, 1990.

Makki Bacho, Ginane. *Afterimage Catalog*. Beirut: Ayyam Gallery, 2013.

Maksoud, Hala. "The Case of Lebanon: Women and the Civil War in Lebanon." In *Arab Women: Between Defiance and Restraint*, edited by Suha Sabbagh, 89–94. New York: Olive Branch Press, 1996.

Malchiodi, Cathy. "Ethics, Evidence, Trauma-Informed Practice, and Cultural Sensitivity." In *Creative Interventions with Traumatized Children*, edited by Cathy Malchiodi, 24–42. New York: Guilford, 2008.

———. "Neurobiology, Creative Interventions, and Childhood Trauma." In *Creative Interventions with Traumatized Children*, edited by Cathy Malchiodi, 3–23. New York: Guilford, 2008.

Manoukian, Aline. "Seta Manoukian: A Chronology." In *Seta Manoukian: Painting in Levitation*, 164–68. Beirut: Kaph Books, 2019.

Manoukian, Seta. *Lebanese Children and the War*. Beirut: Technopress Moderne / Dar al-Farabi, 1977.

———. *Traces rouges et bleues: Exprimées par les enfants durant l'occupation*. Beirut: League for Lebanese Women's Rights, 1983.

Maroun Baghdadi Documentary. Supplement to Maroun Baghdadi, *Ajmal al-umahat*, DVD. Beirut: Nadi La Kol El Nas, 2013.

McKray, George. *The Psychological Impact of War Trauma on Civilians: An International Perspective*. Westport, CT: Greenwood, 2003.

Meskaoui, Zéna M. *Dignity (R)Evoked: Art in Lebanon—a Reading in between Lines*. New York: Atropos Press, 2018.

Morrison, Toni. *Beloved*. 1987. Reprint. New York: Knopf, 2004.

———. *What Moves at the Margin: Selected Nonfiction*. Jackson: Univ. Press of Mississippi, 2008.

Mundus, Hani. *Tariq Tal al-Zaʿtar*. Beirut: Markaz al-Abhath al Filastiniyya, 1977.

Nachabe Taan, Yasmine. *Hilmi al-Tuni: Evoking Popular Arab Culture*. Amsterdam: Khatt Books, 2014.

Nasr, Salim. *Susyulujya al-harb fi Lubnan: Atraf al-siraʿ al-ijtimaʿiwa al-iqtisadi, 1970–1990*. Beirut: Dar al-Nahar, 2013.

Nofel, Mamdouh. *Maghdusha: Qisat al-harb ʿala al-mukhayamat fi Lubnan*. Ramallah: Muwatin, the Palestinian Institute for the Study of Democracy, 2006.

Nuwayhed al-Hout, Bayan. *Sabra and Shatila, September 1982*. London: Pluto, 2004.

Pappé, Ilan. *The Ethnic Cleansing of Palestine*. Oxford: Oneworld, 2016.

Petran, Tabitha. *The Struggle over Lebanon*. New York: Monthly Review Press, 1987.

Quilty, Ben. *Home: Drawings by Syrian Children*. Victoria, Australia: Penguin, 2018.

Ribas-Mateos, Natalia. "Women and Left in the Middle East: The Voice of the Protagonists. An Interview with Azza Chararah Baydoun." In *Communist Parties in the Middle East: 100 Years of History*, edited by Laura Feliu, 282–98. New York: Routledge, 2019.

Rogers, Sarah. "Out of History: Postwar Art in Lebanon." *Art Journal* 66, no. 2 (2007): 8–20.

———. "A Short History of Postwar Art in Lebanon through the Early Work of Walid Sadek and Ziad Abillama." In *Contemporary Art from the Middle East: Regional Interactions with Global Art Discourses*, edited by Hamid Keshmirshekan, 135–56. London: I. B. Tauris, 2015.

Rooney, Caroline, and Rita Sakr, eds. *The Ethics of Representation in Literature, Art, and Journalism: Transnational Responses to the Siege of Beirut*. London: Routledge, 2013.

Ross, Miriam. "The Film Festival as Producer: Latin American Films and Rotterdam's Hubert Bals Fund." *Screen* (London) 52, no. 2 (2011): 261–67.

Rothchild, Babette. *The Body Remembers: The Psychophysiology of Trauma and Trauma Treatment*. New York: Norton, 2000.

Saffi, Walid. Introduction to Seta Manoukian, *Lebanese Children and the War*, ii–vii. Beirut: Tecnhnopress moderne/ Dar al-Farabi, 1977.

Saliba, Therese. "June Jordan's Songs of Palestine." Feminist Wire, Mar. 24, 2016. At https://thefeministwire.com/2016/03/june-jordans-songs-ofpalestine/.

Salibi, Kamal. *A House of Many Mansions: A History of Lebanon Reconsidered*. Berkeley: Univ. of California Press, 1990.

Saneh, Lina [Lina Majdalanie]. *Appendice*. Performed in Beirut, 2007. Copy of script in Zéna Meskaoui's files.

Saudi, Mona. *Forty Years in Sculpture / Quarante ans de sculpture*. Beirut: n.p., 2006.

———. *In Time of War: Children Testify*. Beirut: Mawakef, in cooperation with the Popular Front for the Liberation of Palestine, 1970.

Schulze, Kristen, Martin Stokes, and Colin Campbell. "Communal Violence, Civil War, and Foreign Occupation: Women in Lebanon." In *Women, Ethnicity, and Nationalism: The Politics of Transition*, edited by Rick Wilford and Robert Miller, 130–46. London: Routledge, 1998.

Seigneurie, Ken. *Standing by the Ruins: Elegiac Humanism in Wartime and Postwar Lebanon*. New York: Fordham Univ. Press, 2011.

Seta Manoukian: Painting in Levitation. Beirut: Kaph Books, 2019.

Shabaro, Israr. "لينا بوبس . . . أجمل الأمّهات الثائرات من أجل وطن" (Lina Boubus: The most beautiful of mothers, militants for the nation). Annahar.com, Jan. 23, 2020. At https://www.annahar.com/arabic/article/1110034-أجمل-الأمهات-وأيقونة-ثورة-لبنان-لينا-بوبس-تضارب-أبنائنا-يدمي-القلوب.

El Shakry, Omnia. *The Arabic Freud: Psychoanalysis and Islam in Modern Egypt*. Princeton, NJ: Princeton Univ. Press, 2017.

Shehadeh, Lamia, ed. *Women and War in Lebanon*. Gainesville: Univ. Press of Florida, 1999.

Shibli, Adania. *Masas*. London: AM Qattan Foundation, 2003.

———. *Touch*. Translated by Paula Haydar. Northampton, MA: Clockroot, 2010.

Smith, Andrea. *Conquest: Sexual Violence and American Indian Genocide*. Durham, NC: Duke Univ. Press, 2015.

Sontag, Susan. *Regarding the Pain of Others*. New York: Farrar, Straus and Giroux, 2003.

Stoler, Ann Laura. *Carnal Knowledge and Imperial Power: Race and the Intimate in Colonial Rule*. Berkeley: Univ. of California Press, 2010.

Sukarieh, Mayssoun, and Stuart Tannock. "On the Problem of Over-Researched Communities: The Case of the Shatila Palestinian Refugee Camp in Lebanon." *Sociology* 47, no. 3 (2013): 494–508.

Tamraz, Nayla. *Littérature, art, et monde contemporain: Récits-histoire-m*émoire. Beirut: Presses de l'université Saint-Joseph, 2016.

Tanay, Emil Robert. "Croatian and Bosnian Children's Art in Times of War." *Journal of Art & Design Education* 13, no. 3 (1994): 235–40.

Toufic, Jalal. "Ruins." In *Tamass: Contemporary Arab Representations*, edited by Catherine David, Tony Chakar, and Walid Sadek, 26–39. Barcelona: Antonio Tapies, 2002.

Toukan, Hanan. "On Being the Other in Post–Civil War Lebanon: Aid and the Politics of Art in Processes of Contemporary Cultural Production." *Arab Studies Journal* 18, no. 1 (2010): 118–61.

Traboulsi, Fawaz. *A History of Modern Lebanon*. London: Pluto, 2012.

Weiner, Irving B. "Some Observations on the Validity of the Rorschach Inkblot Method." *Psychological Assessment* 8, no. 2 (1996): 206–13.

Westlich, Cynthia A. "Art Therapy with Culturally Different Clients." *Art Therapy* 11, no. 3 (1994): 187–90.

Wilson-Goldie, Kaelen. "Lebanon Bans Tale of Fighters in Militias." *New York Times*, Aug. 18, 2007. At https://www.nytimes.com/2007/08/18/theater/18perf.html.

Wood, James M., and Scott O. Lilienfeld. "The Rorschach Inkblot Test: A Case of Overstatement?" *Psychological Assessment* 6, no. 4 (1999): 341–51.

Yawmiyyat al-harb al-Lubnaniyya. Vol. 1. Beirut: Munazamat al-Tahrir al-Filastiniyya, 1977.

Zuʿaytir, Midhat. "Aal Zuʿaytir in History, Geography, and Politics." MA thesis, Institute of Social Sciences, Lebanese Univ., Beirut, 1989.

Contributor Biographies

Editor Biographies

Malek Abisaab is associate professor at McGill University, where he teaches in the Department of History and Classical Studies and the Institute of Islamic Studies. His books with Syracuse University Press include *Militant Women of a Fragile Nation* (2010) and *The Shi'ites of Lebanon: Modernism, Communism, and Hizbullah's Islamists*, coauthored with Rula Jurdi Abisaab (2014).

Michelle Hartman is professor and director of the Institute of Islamic Studies at McGill University. She has published two books with Syracuse University Press, *Breaking Broken English: Black-Arab Literary Solidarities and the Politics of Language* (2019) and *Native Tongue Stranger Talk: The Arabic and French Literary Landscapes of Lebanon* (2014).

Author Biographies

Mary Jirmanus Saba is a geographer who uses film and other media to explore labor, agrarian, and working women's movements in the Middle East and Latin America as well as the militant images of both regions and their usefulness for the present. Her feature debut film, *A Feeling Greater Than Love*, won the FIPRESCI International Critics Prize at the Berlin International Film Festival Forum in 2017. Her new collaborative films work at the intersection of labor politics, feminism, and finance capital.

Zéna Meskaoui is senior lecturer in the Department of Art and Design at the Lebanese American University, where her area of academic research is art history and critical theory, with a special interest in Lebanese and regional artistic production. Her book *Dignity (R)evoked: Art in Lebanon—a Reading in between Lines* was published in 2018, and her recent article "The Banal as a Symptom of War" was published in 2019.

Yasmine Nachabe Taan is visiting associate professor at Bilkent University in Ankara, Turkey, and associate professor in the School of Architecture and Design at the Lebanese American University in Beirut. She has published a series of books on Arab artists and designers, including Hilmi al-Tuni and Abdelkader Arnaout, and her most recent book is *Reading Marie El Khazen's Photographs: Gender, Photography, Mandate Lebanon* (2020).

Nova Robinson is associate professor at Seattle University, where she has a joint appointment in history and international studies. Her most recent articles have been published in the *Arab Studies Journal* (Fall 2019), the *Journal of Middle East Women's Studies* (Fall 2021), and *Signs: Journal of Women and Culture in Society* (Spring 2022). Her forthcoming book manuscript is currently titled "Truly Sisters: Arab Women and International Women's Rights." She is also coeditor with Bonnie G. Smith of *The Routledge Global History of Feminism* (2022).

Index